Families for Mobility

Families in Focus

Series Editors

Naomi R. Gerstel, University of Massachusetts, Amherst
Karen V. Hansen, Brandeis University
Nazli Kibria, Boston University
Margaret K. Nelson, Middlebury College

For a complete list of titles in the series, please see the last page of the book.

Families for Mobility

Elite Korean Students Abroad and
Their Parents' Reproduction of Privilege

JUYEON PARK

Rutgers University Press
New Brunswick, Camden, and Newark, New Jersey
London and Oxford

Rutgers University Press is a department of Rutgers, The State University of New Jersey, one of the leading public research universities in the nation. By publishing worldwide, it furthers the University's mission of dedication to excellence in teaching, scholarship, research, and clinical care.

978-1-9788-3266-4 (cloth)
978-1-9788-3265-7 (paper)
978-1-9788-3267-1 (epub)

Cataloging-in-publication data is available from the Library of Congress.

LCCN 2025939360

A British Cataloging-in-Publication record for this book is available from the British Library.

All photos by the author.
This work was supported by the Yonsei University Special Research Grant of 2023 for the Humanities and Social Science Field and also the Yonsei University Research Fund of 2023-22-0099.

References to internet websites (URLs) were accurate at the time of writing. Neither the author nor Rutgers University Press is responsible for URLs that may have expired or changed since the manuscript was prepared.

♾ The paper used in this publication meets the requirements of the American National Standard for Information Sciences—Permanence of Paper for Printed Library Materials, ANSI Z39.48-1992.

rutgersuniversitypress.org

For my three parental figures—my mother, father, and maternal grandmother.

Contents

Note on Romanization and Translations

I use the McCune-Reischauer romanization system for Korean words and names, with two exceptions: widely recognized alternative spellings, such as *Seoul, hagwon,* and *Suneung;* and the names of authors who write in English and use their own preferred spellings. In most cases, I follow the East Asian convention of placing surnames before given names, except for individuals who prefer the Western order.

All translations from Korean are my own.

Families for Mobility

Introduction

Education Abroad as a Familial Strategy

Prologue

Sarah—an intelligent, diligent, and sophisticated young woman—was among the students who responded to my research participant recruitment ad, which was distributed through Korean[1] student associations at several Ivy League colleges. She felt that her transnational upbringing set her apart from many other Koreans. At the beginning of her interview, she remarked, "I always thought someone needed to study people like me."

Although Sarah was born and primarily raised in the Seoul metropolitan area, she regarded the year and a half she spent in California as the highlight of her childhood. Reflecting on her time there, she shared, "I was only eight, so I didn't worry about my life much. I just enjoyed being there. Every day after school, I went swimming with my friends. I loved it! California's weather is perfect for young kids to have fun outside. I had a lot of fun there." These fond memories filled her with gratitude toward her father, a medical school professor who first brought her and her brother to the United States during his sabbatical at a U.S. medical research institute.

Her father played a central role in shaping her life, a theme that recurred throughout her narratives. She noted that he was the one who "got [her] into reading," but his influence extended far beyond instilling a love for books. She explained, "My father's work had a significant impact on me. [...] I shadowed my dad at his hospital in middle school, which sparked my interest in medical science."[2] Sarah felt that her father was intent on guiding her toward becoming the person he envisioned her to be. His influence extended even to her academic choices. "He wanted me to appreciate the beauty of math or physics," she remarked, hesitating slightly, perhaps wary of appearing critical of her father, "although he never explicitly pressured me to choose a specific major."

When discussing her mother, Sarah's tone shifted noticeably. Sarah saw her mother in a different light compared to her father. She described her mother, who had left her job at a foreign embassy in Korea to focus on motherhood, as the "good cop" of her childhood, characterized by her laid-back and humorous nature. Sarah perceived her mother as "indifferent" to significant life decisions, such as her choice of college and major. "My mom didn't weigh in with her opinion," she explained. Refuting the common stereotype of Asian mothers as "tiger moms," she defensively added, "She's a free spirit. She really didn't push me in any way." She recalled how her mother would try to alleviate her stress when she felt overwhelmed by school, taking on more of a friend's role than a parent's. "Now I see my mom as a friend, a very cool friend," she said. During school semesters in the United States, Sarah often had candid conversations with her mother in Korea through texts and video calls, feeling that her father was "lacking empathy." In her narratives, the roles of her mother and father appeared distinct and unequal.

A few months after Sarah's interview, I had the opportunity to meet Sarah's mother in Seoul. She exuded the vibrant energy that Sarah had described. She positioned herself as a "mediator" between Sarah and her husband, whom she sometimes sensed tension between. For instance, she recounted, "Sarah loves to read and does read a lot, but my husband keeps stacking even more books on her desk, even when Sarah doesn't touch them." Despite these occasional conflicts, Sarah's mother felt that her daughter and husband shared much, such as their intellectual interests. Proud of her role, she said, "If Sarah comes to me with complaints about her father, I ask my husband to give her some space. I don't think he means any harm, but my job is to help smooth things over."

Regarding Sarah's education, Sarah's mother downplayed her own ability to contribute compared to her husband's support. Despite this, she believed there was a unique role she could fulfill as a mother. She explained, "Sarah sometimes overthinks about her future, and it stresses her out. The only thing I can do for her now is listen patiently, do some online shopping together, take her to a café, and enjoy something delicious together." She recognized and accepted the division of parenting roles that mirrored Sarah's perspective. "My husband tries to find solutions when Sarah complains, but I don't. What kind of advice could I give her? She's much smarter than I am now," she noted. She characterized her support as gendered work, stating, "What I do for Sarah is something only a mother can do."

I met Sarah's father, the final family member I interviewed, at his office in a university hospital near Seoul. It was adorned with mementos of his children: hard copies of Sarah's school essays, crafts made by her younger brother, and numerous family photos. The interview proved to be highly rewarding, as he spoke for over three hours with detailed enthusiasm about how he guided his children to become "globally competitive." He expressed a firm belief that liberal or hands-off parenting would not benefit high-achieving children. "They [children] are still young. Parents shouldn't let children do whatever they want. They need to be actively involved in their children's growth. They must take concrete actions," he asserted.

Consistent with what Sarah and her mother had shared, Sarah's father appeared deeply invested in his children's upbringing, both in Korea and abroad. Perhaps to counter the negative stereotypes of overly involved parents, he detailed how his hands-on approach benefited both his children and himself, emphasizing that he felt he was "growing together" with them. "I keep learning whether my input was right or not. That's a great learning process," he noted. He did not want his involvement to be perceived as forceful or selfish. "I'm not trying to achieve something for myself through my children. I'm just trying to guide them. It's all about interacting with my kids," he explained.

In his vivid recollections, Sarah's father saw himself as a devoted father deserving of appreciation and respect from his children and wife. "My wife often tells our kids how lucky they are to have me as their father, even though I'm not a great husband to her. [...] She once told Sarah that she could have gone to an Ivy League school if she had a father like me," he said with a laugh, recalling the memory with pride.

The narratives of Sarah and her parents reflect family dynamics shared by many in this book. The children valued their transnational upbringing, attributing much of its success to their fathers. They viewed their mothers as the "cheerleaders" of the family, while their fathers, a group often overlooked in studies, embraced and took pride in their demanding roles as transnational parents. Neither the children nor the parents explicitly criticized or challenged these highly gendered dynamics of their family life and parenting. They recognized the role of class privilege, shaped by the gender achievement gap between parents, as crucial to the transnational upbringing of these high-achieving students.

Sarah's case raises intriguing questions. While conventional views often depict Korean mothers, and Asian mothers more broadly, as providing hands-on, intense, and sometimes excessive support to their children, the role of fathers in such intensive parenting is frequently overlooked. However, Sarah's narratives and those of her parents reveal a notable and substantial investment in care and educational support from her father. Although the increasing involvement of fathers in their children's upbringing has been documented in various societies, the intensive management of children's education has traditionally been more closely associated with mothers, especially in Asian contexts. Sarah's case underscores the need to reassess the role of fathers in parenting dynamics and their broader impact on family involvement in education, particularly for high-achieving students with a transnational upbringing.

Are there many Korean fathers who are as involved in their children's lives as mothers, and how does their involvement compare? Is the "tiger parent" stereotype, commonly portrayed in the media, applicable to all Korean parents? Beyond gender differences, there is limited exploration into the resources and privileges of parents who practice intensive parenting. Additionally, research on how children respond to and interpret this parenting style is sparse. Do Korean children generally resist their parents' hands-on involvement, which some might view as excessive? If not, which children embrace this style and actively engage with their parents, and what motivates this acceptance?

Addressing these questions necessitates moving beyond stereotypical views of Korean and broader East Asian parenting, such as the pathologized concept of the "tiger mom." Sarah's case highlights the need to understand intensive parenting and parenthood on a global scale: How do the global hierarchies of education, language, and culture influence and amplify the practices of intensive parenting within elite Korean families?

Foreign Credential as Class Capital in Korea

Studying abroad must be analyzed from both the supply and demand perspectives. Western countries actively aim to boost their knowledge economies via what is often referred to as "global talent recruitment,"[3] a process embedded within the globalization of higher education. Meanwhile, countries that send students abroad often worry about losing valuable human capital.[4] This implies that student migration is not a neutral process but a power dynamic in which some societies benefit, while others are disadvantaged.[5]

In this, Korea offers a notable example due to its unique position in the global hierarchy. It is a non-Western, non-English-speaking country in Asia, traditionally positioned as a follower rather than a leader in cultural and educational matters but with a relatively advanced economy. In this context, Korean elites are often fueled by a strong desire for global belonging.[6] Their quest for cosmopolitanism, aiming to become "citizens capable of living both at home and in the world,"[7] drives many to seek educational or professional opportunities outside Korea—particularly by pursuing foreign degrees. In this environment, the traditional capitalist class struggle is increasingly being supplanted by competition over educational credentials.[8] With the growing importance of global connections, English proficiency has emerged as a vital asset for Korean elites, recognized as the world's first "global language."[9]

English holds symbolic value not only in Korea but also in many other Asian countries. Because opportunities to study abroad are largely limited to a specific demographic, English proficiency in Korea has become a significant marker of class distinction, symbolizing elite status. Fluent English, a significant indicator of transnational experience, coupled with degrees earned abroad, collectively constitutes a cosmopolitan life in these societies. Within this context, studying abroad, known as *yuhak* in Korean, has evolved into a key form of cultural capital for Korean elites and a powerful tool for class reproduction. It is indeed an "index of cosmopolitan striving"[10] among Koreans.

The academic achievements of Korean students deserve recognition. Reflecting the nation's strong desire for Western cultural capital, Korean students have come to constitute a significant portion of the student population at institutions in English-speaking Western countries, including the United States, the United Kingdom, Canada, and Australia. In most U.S. colleges, Korea has consistently ranked as one of the primary sources of international students, trailing behind only India and China—countries with populations more than twenty times that of Korea. The number of Korean students in the United States experienced a notable surge in the 2000s: Applications from Korea to Harvard University, one of the HYPS[11] colleges highly coveted among Korean students, tripled from 2003 to 2008.[12] In 2015 and 2016, when I engaged with most of the students featured in this book, approximately sixty-one thousand Korean students were enrolled in U.S. schools, surpassing those from any other country except China, India, and Saudi Arabia.[13]

Although the surge of Korean students at elite U.S. colleges has slowed in recent years, they still form a substantial portion of the international student population at many selective institutions. For example, in fall 2023, Korean students made up about 4.5 percent of Yale University's international population, making them the fifth-largest international group after China, India, Canada, and the United Kingdom.[14]

Despite its prominence in the global education market, Korea has a relatively short history of studying abroad. The Korean government did not legally recognize degrees obtained abroad until January 1989. This legal reform aligned with Korea's globalization efforts, marking a fundamental cultural transformation. Following democratization in the 1990s, there was an increasing demand among Koreans for liberal principles such as freedom and individuality. Simultaneously, the state expressed interest in aligning with the modern, democratic, and developed world.[15] Under the presidency of Kim Young-sam (1993–1998), the Korean government actively prepared society for rapid globalization, reflecting both public and governmental aspirations for survival in the global economy.

During Kim's regime, *segyehwa* (globalization) became the central motto of the country. Schools increased the hours and credits for English courses, and corporations began prioritizing applicants' English proficiency in their hiring processes. This social shift triggered the movement of Koreans to study abroad. Those who obtained degrees from elite colleges abroad quickly ascended to the top of the social hierarchy, assuming prestigious roles as politicians, corporate executives, and academics in Korea. In this context, degrees from schools abroad, particularly elite U.S. universities, became a prerequisite for membership in the Korean elite.[16]

The 1997 Asian IMF (International Monetary Fund) crisis triggered profound transformations across various facets of Korean society, leading to the restructuring of roles within Korean families. Faced with widespread unemployment and economic insecurity, individual families found themselves compelled to navigate these challenges. Established norms, including the conventional model of the male breadwinner and the concept of the family wage, crumbled under the pressure of the crisis, giving rise to debates concerning gender roles and the trajectory of modernization.[17] In response to the crisis, Korean families began to place an even greater emphasis on prioritizing children's education. This recalibration acknowledged education as virtually the sole driving force behind the country's rapid recovery and ensuring the survival and upward mobility of families amid the economic turmoil.[18]

The qualitative transformation of the Korean economy also spurred a fervor for studying abroad as a self-development strategy. The restructuring of the Korean economy aimed to align with the demands of the postindustrial, knowledge-based global labor market, necessitating high-skilled professionals proficient in English and possessing a global mindset.[19] This enthusiasm for becoming part of the transnational elite led to the significant rise in applications from Koreans, particularly in elite circles, to schools abroad. A survey revealed striking numbers, showing that 40 percent of Korean adults at the time aspired to pursue education-driven migration.[20]

Aspiring cosmopolitans have also been pushed to seek education abroad due to the remarkable academic achievements of the Korean education system—and the resulting intense competition within Korean schools. In numerous international comparisons, Korean students have consistently outperformed their global peers. In 2015, even U.S. President Barack Obama publicly commended the success of Korean students, crediting it to Korea's national dedication to education and well-funded public schools.[21] He reportedly stated that there was "much to be learned from Korea's approach to education."[22] However, many Koreans found Obama's praise of their education system dubious and uninformed, believing that Korean students' academic achievements do not solely result from the country's public education. No Korean denies that Korean students dedicate long hours to self-study or attend *hagwons* (private cram schools) after regular school hours, facing tremendous pressure to excel or, at the very least, avoid falling behind.[23] These

FIG. 1.1 An advertisement for a *yuhagwŏn* (overseas education agency) on a public bus in the Seoul metropolitan area

after-school programs, including private tutoring, impose both financial and emotional strains on parents, in hopes that they will provide their child with a competitive edge.[24]

Many critics highlight the Korean educational system's reliance on highly standardized tests and an overemphasis on rote memorization as significant shortcomings.[25] These factors are often blamed for stifling creativity and independent thinking among students. In response, affluent parents who seek education abroad for their children aim to provide them with a less intense, more liberal educational experience. The phenomenon of early study abroad, known as *chogiyuhak*[26] in Korean, epitomizes the intense enthusiasm for English and liberal education that has permeated Korean society since the late 1990s, peaking in the mid-2000s. The United States and Canada have emerged as the most popular destinations for Korean students, though English-speaking Asian countries like Singapore and the Philippines are also occasionally chosen.[27] In response to this trend, a thriving industry known as *yuhagwŏn*—agencies dedicated to placing students in overseas schools—has developed, particularly in Seoul and affluent districts beyond the capital. These agencies systematically facilitate students' enrollment in foreign educational institutions, catering to the desires of ambitious parents.

Frequently guided by these costly agencies, students hailing from affluent backgrounds often enroll in overseas schools for several years of their childhood or adolescence. Those harboring aspirations to attend foreign colleges typically leave their home country for either middle or high school or opt for attendance at select high schools in Korea offering specialized programs geared toward preparation for admission to foreign colleges.[28] These students, in pursuing protracted education abroad and a transnational career trajectory, have aspirations distinct from individuals who merely visit Western schools for short-term experiences. Fueled by their parents' financial means, they seek advantages beyond tangible proficiency in English and the acquisition of international credentials. Early study abroad is instead a path toward the cultivation of global affiliations and a cosmopolitan worldview.[29]

Several Korean alumni who attended prestigious boarding schools abroad have written autobiographies recounting their privileged academic experiences. The notable popularity of these literary works reflects not only the promotion but also the idealization of overseas education within Korean society. One prominent example is businessman and politician Hong Jung-wook, the son of a renowned actor, whose autobiography *7mak 7chang* (Seven acts, seven scenes) garnered significant attention following its publication in 1993. In this narrative, Hong vividly details his journey through Choate Rosemary Hall, Harvard, and Stanford, emphasizing his pivotal decision to enroll at an elite U.S. boarding school at the age of fourteen:

> In a book chronicling the life of John F. Kennedy, I gleaned insights into what constituted an ostensibly flawless existence—his education, appearance, parentage, and even marital partner all appeared to surpass the realms of the ideal. Confronted with this portrayal of perfection, I felt compelled to chart a course toward a similarly immaculate life. The prospect of mapping out an ideal trajectory for myself from an early age filled me with enthusiasm, and I embraced the potential to shape my own destiny with contentment.[30]

In his autobiography, Hong extols the virtues of elite U.S. education, yet notably overlooks the class privilege inherent in his and his classmates' experiences. Throughout his narrative, elite U.S. education is romanticized, establishing a stark dichotomy between the developed Western educational paradigm and the developing landscape of Korean education. While Korean education places emphasis on evaluating comparative intelligence among students, elite U.S. education, according to Hong, strives to instill in students confidence and a perception of boundless potential.

Quoting Erich Fromm, Hong asserts that "education is synonymous with helping the child realize his potentialities." While evaluating educational outcomes is undeniably important, Hong emphasizes that a more crucial aspect is guiding students to recognize and embrace their individual potential.

"Through the learning process, students should not only understand their responsibility for personal growth but also acknowledge their role in contributing to societal improvement," he insists.[31]

The resounding success of Hong's publication served as a catalyst, prompting additional autobiographical works from former study abroad students. Wonhee Park, who claimed admissions from ten prestigious U.S. colleges, meticulously chronicled her odyssey from a selective Korean high school to Harvard in her 2004 book titled *Kongbu kudan ogi siptan* (Study at level 9 and persevere at level 10). Following its release, Park's book swiftly gained prominence as essential reading for Korean students aspiring to pursue education abroad. Many students I met for this book cited her work as a significant source of inspiration for their early endeavors to study abroad.

In her narrative, Park emphasizes that her steadfast commitment to academic excellence was the key to her success. She highlights her industriousness by reflecting on her high school years at a prestigious Korean boarding school with a specialized program designed for college preparation abroad: "Have you ever experienced the resonant melodies of grass bugs emanating loudly around 2:00 a.m.? Positioned by my dormitory window, I was privy to their nightly serenades as I devoted countless hours to studying. [. . .] Regrettably, I found myself unable to savor the romantic ambiance of the night, nor did I have the luxury to acknowledge the inherent solitude that enveloped me."[32]

Whether intentionally or not, Park refrains from acknowledging external factors in her academic achievements. However, discerning readers may recognize the considerable impact of her family background—she is the daughter of an ophthalmologist father and a stay-at-home mother who "loved writing poems." Park's memoir downplays the influence of her parents' financial and cultural resources on her success; she attributes her acceptance into multiple Ivy League schools primarily to her own tenacity and passion for learning. This reflects a meritocratic belief, a common among elites, that obscures the class-based context of her academic success.[33]

Immersed in memoirs chronicling the achievements of elite education abroad, many Korean youths, particularly those raised in the 2000s, solidified their aspirations to study internationally and emulate the status of transnational elites like Hong and Park. As early study abroad became a viable educational path—particularly for those with financial resources—numerous magazines targeting mothers began publishing articles offering guidance on securing spots for their children at prestigious overseas institutions. For instance, in August 2015, *Yŏsŏngjungang* (Real Women), a widely read magazine for middle-aged women in Korea, openly endorsed studying abroad as a hallmark of Korean elite tradition, highlighting the pursuit of opportunities beyond Korea's borders:

The tradition of sending gifted children abroad for education is far from a recent development. During the Chosŏn Dynasty (1392–1910), many scholars traveled to China and India for their studies. [...] The motivations of these historical figures mirror those of today's students: the belief that international education provides invaluable exposure to diverse cultures and civilizations. The core rationale remains unchanged—to gain the knowledge and empathy required to enrich and advance one's own homeland upon returning. Thus, the pursuit of studying abroad continues to be a vivid expression of a profound commitment to learning.[34]

The article further underscored the significance of prestigious U.S. boarding schools and offered comprehensive guidance for mothers aspiring to enroll their children in these institutions from an early age:

> For parents contemplating sending their young children to schools in the United States, it is crucial to gather thorough information about U.S. boarding schools. [...] An emerging trend shows that more children are beginning their educational journeys abroad before even finishing middle school. This has led to increased interest in junior boarding schools in the United States, which offer advantages such as early English proficiency, adjustment to dormitory life, and a head start in the college admissions process. [...] To ease the transition, consider enrolling the child in summer camps associated with the preferred schools before they complete elementary school.[35]

The article concludes by highlighting that while attending boarding schools away from home can be challenging for young children, those who find joy and value in U.S. education can reap significant benefits from using these institutions as stepping stones in their global educational journey. It implicitly observes that Koreans with a strong commitment to education often establish transnational family arrangements. Some affluent parents permit their children to study abroad independently, while others choose a geographically split family arrangement: One parent, typically the mother, accompanies the children abroad, while the other parent, usually the father, remains in Korea to provide financial support. This reflects a broader trend among Koreans, showcasing a nationwide enthusiasm for and competition over foreign degrees and transnational cultural capital.

Education-Driven Asian Migration and Korean Wild Geese Families

Korea serves as an exemplary case study for understanding how the family, functioning as an economic unit, perpetuates class privileges across generations through the vehicle of children's education, both domestically and internationally. The pursuit of cosmopolitan aspirations has led Koreans to view early study abroad as a pivotal step in the intergenerational transmission of privilege. Consequently, Korean families have become increasingly diverse, fostering intricate family arrangements to facilitate migration driven by educational pursuits.

Affluent parents in other Asian countries—including Hong Kong, Singapore, Taiwan, and notably China—share a comparable enthusiasm for their children's education abroad. Since the 1980s, a demographic known as the "new rich" Asians has emerged and thrived, comprising skilled professionals in managerial, financial, legal, technical, and commercial services.[36] Endowed with both wealth and the capability to navigate global opportunities, they have sought improved job prospects, economic prosperity, and political autonomy. For many ethnic Chinese in Hong Kong and Southeast Asia across class, strategies of accumulation often begin with the acquisition a Western education.[37] They constitute the elite Asian diaspora who are "some of the best educated, well trained, and highly skilled" with "considerable wealth."[38]

In examining the transnational mobility of "new rich" Asians, Pierre Bourdieu's conceptualization of capital proves particularly useful. Bourdieu's three forms of capital—economic, cultural, and social[39]—manifest in the multipurpose migration of "new rich" Asians. Through migration, Asian entrepreneurs acquire a range of symbolic capitals that "facilitate their positioning, economic negotiation, and cultural acceptance in different geographical sites."[40]

The emergence of the Asian "new rich" calls for a distinct perspective on recent Asian diaspora and transnational families compared to earlier Asian migrants, whose primary objective was often basic family survival. In earlier literature focusing on the cultural logics of contemporary Asian migration,[41] education per se has been considered a peripheral motivation behind the increasing number of Asian transnationals.[42] However, an increasing amount of scholarly attention is directed toward understanding how education functions as the primary driving force and a conduit for the manifestation of cosmopolitanism among affluent Asians.

The diverse approaches of Asian parents to education-driven migration have been extensively documented as deliberate family endeavors aimed at perpetuating class status. Numerous terms have been coined to encapsulate these phenomena: The "astronaut family,"[43] predominantly associated with Chinese families, denotes those whose members reside in various countries worldwide. "Parachute kids"[44] represents children sent abroad, often independently, for educational purposes while their parents remain in their home country. "Study mothers,"[45] who accompany their children abroad, have garnered the most academic attention, underscoring the gendered division of parenting in transnational contexts. Conversely, fathering and fatherhood in similar circumstances remain relatively underexplored in scholarly literature.[46]

Among the diverse family arrangements centered around studying abroad children, Korean wild geese families stand out. These typically comprise children studying abroad, an accompanying mother, and a father who remains in Korea to provide financial support to the family members abroad. Analogous to geese daring to relocate to create an optimal environment for their offspring, Korean wild geese parents endure a transnational family structure for the sake of their children's education, often incurring significant sacrifices.

This phenomenon has become increasingly visible since the mid-1990s, coinciding with the Korean government's vigorous pursuit of globalization to attain advanced world nation status. Before this era, education abroad, primarily for graduate degrees, was monopolized by affluent families or a limited group of intellectuals.[47] In tandem with the widespread societal enthusiasm for globalization and the nation's economic growth, education-driven transnational family arrangements have become prevalent not only among upperclass elites but also within the middle class.

Wild geese families are often seen as emblematic of broader societal issues, particularly in education. A Korean college professor is quoted in a news article describing wild geese fathers as "poor Korean souls who essentially sacrifice themselves for their children's better education."[48] The article highlights the emotional and financial toll on fathers within this family structure, stating, "The unnatural phenomenon of 'wild geese' daddies is a clear sign of something wrong in our society. [...] If South Korea were a better place to live, fathers would not be suffering, and children, accompanied by their mothers, would not be leaving the country."

The wild geese family model represents a strategic adaptation among Korea's middle class, aimed at leveraging global resources and opportunities. This family arrangement involves inherent contradictions, as these families aim for stability while contending with an unstable marital life.[49] Some describe it as "an ironic form of family that sacrifices togetherness."[50] Consequently, the division in wild geese families—where mothers and children are abroad while fathers remain in Korea—has garnered significant academic and media attention, often facing scrutiny.

Family studies often emphasize the importance of geographical proximity for interaction and connection while overlooking the dynamics of families spread across national borders.[51] Many have sought to understand wild geese parents' intense commitment to fulfilling their parental obligations, sometimes at the expense of marital stability. The unconventional family split inherent in their family arrangement has sparked debates regarding their utility and significance, with many considering them to be financially and emotionally burdensome. Public concerns often focus on potential psychological challenges, such as increased levels of depression and loneliness, marital discord, and financial strain.[52]

These perspectives can stigmatize wild geese families, suggesting that their geographical separation and the resultant independence from the father undermine traditional Korean family values.[53] Some argue that the physical distance from fathers may lead to diminished respect for paternal authority and greater independence in children, implying that the family members "don't need each other."[54] This arrangement tests the relevance of different family bonds to overall well-being. In wild geese families, the parental bond is often prioritized over the marital bond, leading to questions about the validity of marital bonds as the foundation of the modern Korean nuclear family.[55] While public opinion may be skeptical, recent research tends to be more optimistic about the cohesion of wild geese family ties.[56] Despite varying viewpoints, wild geese families highlight the cultural differences between child-centered Asian families and couple-centered Western families.[57]

On the surface, the prevalence of wild geese families reflects the competitive and academically focused parenting style typical of Koreans, often exemplified by the stereotype of "tiger parents." However, the implications of Korean wild geese families extend beyond this stereotype. These families also embody East Asian familism, where the family unit plays a central role in economic and political spheres, as well as the persistence of patriarchy and the gendered division of labor. In wild geese families, this gendered dynamic is particularly evident. Mothers typically assume the primary caregiving role by accompanying their children for education abroad, while fathers remain behind as the primary breadwinners. This arrangement underscores the gendered nature of Korean family structures, where traditional roles are maintained despite the geographical separation.

Furthermore, the wild geese family arrangement highlights the hierarchical and unequal dynamics between English-speaking developed Western societies and the East. For many wild geese parents, the primary goal is to cultivate global citizens through English proficiency and exposure to Western education.[58] While the educational enthusiasm and gender division of parenting in wild geese families have garnered considerable academic attention, there remains a notable gap in the exploration of other forms of education-driven transnational families. Specifically, families that employ flexible arrangements, rather than adhering to the conventional model of separating the mother and children abroad while the father stays in Korea, have been underexplored.

A select group of more advantaged families can bypass the pathologized wild geese model while still nurturing their children as transnational elites. These families often choose to send their children abroad alone, typically to prestigious boarding schools or host families, while striving to keep their family unit intact in Korea. Their more costly approach frequently involves both parents making regular international visits between their home in Korea and their children's school abroad, as well as the children returning home periodically.

Given the considerable financial and cultural resources involved in such transnational parenting, a more thorough and nuanced examination is essential. What distinguishes these families from other education-driven families? How do they leverage their resources differently or similarly compared to other parents in raising their children within a transnational context? How do class and gender dynamics interact to shape their approach to parenting and parenthood? Furthermore, what criteria do they use to evaluate the effectiveness of their transnational family arrangements? These questions underscore the need for a deeper exploration to fully understand the complexities and diversity within education-driven Korean, and more broadly Asian, transnational families.

About This Book

Families for Mobility aims to provide a nuanced description and analysis of elite Korean parents and their high-achieving children abroad, who are often stereotyped as intense and excessive, usually labeled as "tiger mother" and "model minority." This work addresses a gap in multiple academic disciplines: Family literature often portrays Asian families and parenting as authoritarian, top-down, and occasionally detrimental to children's psychological well-being.[59] Migration scholars, while focusing on specific transnational family arrangements such as the wild geese family, tend to overlook the diversity within Korean or Asian transnational families. Asian American studies have generated insightful discussions on the cultural context of Asian achievements but have not extensively explored how Asians perceive and practice migration as a temporal, flexible, and expensive strategy for reproducing class privilege rather than viewing it solely as a means of settlement and financial success in destination countries.

This study of elite Korean transnational families, representing a numerical minority, employs a "strategy of the extreme case"[60] to document highly resourceful agents and identify any structural constraints limiting them. With few exceptions, parents and children in this book occupy the upper echelons of the hierarchy among Korean students abroad and their parents, boasting ample financial resources and a cosmopolitan habitus. The exploration delves into the parenting and parenthood of those who aspire to global membership and cosmopolitanism for themselves and their children. In many instances, their study abroad experiences aim to fulfill a cosmopolitan ambition rather than merely gaining a competitive edge in the job market. Driven by a belief in the cultural value of transnational mobility, they seek to transfer their own mobility to their children through a similar educational trajectory. The intergenerational replication of mobility demands close attention due to its unique implications within the highly classed context of Korean parenting in the globalized world.

This book introduces a fresh perspective on Asian parenting, challenging the prevailing stereotype of strict disciplinarian Asian parents. The broad application of this and the "model minority" and high-achiever stereotypes to nearly all Asians in Western societies results in a one-dimensional perspective. This perspective praises academic prowess and occupational success while pathologizing these achievements as outcomes of absurdly high parental expectations and strict parenting. Unfortunately, few studies have endeavored to unravel the complexity of Asian family and parenting dynamics. This book challenges the simplistic portrayal of Asian, particularly Korean, families by examining their intensive parenting, within the context of children's education abroad, as an exclusive family endeavor aimed at class reproduction.

A thorough exploration of the desires, aspirations, and expectations of high-achieving Korean student migrants abroad, alongside their parents, highlights the significant role of parental resources—financial, cultural, and linguistic—in shaping various aspects of parent-child relationships and family cohesion. This scrutiny extends to encompass family dynamics, parental role satisfaction, self-assessment, and the sense of filial duties. By highlighting both the commonalities and disparities within the cohort of elite Korean families sending their children to schools abroad, this book challenges the prevailing misconception that assumes near-universal high academic achievement among Asian students and uniform intensity among their parents.

Methodologically, this book contributes to the existing literature in two significant ways. Firstly, adopting a "studying up"[61] approach to examining elite families expands the scope of family studies beyond its conventional focus on working-class and middle-class experiences. Secondly, it offers a multidimensional analysis of elite families by triangulating the perspectives of young adult children, mothers, and fathers, revealing how family and parenting dynamics can be interpreted differently depending on each person's position within the family.

This book also offers valuable theoretical insights into the gendered dimensions of elite Asian transnational parenting. The privileged context of the families featured in the book provides a unique opportunity to examine how upper-middle- and upper-class parents with mobility either challenge or reinforce traditional gender divisions in parenting. This book positions parenting as a vital analytical lens to explore how the gender achievement gap influences the creation, reinforcement, or reduction of disparities within couples. It delves into the role of gendered resources within the framework of transnational parenting for high-achieving children, emphasizing gendered parenting as a key force in the intergenerational transmission of mobility.

By investigating the intersections of gender and class, the book reveals the specific gendered dynamics through which Korean parents and their children sustain transnational mobility and nurture cosmopolitan aspirations through education abroad. Moreover, it enriches the literature on transnational families, which has traditionally focused on working-class migrant families from developing countries, by adding the perspectives of elite families.

Children and Parents in This Book

This book narrates the experiences of Korean daughters and sons, along with mothers and fathers, in education-driven transnational family arrangements. It not only presents the stories of mothers, which have been extensively explored in other contexts, but also highlights often-overlooked paternal involvement, both financial and nonfinancial, and young adult children, a group frequently omitted in academic discussions of migrant or transnational families. The rarity of interviews with children is considered one of the significant gaps persisting in the scholarship on transnational families.[62] The Korean young adult children featured in this book, who are fully capable of articulating their perspectives and evaluations of their experiences, offer a valuable lens through which to explore education-driven migration and elite education abroad.

By triangulating the perspectives of children, mothers, and fathers, this book not only sheds light on the same issues from three distinct viewpoints but also reveals how parental perceptions influence and shape children's understandings and aspirations. For this study, I conducted interviews with 74 children (38 daughters and 35 sons) and 34 parents (24 mothers and 10 fathers) at ten selective U.S. colleges, predominantly Ivy League schools. Among the 34 parents interviewed, 29 were the parents of the participating children (I did not have the opportunity to interview the children of the remaining 5).

With IRB (Institutional Review Board) approval, I conducted interviews with participants between 2015 and 2018, primarily at or near their residences. For most of the young adult children, our meetings took place near or within their U.S. colleges during the school semesters. My previous experience as a doctoral student at a university in the Northeastern United States greatly facilitated my visits and in-person interviews around their campuses and residences. As for the parents, despite their frequent international travels, I primarily met them in the Seoul metropolitan area where they lived.

For recruitment, I initially contacted the Korean student associations at seven elite U.S. colleges—Harvard, Yale, Columbia, Dartmouth, Brown, Cornell, and Amherst College. The first-round participants who responded to my recruitment email assisted my snowball sampling by connecting me

FIG. 1.2 A coffee shop in the Northeastern United States—the setting for interviews with child participants

with their Korean friends or colleagues at their schools or neighboring colleges whom they thought shared similar upbringings. Through these introductions, I interviewed 3 students from the following institutions: the University of Pennsylvania, the Massachusetts Institute of Technology, and the California Institute of Technology. To minimize selection bias, I limited participants recruited through respondent-driven sampling to no more than 3 students recommended by any individual.

To understand gender impacts, I aimed to recruit an equal number of daughters and sons, ultimately interviewing 38 daughters and 35 sons. Instead of using *male* and *female*, which are biological categories, I employ *man/ men* and *woman/women* as adjectives when referring to participants' gender. Regarding nationality and national identity, all the young adult children identified themselves as Korean, although not all were legally Korean. Approximately 40 percent of the children held citizenships other than Korean, having been born in the United States or other Western countries while their parents, typically fathers, were studying or working abroad in those countries. For them, being Korean was more about their ethnic and cultural identity than their legal status. I recruited respondents without strict control over the children's citizenship, as long as they identified culturally as Koreans. The cases where children are not Korean citizens highlight essential aspects of the intergenerational transfer of mobility among Korean elites, a topic I explore further in the following chapters.

Regardless of their citizenship, nearly all children were raised in a highly transnational manner. Half of them (37) graduated from high schools abroad, predominantly in the United States and Canada. The other half (37) completed high school in Korea after attending schools abroad for a period, often during their fathers' appointments as expatriates or visiting scholars.

While most young adult participants perceived their families as well off and privileged in many respects, fewer than 15 considered themselves a class minority among Korean students at elite U.S. colleges. In this book, I refer to them as "less affluent" only in comparison to the majority. Among those considered less affluent, 4 children—2 daughters and 2 sons labeled as "migrant children"—relocated to the United States with their parents during childhood, primarily for educational reasons. The downward mobility experienced by their families after migration sets these children apart from others in terms of their relationships with their parents, the frequency and content of their conversations, as well as their career and family aspirations.

For parent interviews, I initially asked my young adult participants to help recruit their parents, ideally both. Except for five cases where parents were recruited by other parents, I engaged with all mothers and fathers through this participant-driven recruitment process. Most interviews were conducted face-to-face during summer breaks in Seoul or nearby regions. I typically met father participants in their offices or at coffee shops near their workplaces, while interviews with mothers were primarily conducted in their homes or at nearby coffee shops. There was only one exception, where an employed mother chose her office for the interview. The predominance of mothers in my parent sample suggests that both the children and I found it easier to recruit mothers than fathers. This may be due to the perception that discussing family and parenting aligns more closely with mothers' responsibilities for their children's well-being rather than with fathers'.

With only a handful of exceptions, all parents featured in this book were affluent and highly educated, often having attended schools abroad. Due to their prestigious transnational background, I refer to them as elite transnational parents. Out of the 24 mothers I interviewed, half (12) were employed, all in professional occupations, while the other half (12) were stay-at-home mothers who (claimed to have) chosen to opt out of the workforce to prioritize motherhood. All mothers, except for 1, had advanced beyond college, with 4 pursuing graduate degrees from either Korean or U.S. colleges. Despite their limited number, the 10 fathers in the book epitomized elite professional parenthood in many ways, given their uniquely advantaged educational and occupational backgrounds: 8 of them had extensive experiences studying or working

FIG. 1.3 Two mugs for parents at college bookstore, discovered during interviews in the Northeastern United States

abroad, while the remaining 2 were Korean local elites. All the fathers, except for 1, perceived themselves as earning comparably well relative to most other Korean fathers.

Many of the mothers and fathers featured in this book had personal experiences living in the United States or other developed Western societies at different points in their lives, often during their formative young adulthood and sometimes even in childhood. Given the relatively recent history of Koreans' involvement in international education, it is likely that these individuals were raised in privileged family environments marked by higher affluence and exposure to transnational settings compared to the average Korean household. To emphasize the continuity of upward mobility across generations, I adopt a life-course perspective by utilizing the narratives of parents.

Furthermore, the high tuition fees of elite schools abroad and the substantial costs associated with maintaining transnational family arrangements underscore the class background of the families discussed in this book: typically upper-middle or upper class with the financial means for transnational mobility. Parents' ambitions for their children's careers also serve as significant markers of class status. The "symbolic potency"[63] of overseas education is often seen as fully realized when students return home, gaining a competitive advantage in the local job market over peers educated solely in Korea. However, most parents in this book expressed a preference for their children to remain abroad and establish successful careers there, ideally in transnational fields, rather than returning home to become local elites. This class homogeneity has led me to categorize the participants' backgrounds in a relatively loose but distinct manner, distinguishing them from middle-class Korean parents, including most wild geese families.

Given the class homogeneity of the sample, I aimed to capture the subtle distinctions between families with extensive transnational experiences and those with fewer. A significant number of these families included parents—and in some cases, grandparents—who had studied or worked abroad, with their children following similar educational paths. However, a smaller number of families had limited exposure to foreign cultures, with the exception of their children who were studying abroad at the time of the interviews. Given this context, I use the terms *class* and *transnational mobility* interchangeably in my analyses, as the breadth and depth of parents' and children's experiences studying or working abroad were key factors that distinguished more privileged families from less advantaged ones. In the following chapters, I generally categorize the families into two groups: one consisting of cosmopolitan parents with extensive transnational experience and the other comprising more locally rooted, often less affluent parents, despite being fewer in number. It is important to note, however, that nearly all the children and parents featured in this book were upper-middle and upper class and had relatively high levels of education.

All interviews were conducted face-to-face, lasting between 90 and 180 minutes. Only two couples (comprising 2 mothers and 2 fathers) requested joint interviews, offering valuable insights into their couple dynamics throughout the conversations. All children and a considerable number of parents were fluent in both Korean and English, as was I, allowing interviews to be conducted in either language based on the participants' preference. After transcribing the digitally recorded interviews, I read the transcripts multiple times and initially coded them literally, based on the main questions of interest in the study. Subsequently, I progressed to more focused coding, where I compared participants' narratives to one another and related them to themes in the existing literature on motherhood, fatherhood, study abroad students, and education-driven migration. The focused coding process facilitated the development of the themes upon which the following chapters are based. I translated all interview quotes presented in this book from Korean to English myself, except for those that were originally conducted in English.

All names used in this book are pseudonyms. When introducing the accounts of students—or young adults—in this book, I intentionally use the term *children* to emphasize that both their perspectives and my focus as the author center on reflecting and interpreting their family dynamics.

When presenting accounts from parents, I refer to participants using the titles "mother" and "father," alongside their children's English names, such as "Jennifer's mom" or "David's dad." This choice to include the children's English names is intentional, reflecting both the cosmopolitan aspirations and the actual naming practices prevalent within their social circles. It also aligns with how Korean parents commonly refer to one another within their communities, often using their children's names after becoming parents, particularly mothers. This naming convention is widely adopted by scholars in their writings and is not intended to diminish the identities of parents beyond their roles as caregivers.[64] Rather, it aims to mirror participants' everyday language usage and underscores the analytical focus of this book on parenting and parenthood.

The lack of longitudinal data on children's life trajectories after college may be seen as a limitation of my study. However, my focus is primarily on exploring how children envision their future careers and families.[65] Aspirations and expectations play a crucial role in shaping individuals' behaviors and can arguably enhance their achievements.[66] By closely examining the aspirations and expectations that children and parents hold for one another, this book offers valuable insights into how transnational education serves as a powerful tool for class reproduction among Korean elites.

My Ambivalent Positionality: An Insider-Outsider

In many ways, my positionality as a Korean-born doctoral student at a U.S. university during data collection significantly aided in conducting interviews by conveying an "outsider privilege."[67] Insider researchers are typically members of the group they are studying, while outsider researchers remain relatively detached, as they are not part of the group under examination.[68] By that standard, I was mostly an outsider during my fieldwork. My positionality as someone who did not grow up in an elite transnational family enabled me to maintain an outsider researcher perspective, with fresh perspectives and few preconceived notions.[69]

My experience of studying abroad was notably distinct from that of most participants, primarily because of class differences. Across two phases of study in the United States, one as an undergraduate (for approximately one year) and the other as a doctoral student, I primarily resided abroad alone while my parents remained in Korea. My familial background set me apart from most children and parents discussed in this book: Neither of my parents graduated from four-year colleges nor did they hold elite professional occupations. They did not frequently travel internationally between continents during my study abroad due to inability and other constraints. The cosmopolitan lifestyle that many of my participants experienced did not characterize my own childhood and adolescence. In that sense, I was largely an outsider during my interview data collection.

My outsider status proved valuable, allowing me to notice aspects that might be taken for granted by those who grew up in a similarly privileged context. Moreover, it reduced the risk of assimilation into the culture I studied, ensuring I maintained a necessary degree of distance for a critical analytic lens. Surprisingly, being an outsider often facilitated greater openness from participants, especially parents, who seemed hesitant to disclose certain information due to concerns about judgment or repercussions within their exclusive, closed elite community.

Simultaneously, my educational background occasionally provided me with a level of "inside knowledge"[70] about the lives of the children I encountered. Having pursued my studies abroad, predominantly at the graduate level with a brief stint as an undergraduate student, I established a good rapport with the child participants, significantly easing our conversations. I often found common ground with the children regarding their cosmopolitan aspirations and could empathize with some of their experiences with prejudice as international students. This empathy helped me craft detailed yet tactful interview questions about their experiences both within and beyond the school environment in a Western society.

Being a doctoral student pursuing an academic career also played a significant role in recruiting parent participants. A considerable number of parents I interviewed were engaged in academia as professors or researchers, with many having completed their degrees in the United States. The shared academic background often led them to perceive me as a junior colleague. I even interviewed a couple of parents who attended the same Korean college as me, whom I could address as *sŏnbae*, a Korean term meaning "senior," commonly used to refer to a student older than oneself at school. That shared academic connection not only facilitated our conversations but also fostered a comfortable and friendly environment for the interviews.

Acquiring transnational experiences and resources primarily through my doctoral studies in the United States granted me a perspective within the circle of Korean transnational elites I studied that was at once insider-like yet fresh. This ambivalent positionality enabled me to "credibly function as both an insider and an outsider."[71]

Overview of the Book

The central five chapters of this volume explore the multifaceted aspects of education-driven Korean transnational families with children at elite U.S. colleges. The focus is both children's perspectives on, and parents' evaluations of, the transnational parenting and parenthood they practiced or experienced. Chapter 1, "Children Recount Public Fathering and Private Mothering," illustrates how children, often unheard in the academic discourse on intensive parenting within transnational families, ascribe meaning to their parents' involvement in their transnational upbringing. It examines how this involvement aligns with and deviates from the gendered expectations placed on mothers and fathers. Chapter 2, "Who Learns to Become Cosmopolitan Better?" focuses on the career and family aspirations of these children, which strongly mirror their upbringing. It delves into how gender, in interaction with familial background, shapes the life values, goals, and plans of high-achieving Korean young adults abroad, revealing discernible differences within this cohort.

Shifting the focus to the narratives of the parents, who comprised a predominantly homogeneous elite group, chapter 3, "When Class Trumps Gender: Korean Parents' Views," underscores the nuanced disparities and inequalities among parents in terms of their motivations and strategies for elite transnational parenting—a venture that demands substantial financial and cultural resources. Chapter 4, "What Makes for a Perfect Transnational Mother?" and chapter 5, "Emerging Extensive Transnational Fatherhood," illuminate how mothers and fathers, respectively, construct their ideal forms of transnational parenthood and pursue these ideals using their classed and gendered resources. The empirical findings and theoretical implications of my analyses are synthesized in the conclusion, which also includes recommendations for future research on related topics.

1

Children Recount Public Fathering and Private Mothering

Gender exerts a significant influence across various social institutions, particularly in shaping the formation and evolution of families and households. In the realm of parenting dynamics, it plays a crucial part in defining the roles and involvement of mothers and fathers in raising their children, influenced by societal norms deeply rooted in gender expectations. In many cultures, the primary responsibility for nurturing children is assigned to mothers, while fathers are primarily evaluated based on their roles as providers of financial support to the family. This gender-based division perpetuates an unequal distribution of familial resources between mothers and fathers, which in turn impacts how children attribute recognition and respect to each parent.

Many Korean parents comply with these gendered expectations and, in turn, experience divides and inequalities in parenting. Across education levels and employment statuses, Korean mothers are expected to be the primary caregivers for their children and experience a great deal of social pressure regarding their children's educational achievements.[1] This has resulted in a norm for *intensive mothering*,[2] which calls for prioritization, self-sacrifice, and devotion. Korean mothers often willingly take on the role of "education manager," believing it is a requirement for "good" mothering.[3]

On the other hand, the active, daily participation of Korean fathers in their children's education is reportedly minimal. The predominant emphasis continues to be on fathers' roles as breadwinners, despite the emergence of "new age" fatherhood.[4] A popular Korean joke succinctly captures this gender disparity in parenting: "To raise high-achieving children, you need the cooperation of well-informed mothers, uninformed fathers, and well-off grandparents."[5]

Scholarship on parenting and families, especially regarding migrant or transnational families, has primarily focused on the perspectives of parents, thereby neglecting the viewpoints of children. This chapter seeks to address this gap by shifting the focus to young adult children who have lived through transnational family arrangements for an extended period. The narratives of seventy-four Korean undergraduate students at elite U.S. colleges offer insights into how these individuals construct and interpret their experiences in relation to the gendered expectations placed on mothers and fathers. This analysis leads to a discussion on how their expectations, influenced by class and gender norms, perpetuate the gendered division of parenting in how they attribute varying levels of gratitude and respect to their parents.

Extensive Yet Undervalued Maternal Involvement

Maternal Educational Support: Early Stage and Collaborative

The majority—significantly more than half—of the children featured in this chapter were raised by stay-at-home mothers who opted out of the labor force to prioritize motherhood. These children generally viewed their mothers' unemployment or interrupted careers as commonplace, with only a few daughters expressing a sense of sympathy toward their mothers' "unfulfilled dreams."

Jack, who left Korea at a young age for a U.S. prep boarding school, thought that his mother "naturally" assumed the role of a stay-at-home mother. He cited his father, stating, "My dad said he wanted my mom to stay home and focus on children because he considered children's education more important than additional income." Another son, John, believed that the neotraditional family[6]—a heterosexual nuclear family with gender-differentiated roles and a focus on child-centered concerns—was the ideal family arrangement, given his father's successful yet time-consuming career: "My dad has been working for one company [a famous Korean conglomerate] for many years. Because his job provided sufficient support for the family, he believed it was best for everyone if my mom stayed at home to raise and educate me and my sister, even though she was fully capable of working outside the home." John, like many other children, took the man-breadwinner model for granted and perceived it as beneficial to his family. He neither questioned nor expressed sympathy for his college-educated mother's unrealized career ambitions.

Children shared a collective understanding of intensive mothering as a societal norm and believed that their mothers diligently fulfilled this duty, particularly during their childhood. What led them to view their mothers' involvement as exceeding society's conventional understanding of intensive mothering was their mothers' meticulous and wide-ranging management of their early education. I refer to this form of mothering or parenting as *extensive*, both in this chapter and throughout the book.

My use of the term *extensive* expands its meaning from previous literature by considering the context of Korean middle-to-upper-class parenting. In earlier studies, extensive mothering described strategies (Western) mothers use to maintain intensive care and involvement in their children's lives when they cannot provide constant, direct attention.[7] While this definition emphasizes indirect, yet deeply engaged, forms of mothering, *extensive parenting* in this book refers to a broader, more all-encompassing form of parental support typically practiced by middle-to-upper-class parents who aim to reproduce their social class through their children's education. Reflecting the gendered expectations and practices tied to parenting, *extensive mothering* signifies a mother's comprehensive sacrificial commitment to providing exceptional care. This care encompasses not only personal well-being but also educational development.

Numerous daughters and sons recalled their mothers being extensively involved, sharing stories of how their mothers taught them various subjects, with a particular emphasis on languages. Yvonne, who spent her childhood in the Middle East, shared a memory of her mother's educational efforts in a foreign environment: "I remember how my mom always pushed me to study hard during elementary school. She had me work on math and science workbooks every day after school and made sure I read plenty of books. I believe she ordered these Korean-language books from Korea and had them sent via air mail." Despite receiving intense educational support, Yvonne hesitated to label her mother as an overinvolved "tiger mom." Instead, she believed that this assistance—whether in learning English or participating in extracurricular activities—was essential for her growth. Like many other children, she considered hands-on education of young children by mothers to be normative and even appropriate. From this perspective, an involved mom was a "good" mom.

Reflecting Korea's high worldwide ranking in terms of the share of private expenditures spent on educational institutions,[8] a central feature of a "good" mother involves arranging ideal *hagwons* (private cram schools) and tutors for her children. Children's childhood memories of private education recalled the intense management of early education by mothers. Many shared vivid memories of a wide range of extracurricular activities during their early days, including sports, music, arts, debates, and language courses.

David, who spent his childhood in Seoul, reflected on his "busy" days in elementary school: "I took advantage of every opportunity available in the neighborhood, from Taekwondo and drawing to piano lessons. People often tell me how shy I was. They remember me being unable to speak in front of others. To fix that, my mom even signed me up for public speaking classes. I ended up learning a lot from all these experiences." Rather than being critical, David sought to understand why his mother was sometimes "obsessive" about his early education. He ended up justifying his mother's intensive management of his extracurricular activities by aligning it with his own ambitions: "I believe it is crucial for every child to discover something they love and excel at. Look at famous figures like Yuna Kim [the Korean Olympic gold medalist in figure skating]! My mom shared this belief and wanted me to find my own passion. That was why she enrolled me in so many different lessons."

Another son, Greg, similarly described heavy maternal management but in a more critical tone. He mentioned that his mother filled his time after school with various lessons, including piano and swimming: "My mom wanted me to become a concert pianist because she believed I was a prodigy. But I didn't enjoy playing the piano. Instead, I swam until I was exhausted, not just because I loved swimming but also I wanted to avoid practicing the piano. When my mom saw how tired I was, she allowed me to stop the piano lessons." Greg, however, refrained from placing much blame on his mother. He didn't perceive his childhood as unusually busy and stressful. Instead, he normalized such intense early education as typical. Similarly, many children attempted to rationalize how their mothers leveraged the value placed upon early education. They bought into the normalization of intensive maternal involvement in children's upbringing, at least during the early years.

While most children acknowledged the educational support from their mothers during their younger years, fewer than five specifically credited their working professional mothers for supporting them academically in later years. Greg stands out as an interesting case, as his professionally employed mother had studied and worked abroad. In contrast to most young adult participants, whose local mothers did not have degrees from abroad and who seemed to "take the back seat" after their children entered college, Greg began to perceive his mother differently later in his education. "My [locally educated] dad seemed to take his hands off from advising me after I left Korea. [It was because] my mom knows so much [about studying at a U.S. college]," he explained.

Greg attributed his mother's educational zeal to his family's cultural and legacy ties. "There are so many relatives on my mom's side who studied abroad, including my grandfather, who studied in Japan during the Japanese colonial period," he explained. With a mother holding a U.S. PhD and a father who only studied in Korea, he noted that he naturally shared more details of his college life in the United States with his mother than with his father. Here, it was the experience and degree obtained abroad, rather than solely gender, that determined who his "go-to parent" was when it came to discussions about his higher education: "I inform my mom about the courses I choose each semester and share my concerns about my GPA with her. Since she has a background in social science, I also sometimes consult her for help with statistics." He added, "There are many children like myself [around me] because my mom's friends and colleagues [in academia] are similar to my mom." However, among the young adult children I met for this book, he belonged to a minority with a mother who studied abroad and a father with national education. This unique division of parenting stood in contrast to many other families.

Intensive mothering in Korea, instead of being a solitary endeavor, was very much a collective enterprise. According to many children, their mothers engaged in "concerted cultivation,"[9] often with the assistance of gender-segregated networks known as "mothers' groups." Many children recalled their mothers participating in multiple mothers' groups to support their education. This collaborative approach to managing children's education appeared to persist for an extended period, continuing through their high school days.

The children recalled that their mothers cooperatively managed their extracurricular activities within these mothers' groups. These activities included volunteer work, internships, and tournaments, which the children believed largely determined whether their college applications were considered "good" or not. They believed their mothers carefully formed a "team"—a small, exclusive network of mothers and their children who shared the same tutors and collaborated on extracurricular opportunities. Within a team, children observed their mothers searching for and hiring private tutors for their Advanced Placement (AP) or SAT courses. Given the limited number of Korean high schools providing systemic assistance for foreign college applicants,[10] many children considered such mother-led team tutoring helpful and even necessary in their elite circle. Mothers' collective management of children's college applications was thus tailored to the particular needs and context of the children.

Despite the potential benefits of collective management, some children used the term "mothers' cartel," reflecting an overall ambivalent view toward the networks. The term implies that, while children acknowledged the beneficial effects of mothers' groups on their achievements, they also felt that the groups were too intrusive. This was especially true among those students who attended boarding schools abroad. Due to the distance between their schools abroad and Korea, they often felt subjected to their mothers' collective parenting practices in Korea during school semesters. They believed that the mothers' networks exchanged information about their schooling and daily lives, including their dating lives. They perceived this exchange of information among mothers as nosy and gossipy, considering it a form of covert surveillance.

Some boarding school graduates blamed these tight-knit networks for conflicts with their mothers. For example, James explained why he did not fully appreciate his mother's membership in multiple such groups: "My mom is active in several parent groups, including ones from my middle school, boarding school, and college. [...] When I was in high school, she found out about my girlfriend from other mothers before I had a chance to tell her. It made our conversations a bit awkward afterward." He tried to understand his mother's participation in these groups as an essential part of her socializing, given her limited social life as a stay-at-home mom. However, concerning his objections to the supervision of his private life, he couldn't help but blame mothers' networks as a primary source of the conflict.

In this way, the overall perspective of the majority of children toward mothers' groups was ambivalent. While they acknowledged the effectiveness of these groups, they simultaneously found such networks sometimes overly controlling, especially when impacting nonacademic matters where their privacy was at stake.

Not all children harbored resentment toward mothers' networks; a minority did not have the opportunity to develop such ambivalence, and some resented the lack of participation by their mothers in such networks. Yoana, who described her mother's parenting philosophy as "too hands-off," expressed her frustration with her mother's handling of extracurricular activities, relating it to the lack of network participation: "I think I was a competitive kid, so I wanted to try everything my friends were involved in, like debates and dancing. But when I asked her to enroll me in these activities, she often dismissed my requests, so I felt disappointed. In high school, many of my friends had mothers who facilitated all sorts of extracurricular opportunities, but my mom didn't provide that kind of support." Instead of questioning the value of collective work by mothers, Yoana actively embraced such work and even envied those who, in her belief, greatly benefited from it. She added, "If my mom had socialized more with my friends' mothers, my college application process might have been much easier."

Megan, whose parents attended elite Korean colleges but did not study abroad, observed a disconnect between her mother and those of others in terms of their level of engagement in mothers' groups. She perceived that other mothers—and their families as a whole—had more extensive transnational experiences compared to her own, which she felt created a psychological distance between her mother and the others: "Some of my friends' mothers went to Harvard or other prestigious U.S. colleges, and they also had cousins at Ivy League schools. Seeing that, I felt discouraged and sometimes envious too. I thought, 'My family is so uninformed [about elite U.S. colleges] compared to them!' The competition was quite intense, and it was hard not to feel jealous of those friends." Megan did not hesitate to express her disappointment regarding her mother's peripheral position in mothers' networks: "Sometimes, I found those mothers' groups to be very select and exclusive. At first, I thought they were just made up of students whose mothers were close friends, but it turned out it was more about families with similar backgrounds." Her remarks highlight the divides and inequalities within the circle of Korean students who aspire to study abroad. Instead of strongly criticizing the exclusivity of mothers' networks, she expressed a wish that her mother could have engaged more with transnational mothers, believing it could have made a significant difference for her.

Unlike Megan, who openly discussed the impact of mothers' groups, a few children chose not to elaborate on their mothers' involvement in these networks, likely due to the societal stigma surrounding "overinvolved" mothers. Sam was one of them. When asked if his mother joined any "team" for his education, he answered defensively: "My mom attended a few mothers' meetings, but the other mothers were far more assertive. They attended every available college admission briefing, whereas my mom wasn't like that and didn't really get along with them." His endeavor to differentiate his mother from others was noteworthy. Concerned about the potential perception of his mother as a "tiger mom," Sam endeavored to downplay her involvement in mothers' groups, saying, "My mom usually spent time with other laid-back mothers like herself. Whenever they came up with plans for extracurricular activities, I naturally joined in with their children." Sam described his mother as "chill" and "not that intense," terms he saw as contrasting with the typical image of a Korean mother.

The enduring and highly gendered Korean term *chimatbaram*, which literally translates to "the wind caused by a fluttering skirt," is conceptually akin to the Western notion of a "helicopter mom." This term pathologizes the extensive "status production work" undertaken by mothers, characterizing it as excessive.[11] Criticisms associated with this concept presuppose that children raised under intensive mothering will become overly reliant and docile. Consequently, this stigma prompted many children in this chapter, whether consciously or unconsciously, to downplay their mothers' involvement in maternal groups. They did so by emphasizing their mothers' "mere support" in handling assignments or participating in extracurricular activities.

Instead of attributing their academic achievements to their mothers' support, many children highlight their individual efforts, portraying themselves as sufficiently independent. This unintentionally reinforces society's negative view of intensive motherhood, as children often emphasize the drawbacks of their mothers' collective involvement in their education.

Motherly Support: "Great Cooks" and "Emotion Experts" at All Stages

In a family adhering to a traditional division of labor, mothers, often designated as the "emotion experts,"[12] typically shoulder the majority of emotional labor. Women are inclined to "monitor the tenor of the marital bond" and are regarded by both partners as more "intimately and emotionally connected to the children."[13] The children in this chapter reinforced this gendered division in parenting, recounting vivid memories of their mothers tending to both their physical and emotional well-being. They recalled spending more time with their mothers than with their fathers throughout their upbringing and, despite occasional conflicts, felt a profound and close connection with their mothers.

Aaron, who departed Korea at the age of eleven to attend a Canadian middle school, recalled his mother assuming the role of a temporal wild goose mother until he entered a U.S. boarding high school. He elaborated on how his mother wholeheartedly dedicated herself to supporting extracurricular activities, which he identified as the most distinctive memory of his early education abroad:

> I'm amazed at how my mom supported me through all the rowing practices I had in middle school. We sometimes practiced at 4:00 a.m., three times a week. She woke up earlier than me to get me up, prepared a good breakfast, encouraged me to eat, and drove me to the practice location. [. . .] She always stood by the riverside, watching me practice until the very end. Many of my teammates' mothers did the same, but I still think it was a significant effort for anyone.

Aaron acknowledged the considerable physical sacrifice his mother made to support him. Despite this, he chose to interpret her actions as emotional support,[14] finding comfort in the sense that she was "always there" whenever he needed urgent assistance. The competitive environment that shaped the upbringing of many children, whether in Korea or abroad, led them to attribute substantial credit to their mothers for providing this emotional backing.

Many children emphasized the unwavering care and effort their mothers invested in ensuring their physical and mental well-being. They noted that their mothers' commitment remained strong even during periods of physical separation, such as when they were studying abroad. For example, Walter described his mother's primary focus as his well-being, saying, "My mom pays close attention to how I'm doing. She wants reassurance that I'm taking good care of myself." Similarly, Jake mentioned that his mother's frequent calls from Korea were primarily concerned with his health and welfare, noting, "Most of her calls are to inquire about my health and well-being."

Intensive food preparation emerged as the cornerstone of maternal care, a service distinctly provided by mothers and not commonly received from fathers. Heather began her education abroad relatively late, during college, and fondly recalled her mother's dedicated efforts in preparing delicious meals for her and the entire family throughout her upbringing. Heather noted that her mother invested almost all her energy into creating tasty dishes, often encouraging her to explore various culinary delights. When asked if this ever bothered her, Heather responded, "Um . . . not really, it's my mom's way of expressing love." For Heather, well-prepared food epitomized the essence of maternal care.

For many other children, too, their mothers' cooking symbolized a form of emotional care, especially when their mothers were employed outside the home. Henry fondly reminisced about how his mother cooked every day after returning from work, recalling, "It was her routine. As soon as she came home, she took a thirty-minute nap to conserve energy needed for preparing dinner." He expressed a hint of melancholy in his tone. Similarly, Sean, whose parents operated an education company together, affectionately acknowledged, "I know my mom is always busy, but whenever she has time, she cooks for my brother and me. It makes us feel her care."

In most cases, children clearly distinguished between their mothers and fathers in terms of emotional caregiving. Many portrayed their mothers as nurturing and sensitive, while only a few used comparable terms to describe their fathers. Reflecting on her childhood, Hazel expressed a closer bond with her mother than her father, describing her father during those days as "quiet" and occasionally "abrupt," often preoccupied with work. Similarly, Jenna perceived her mother as "like a friend," contrasting with her view of her father as "more like a distant uncle." While Jenna appreciated her father for his sporadic yet valuable advice, she emphasized the greater impact of her mother's comforting words: "When I'm down, my mom tells me, 'You can come home anytime.' That is so comforting." Her appreciation for her mother's emotional support was widely echoed among daughters and sons, many of whom cited it as their mothers' most significant contribution during their college life abroad, which they sometimes found stressful and lonely.

The Worth of Mothers' Emotional Support

Children expressed even greater appreciation for their mothers' emotional support, such as warm words of encouragement, after entering college abroad. Mia, the daughter of an Ivy League–educated couple, reflected on her high school days overseas: "I shared every detail of my life with her [over the phone], including information about all my friends. I hid nothing from her. Since my mom majored in psychology, it probably helped her become such a good listener. [. . .] She understands me so well that talking to her always puts me at ease." Mia regarded her mother as the world's best counselor, not only because of her mother's constant availability to lend an ear but also because of the valuable advice she provided: "My mom doesn't just listen. She offers her opinions while remaining supportive. That's why I cherish our phone calls. They were the biggest source of support for me during my high school years."

Mia found her mother's role to be distinct from her father's. She believed that her mother's gender influenced how they communicated: "Sometimes you need complete empathy, not advice or feedback. Friends and even my boy-friend might not provide that, as he often gives the same responses as my dad. That's when I call my mom to get the understanding I truly need." Mia said she shared specific details of her college life abroad only with her mother, trust-ing her to be the most understanding and supportive person for discussing sensitive matters. She referred to her mom as "the figure whom I can rely on anytime": "Honestly, I'm not sure if I'm handling my internships well. When I expressed my insecurity to my mom, she said, 'I'm so happy my daughter is doing her best. I'm OK as long as you're happy.' I wonder if I'll be able to offer that same level of support to my daughter in the future." She expressed appre-ciation and sympathy for her mother, stating, "Sometimes I think about how stressful and lonely my mom must feel [as a counselor]." Such empathy seemed to lead her to appreciate her mother's efforts for emotional support.

Rachel echoed a similar sentiment regarding the gender differences between her parents. She perceived that her parents had distinct talents and characters aligned with gender stereotypes, which made her feel more com-fortable talking to her mother than to her father: "My mom is good at getting to the heart of the matter. It's not that she provides logical explanations. She just understands what I'm trying to convey. She has a knack for guiding my thoughts and opinions, which she does much better than my dad." The hon-est relationship Rachel shared with her mother provided a rationale for her to seek emotional support from her mother rather than from her father: "Per-haps it's because I feel more comfortable expressing my feelings with my mom. I spend more time with her during summer breaks [in Korea] because she's usually around, while my dad is at work."

While daughters were more explicit than sons in expressing their apprecia-tion for their mothers' emotional support, Ethan also felt profound gratitude toward his mother for a unique form of emotional care. "My mom's job is to pray for me every single day. She has done so since I was very young," he said. Ethan viewed his mother's prayers as a tangible expression of her love, con-sidering it the most meaningful way she could support him. He felt this form of support contrasted sharply with rationality, emphasizing the emotional aspect. "My mom is not an analytical person," he added. Despite both parents supporting his aspiration to become "world famous," he perceived them as occupying different roles based on gender. "My dad provides both financial and emotional support, whereas my mom focuses solely on emotional sup-port, which she offers more extensively than my dad," he concluded, position-ing his mother within the feminine domain.

The advancement of communication technology played a crucial role in facilitating connections among families across two continents. Almost all children reported that their mothers took the initiative more frequently than their fathers in initiating overseas phone calls, video chats, and text messages to maintain connectivity. Such maternal efforts were often taken for granted, as mothers were viewed as the "messengers" of their families—a role inherently associated with motherhood. While no child perceived their fathers as excluded from transnational family communication, many acknowledged their mothers' greater proactivity in initiating contact, considering it a normal aspect of maternal responsibility.

Sam, who began his transnational education at fifteen, highlighted the routine nature of talking to his parents on the phone, a practice that persisted into his college days. "I talk to my parents almost every day. I talk to them more often than I did in high school," he remarked. Additionally, he said he actively participated in "family group texts," where he observed his parents assuming distinct roles. He found his father typically taking the lead and making important decisions, while his mother played the role of a careful listener who responded thoughtfully to his concerns.

Sam was not the only child heavily reliant on international communication with parents during school semesters. Maintaining close contact with parents emerged as a characteristic feature of many families presented in this book. These parents exhibited a particular focus on their children's academic performances and well-being, with the children expressing a desire to regularly update their parents on their progress.[15] However, some children raised questions about their mothers' motivations for initiating contact, perceiving that their mothers occasionally delved into their private lives, particularly inquiring about relationships.

Hailey, who introduced her mother as one of her "best friends," confided in me about the ambivalent feelings she often experienced during overseas calls with her mother: "In ninth grade [at my U.S. boarding school], I felt like my mom was too intrusive. [. . .] I couldn't understand why she needed to know every detail about my life, especially about my friends. Even in college, she still asks a lot about my friends, like whether I go out for drinks with them after classes." She tried to understand and excuse her mother's surveillance as an inevitable aspect of transnational mothering. However, she couldn't help but express her displeasure.

The narratives of children elucidate how mothers sought to ensure a "smooth" and "proper" transition to adulthood for their children, as perceived by both the mothers themselves and others in their social circles. This endeavor involved monitoring their children's personal lives from overseas, a key aspect of "status production work."[16] However, this aspect of maternal involvement was often criticized by the children as being "too much." Daughters, more frequently than sons, shared their sentiments about this scrutiny. They particularly believed that they had stricter curfews and more parental supervision, revealing a double standard that imposes harsher judgments on women's casual relationships compared to men's.

To some extent, the management of their children's private lives served as compensation for the diminishing influence mothers had on their children's college education and career preparation. Upon the commencement of their education abroad, especially in college, children often perceived their mothers, particularly stay-at-home mothers, as stepping back from making significant decisions about their lives, deferring this role to their fathers. Many children found this shift unsurprising, viewing their mothers as lacking the cultural capital to be "good advisors." They believed that their fathers, with higher earnings and a more cosmopolitan outlook, naturally assumed this role.

Jamie, who chose to attend a U.S. boarding school at her father's urging, drew a sharp contrast between her mother and her father in this regard: "My mom hasn't given her opinion on my education [since I left Korea]. That's mainly my father's role. I sometimes discuss my grades or job plans with her, but only briefly. Our conversations usually stay casual and focus on everyday matters rather than anything serious." Jamie genuinely appreciated the strong bond she had with her mother. Simultaneously, however, she seemed to undervalue her mother's support in later stages by characterizing it as related to "trivial things." In contrast, she defined her father's advice as valuable, focusing on its application to the "more important" aspects of her life, such as her college education and career.

Children with one or more parents who had not studied or worked abroad often tended to overlook or undervalue the advice of these parents. David, a first-generation international student with parents who had never lived abroad, admitted that he did not communicate with them as much as his transnational friends did with their parents who had. "My mom sometimes calls me. My dad rarely calls me because he just believes that I'm doing well most of the time," he remarked.

During phone conversations with his mother, David appeared to receive more stress than comfort. He believed that it was challenging for both his mother and father to provide him with advice related to college or his career: "My mom occasionally asks about my grades, but she doesn't really understand the classes I'm taking [at my Ivy League college]. She's not familiar with my college life or the job market preparations I'm involved in, so I tend not to discuss those topics with her on the phone." He struggled to establish a rapport with his mother after leaving Korea for college, feeling that he had started to speak a "different language" than that of his parents: "If I need to discuss job market preparation with her, I have to simplify my language to terms she can understand, which can limit the depth of our conversation. For example, I doubt she would understand a term like *private equity fund*." He downplayed his mother's care accomplished via international calls, stating, "My mom calls me often and asks if I ate well, slept well, or took vitamins, and so on. [...] My mom always talks about my health. That's all."

Similarly, Emily, a daughter who considered herself very close to her mother, believed that her stay-at-home mother was unaware of the details of her career preparation, even when she provided a thorough explanation. "My mom always tells me, 'Do your best.' What else can she say to me? I know that she tries to understand what I'm doing as much as possible and [to] always be supportive," she said with a slight sense of frustration.

Hilary, who completed her schooling in several countries, offered a dual perspective on her parents' involvement, particularly when evaluating the roles of her father and mother. On one hand, her father took the lead in discussing important decisions. She mentioned that she "had to go through" her father's approval for crucial choices regarding her education and private life, such as trips with friends. "I need my dad's approval for almost everything, so that's why I talk to my dad first," she explained.

Given her father's extensive experience abroad as a businessperson, Hilary did not question his deep involvement in her adult life. Simultaneously, she positioned her mother in a secondary role and perceived her mother's input as minor or merely supportive. "After explaining everything to my dad, I usually feel exhausted, so I don't reexplain everything to my mom. So my mom gets to know the result only at the end," she confessed. According to her, her mother was someone with whom she could share "fun moments." She elaborated, saying, "I go shopping with her when I'm home [in Korea] for the summer. That's how we interact."

Mothers' Supervision of Children's Private Lives

Children saw their close relationship with their mothers as both beneficial and challenging. Some mothers were criticized for how they managed their children's daily nonacademic lives. Maternal calls, texts, and emails included not just words of encouragement but also concerns and advice about their children's health, which some children found overly detailed and repetitive.

Aaron, like many other sons, had mixed feelings about the emotional care he received from his mother during his study abroad. While he genuinely appreciated her "cheerleading," he often disregarded her advice and couldn't help but complain about certain aspects of their conversations: "She still asks me if I'm eating well while I'm in college. It's the main topic of our conversations these days. Honestly, I don't think she needs to ask about that anymore since I'm all grown up now!" He understood his mother's messages as a sign of sincere love and care, but at the same time, he found them somewhat intrusive to his adult life. Considering himself capable of taking care of himself after studying abroad for a long period, he felt he no longer needed such close supervision.

Health was not the only topic of "long lectures" from mothers. Sometimes, these conversations reflected maternal surveillance applied to manage children's friendships. Rachel, recalling her days at a U.S. boarding high school, discussed how her mother supervised her social network: "My mom was worrying about me quite often. She didn't like some of my friends, who she thought were not that diligent. She once called one of my teachers and asked if they affected me in any negative way. I did not think any of my friends were a bad influence. I just wanted to have some fun with my friends in our free time."

Henry was another child who felt his mother sometimes tried to exert tight control over his free time even after he entered college. "She constantly tells me [on the phone] not to do drugs or cigarettes. [. . .] Oh, she also tells me not to cheat on my girlfriend," Henry shared, laughing. He considered this advice unnecessary, believing that he behaved well enough.

Although he sometimes found it uncomfortable, Henry tried to frame his mother's advice as useful guidance for his private life, distinguishing her role from his father's. He didn't question the division between his parents' roles, stating, "My dad gives a lot of advice on my career path, so she naturally takes care of other things. I think they have a perfect balance."

When talking about dating, many children took a defensive approach, often avoiding "too-specific" discussions about their lives abroad with their mothers. For instance, Henry, despite valuing his mother's "cheerful voice" during their calls, was careful about what he shared. He explained, "In phone calls with my mother, I generally mention aspects of my private life, including the person I'm dating, but I avoid going into details. I try to keep those conversations brief."

Greg, an only son who took pride in his close relationship with his mother, recounted a more detailed conflict that arose regarding dating: "[Back in high school,] I flunked an AP exam because I was spending way too much time with my girlfriend at the time. My mom had always joked that I should never, ever have a girlfriend during high school, so she had no idea about my then-girlfriend. When she finally found out, I was just glad she didn't flip out. [*Laughs.*] She didn't like my ex-girlfriend much, but she really likes my current girlfriend." Greg knew exactly how his mom felt about his dating life. "My mom is pretty straightforward about my girlfriends. She doesn't hesitate to say, 'I don't like her,'" he said.

Children often described the discerning attitudes of mothers toward their children's dating partners and social circles. George, for instance, contrasted his parents' perspectives on his future partner, saying, "My dad advises me to find someone I truly love. [. . .] My mom insists on finding someone who can handle my temper. She believes I need that kind of support from a part-ner." Despite this, he felt his parents were relatively open-minded compared to his friends' parents. For instance, he mentioned that some parents strongly expected their children to find someone who had a similar educational experi-ence abroad, a requirement he found excessive.

More daughters than sons expressed frustration about their mothers' guid-ance or supervision of their private lives. Emily, for example, disclosed that she didn't share much about her college life abroad with her mother. She felt her mother's concern had intensified since her departure to the United States and described their phone conversations as "increasingly nagging." With a chuckle, she noted, "She doesn't like me walking around at night. But at the same time, she wants me to have a relationship!" Emily lightened her response by framing it as a "joke," her way of understanding such advice as a reflection of her mother's care. She added that her father rarely inquired about her private life, seeing it as a sign of his "coolness."

Another daughter, Jennifer, an Ivy League student in New York, also voiced her unease with her mother's tendency to monitor all the details of her relationships. "Whenever I go out [during breaks in Korea], I have to report who I'm meeting," she noted. She felt her mother was especially sensitive about her dating life, likely because she was her daughter rather than her son. Her comment reflected the prevalent belief in Korean culture that marriage holds greater significance for women than for men: "My mom doesn't outright tell me, 'Don't date anyone,' but if she finds out about my boyfriend, she'll say something like, 'You guys seem like good friends.' Then I'll tell her, 'Mom, we're actually in a relationship.' And she'll just respond, 'Oh, well, you're still young, so it's more like a friendship anyway.'"

Jennifer shared the kind of partner her mother envisions for her future. "My mom always tells me to find a Korean guy here at college who's completed his military service,"[17] she said. She even shared one of her mother's "not-so-funny" jokes that she felt revealed her mother's true feelings: "Sometimes, my mom jokes, 'Don't date anyone who goes to any other colleges in New York besides Ivy League!'"

Many mothers seemed to use the strategy of exposing their children to simi-larly educated friends and potential partners as a way to perpetuate privilege across generations. Interestingly, this role was more often taken on by moth-ers than fathers. For instance, Jennifer recognized that her mother's interest in her dating life was aimed at maintaining and advancing class privilege. Despite this clear understanding, she did not show a strong inclination to challenge or reject her mother's efforts.

Unusually Tangible Paternal Involvement

Fathers' Early Involvement as "Good Cops"

While there were few instances where children described their fathers as deeply involved in their early education, fathers were generally not criticized for this in children's memories. Some children recalled their fathers teaching them subjects such as math or science, tasks their mothers rarely took on. However, in most cases, children remembered their fathers as being "too busy" to be extensively involved in their early education, a reality they accepted without much question. This mirrors societal norms that place primary responsibility for children's education on mothers. Consequently, many children did not express surprise or disappointment at their fathers' more passive role in their early education.

Children perceived their fathers as fulfilling the role of the "good cop," in stark contrast to their mothers, who played the "bad cop" by diligently, and sometimes excessively, managing their daily schedules during childhood. Critiquing his mother's approach to his early education, Ethan said, "I was quite stressed out because my mom pushed me quite often. I think she expected a lot from me." Conversely, he described his father as "much more chill," stating, "My dad wanted to teach me how to stay healthy, so he asked me to work out constantly. That was all. Except for that, he didn't give me any specific guidance."

Daughters expressed similar sentiments. Fondly recalling her father's sympathetic words, Jennifer said, "My dad didn't like me studying until late at night. Whenever he saw me tired, he would say, 'Hey, don't study too hard. You will do well on the test no matter what.'" She believed her father's role was to relieve her from the "pressure of perfection" that she had felt from an early age. While her mother managed her rigorous schedule of *hagwons* and tutors, she viewed her father's conciliatory role as a way to prevent potential conflicts between herself and her mother.

Children tended to perceive their fathers' "good cop" role as generous and humane, especially when they felt their mothers were "too intense" about early education. Emily, who attended elementary school in California for a few years due to her father's overseas assignment, recounted the "special" private education her mother arranged for her upon their return to Korea: "After I came back [from the United States], I went to an English supplementary school just for returnee kids. Oh, I hated it! Everyone there had spent several years abroad, so their English was way better than mine. The classes were just too intense." She compared her mother and father in terms of their reactions to her "sniveling." "My dad finally understood how much I hated it, so he told me to quit immediately. My mom disagreed with him, but he reassured me that it was OK to quit if I didn't like it," she said. Although she did not perceive either of her parents critically, she credited her father more for alleviating her mother's educational fervor, something she genuinely appreciated.

In children's narratives, the role of disciplining was more often attributed to fathers than mothers. Many children recalled that even their "good cop" fathers could be strict at times, yet few harbored any resentment about the discipline they received. Instead, they interpreted it as their fathers teaching them good manners or promoting a healthy lifestyle: getting up early, working out regularly, and behaving well toward others. They appreciated their fathers willingly taking on that disciplinary role, seeing it as a responsibility typically associated with a parent who had ample experience in society rather than one confined to the home.

Julia fondly recalled her father's generosity, stating, "My dad rarely disciplined me, even when I did poorly on a test. He was happy if I did my best." Her only memory of a father-daughter conflict suggests that she perceived her father's discipline as limited to moments of moral guidance: "When I lied about something, he lectured me on the importance of honesty. But that was the only time he was mad at me. Other than that, he never disciplined me."

Using similar terms, Eric elaborated on his father's "tiger-like" characteristics. In his narratives, the term "tiger" connoted resoluteness and authority rather than pressure or violence. He did not feel his father pushed him to study hard; instead, he remembered his father being strict about manners for a good reason. He said, "My dad was kind most of the time, but he disciplined me firmly when I misbehaved. He only got upset with me in those situations." Eric highly valued such discipline, stating, "It was very effective." In this way, Eric naturally attributed the role of moral teacher, which is commonly associated with male household heads, to his father.

Children from relatively less privileged families, with parents who had never studied abroad, shared a similar perspective. David, who began his education abroad relatively late at twenty, did not recall his father's significant involvement in his early education. He even perceived himself and his father as "not that close." Nevertheless, he expressed great respect for his father, noting, "[My father] made me a decent person." David added, "My father wanted me to be a good person more than a smart one. He never pushed me to be successful or famous. His only wish was for me to grow up with strong character." While David's admiration for his father's integrity resonated with the values of his more affluent peers, he rarely cited his father's academic or career accomplishments as a defining example. This distinction set him apart from many of the other children in this chapter.

Fathers as "Study Abroad Counselors"

Children acknowledged that their fathers' academic involvement increased as they began their education abroad. Many stated that at this time, their fathers, rather than their mothers, took the lead in preparing for school interviews and occasionally communicated with school administrators or teachers. To a significant extent, children believed they needed direct support from their fathers to gain admission to elite U.S. colleges, especially when preparing their applications in Korea. This went against the public perception of "education manager mothers" meticulously overseeing their children's education—a role typically associated with women in Korean families, not men.

Jennifer, whose father attended a U.S. graduate school, discussed how her father took the lead in initiating her and her brother's education abroad: "One day, my dad asked us if we wanted to go to a U.S. boarding school. At first, we said no. But he didn't give up and kept persuading us. He even gave us a book titled something like *America's Top 100 Boarding Schools*, and it was all marked and underlined with the schools he had picked out." The suggestion surprised her, and perhaps her brother too, but she tried to rationalize it, seeing it as a natural consequence of her father's transnational life trajectory. Eventually, she grew to appreciate her father for actively guiding her toward pursuing education abroad.

Jake was another child who accepted his father's increased involvement without question. He observed his father becoming more engaged in his education than his mother upon his departure to the United States. He attributed his father's this to the educational gap between his father and mother: His father had earned an MBA from a U.S. university, whereas his well-educated mother had studied only in Korea. He explained, "My dad speaks English much better than my mom does and knows more of my teachers. My mom can speak a little English, but my dad travels abroad frequently for work, so he's more familiar with life overseas. When they visited my school for parent weekends, my dad handled the big important matters while my mom took care of the smaller details." Here, Jake drew a sharp contrast between his parents, framing his father's transnational resources such as fluent English and knowledge of the U.S. school system as valuable parental assets. In doing so, he normalized and justified his father's increasing involvement in guiding his education abroad. At the same time, he perceived his mother, who had never studied overseas, as less qualified to be involved. To Jake and many other children, the parent with more firsthand transnational experiences was seen as the "better guide" for navigating studying abroad.

Jake's family was not the only case illustrating father-led advocacy for overseas education. Henry, whose professor-father had taught as an exchange professor at a U.S. college, identified him as the best help for his U.S. college applications, especially since his selective Korean high school "did not help [him] boost [his] résumé." When Jake had to enhance his application on his own, his father, with his high English proficiency, provided him with substantial assistance: "Most of the information [about extracurricular activities] was online, so my dad did a lot of research for me. I was swamped with AP classes and didn't have time to look it all up myself. He discovered application deadlines and made sure to remind me about them." Henry found his father's direct support proactive and productive, whereas he felt his mother usually gathered education-related information from other mothers. Despite genuinely appreciating both parents, he attributed more credit to his father's firsthand knowledge compared to his mother's reliance on secondhand information.

Mia elaborated on her father's assistance with her U.S. college applications, contrasting it with her mother's involvement:

> My dad's help is very precise. For instance, after I met with a college counselor in high school and got some feedback on my SOP [statement of purpose], I talked to my parents that night about what the counselor suggested. My mom comforted me with a pat on the shoulder, saying, "You're doing great. It's all part of the learning process." She even shared some of her own experiences that might be relevant to my situation. Meanwhile, my dad was all about specifics. He gave me a clear timeline for what needed to be done next and asked, "What's the next step? When should the new deadline be?" That's just how he operates in his own life. He's incredibly organized.

Mia normalized the difference between her parents by framing it as an intrinsic and unchangeable gender disparity. Despite appreciating her mother's empathy, Mia credited her father more for her academic achievements.

The father's increasing educational involvement appeared to smooth out the father-child relationship. William described how this hands-on educational support strengthened their father-son bond. He vividly recalled how his father assisted him with his application for admission to a U.S. boarding school, speaking with a nostalgic tone: "While applying to multiple U.S. boarding schools, my father was a huge help, and we ended up talking a lot. He took me on all the school tours. Although we had an aunt in the U.S. who joined us for part of the tour, she got busy, and my dad and I finished the rest by ourselves. That's when I really felt close to him." William believed that his father's experience abroad, particularly with U.S. schools, offered both practical guidance and emotional support during his application process. School tours abroad, which many children went on with their fathers, were the most representative events in which they could vividly feel their fathers' care and support. Like William, many children recalled these tours as being led by their fathers rather than their mothers, suggesting their dualistic perception of their parents' roles in their educational journeys.

Fathers' Influence on Children's Career Plans

The career success of their fathers as elite professionals led high-achieving children in this chapter to deeply value their fathers' career-related advice. Many children described their fathers as their closest role models. This admiration often began early in life. Sarah, who majors in cognitive science, explained why she aspired to follow the same career path as her father: "My dad is a brain specialist, and his work sparked my interest in neurology. Back in elementary school, our school offered a lot of hands-on learning activities, like shadowing our parents at work. I used to visit his lab [at his hospital] frequently and play with brain models, which really fueled my curiosity about the field." As Sarah grew older, she began to grasp the challenges of achieving the same level of success and "hard work" as her father. Still, despite genuinely appreciating her mother's care, Sarah did not include her mother, who opted out of a career, among her role models.

Several children referred to their fathers as competent and capable. For instance, Hailey described her father, the CEO of an IT company, as "innately hardworking." She mentioned, "He is quite passionate about his job. He even sketches new product ideas on weekends." Hailey did not perceive her father's dedication to work negatively. Instead, she admired it as a key factor contributing to his success: "It's fascinating to see how dedicated my dad is to his work. I used to think he was easygoing and laid-back, but he's actually quite the opposite. He's passionate about his job, especially when it comes to collaborating with his team and achieving goals together."

More sons than daughters explicitly idolized their fathers as their role models. Ethan, a would-be start-up CEO, expressed that his father was "one of [his] biggest supporters." "My father always wishes the best for me, standing behind me rather than leading me from the front," he remarked.

Ethan further explained his eagerness to learn from his CEO father, who managed his business operations in both the United States and Korea: "He has faced many challenges and experienced both the highs and lows of life. I truly admire his perseverance. Even though he's getting older, he continues to work tirelessly. He has a big vision and always looks ahead, with a keen sense of where investments and resources are heading." He added, "I grew up thinking my father was so cool" and expressed deep respect for his father, whom he described as a "self-made" businessman. Ethan admired his ambition and diligence, which he believed were key traits contributing to his father's business success, and he aspired to emulate these qualities himself.

Sam also deeply appreciated his CEO father's influence, crediting much of his academic success to the lessons learned from him. "My father built his business through numerous challenges. Even during his doctoral program in the United States, he juggled multiple jobs to support me and my mom," he explained. Sam regarded his father's achievements as a motivating factor for his own future. "When I look at him, I see the true meaning of hard work. He's the reason I put in so much effort in school," he added.

As children transitioned into adulthood, they increasingly recognized the significant impact of paternal support on their lives abroad, particularly their career pursuits. Children recounted the significant role their fathers played in assisting with their career preparation, such as guiding them in choosing a field of study or securing internships. Fathers' guidance—communicated through daily conversations via calls, texts, and emails spanning geographical distances—frequently shaped the career paths chosen by their children.

William, for example, attributed his career choice largely to his father, an executive member of a Korean conglomerate, who had a substantial impact on his decision-making process: "My father had many friends and acquaintances in the consulting field. Even though he worked in general affairs, he was always interested in consulting. He often talked to me about the consulting world and his aspirations in that area." William held his father's career in high esteem and his father as a valuable source of advice for shaping his own future path. He perceived the career achievement gap between his parents as pivotal, considering his father a superior advisor due to his active professional engagement. Conversely, he minimized the influence of his stay-at-home mother on his career choice, noting, "My father's input carries more weight than my mom's because my father is still actively working, whereas my mom is not."

Yoana, another child who detailed her father's career-related assistance, confided that her doctor-father helped her secure an internship by leveraging his professional connections, even in a field outside his own expertise: "How can students like me find a good internship on their own? Initially, I was frustrated when I didn't have any help with my search. [. . .] I eventually found one with my dad's assistance. He had a friend working in finance who helped me out." She genuinely appreciated the hands-on support in career preparation from her socially successful father. Her remark also implies that, to some extent, children in her social circle consider paternal career-related assistance almost inevitable and necessary.

This career-related support frequently depended on fathers' extensive, predominantly male-centered networks. Like Yoana, many children confessed that their high-status professional fathers introduced them to contacts who could offer internship opportunities or provide detailed career advice. Children viewed this paternal support as an exceptionally valuable "bridge."

Rachel, whose father held an executive position in a major Korean corporation, openly elaborated on the career-related support she received from him: "My dad knows a lot of businesspeople and executives, so he reaches out to them on my behalf. [. . .] When I was looking for internships, he was a huge help. Although he wasn't thrilled about my choice to work at a small start-up, he kept supporting me and eventually helped me [land an internship there]." Rachel wanted to explore job opportunities in either the United States or Korea. Her father, who had connections in workplaces in both countries, seemed to be the "go-to person" for practical and emotional career-related assistance.

Hailey, another daughter who highly valued her father's career-related support, didn't delve much into her mother's role as a job counselor with a doctoral degree from a U.S. university. Instead, she highlighted how her CEO father facilitated her mother's work: "My dad is in the IT field, so he is proficient in using SNS [social networking services]. He recommended my mom to use SNS for her work." Work-related discussions in the family, for her, were primarily led by her father rather than her mother, despite her mother's extensive work experience.

If children felt they had not received enough paternal support, they pitied themselves. Walter was among the few who sensed this lack, despite respecting his father's successful career as a prosecutor. He said, "Even when I talk about what I'm thinking about for my future job, he doesn't seem to be able to relate to me. I can't learn much in such circumstances. [. . .] I wish I could hear more about his own work instead."

Owen was another son who felt less supported by his parents during the college application process, despite both of them being teachers themselves; his father taught at a Korean university, and his mother was a former high school teacher: "Some of my friends got to join research projects with their professor-fathers or their father's colleagues as assistants. [. . .] I managed to find some opportunities on my own, like starting a new club as chair, but I always wished I had more support from my parents [for extracurricular activities]." He added, "I sometimes felt defeated." Owen expressed that while he found neither of his parents helpful for his résumé, his frustration seemed to be directed more toward his father than his mother. This sentiment might stem from the common trend among children, including himself, to appreciate their fathers' support more than their mothers' in later stages of their education. He admitted that his parents' limited involvement in his extracurricular activities occasionally led to parent-child conflicts, albeit not overtly. He perceived direct parental support for college applications as standard, if not expected.

Emotional Support from Fathers: Diverging Views

Children presented diverse views about emotional support from fathers, with about one-third elaborating on how much their fathers loved and cheered them up (comparable to the way they described their mothers). Henry was a child who found himself emotionally well-connected with his father. He spoke about how his professor-father demonstrated his deep love for his family despite his busy work schedule: "My dad spends a lot of time at his office, which is quite far from home. When he's really busy, he even sleeps there sometimes. Recently, when I visited his office, I noticed he had a bunch of old family photos on the wall. He also occasionally sends us pictures of his office through texts." Henry believed that his father's academic job allowed him to maintain a family-oriented lifestyle more easily compared to fathers with stricter schedules. "He could use his time relatively flexibly, so if he wanted to be involved, he had time for that," Henry said. This flexibility led him to view academic jobs positively.

Yoana's narrative about paternal love was more detailed. She fondly recalled her father's warm words of encouragement regarding her ambition to attend an Ivy League college:

> He always encouraged me to follow my own path. [. . .] When I was anxious about the tuition for an Ivy League school, he reassured me not to worry. He said he would cover the cost and insisted that I shouldn't stress about it. He even told me, "I'd be happy if you decided to be a stay-at-home mom after graduating from an Ivy League school. Your college experience will make you a very special stay-at-home mom." He was so confident that I'd enjoy the Ivy League experience.

Yoana appreciated her father's warmhearted character and saw it as a major source of his unwavering support for her Ivy League education, perhaps even more than his financial capacity to cover the high cost of college. In line with how children viewed their fathers as "good cops," she valued her father's approach of not explicitly stating expectations for her career achievements.

Children of fathers who had studied or worked abroad often viewed their fathers' overseas experiences as essential sources of both academic and emotional support. Hailey, whose CEO father earned his undergraduate and graduate degrees in the United States, discussed which of her parents understood her life abroad better, especially off-campus. "My mom isn't aware of how often U.S. college kids drink and party, but my dad understands because he also attended a U.S. college," she explained.

While criticizing her mother's monitoring of her activities outside of classes, Hailey praised her father's "good cop" role, which she attributed to their shared experience of attending college in the United States: "Whenever my mom and I clash over drinking and partying, my dad always supports me. Having worked outside the home for so long, he gets why socializing and going to parties are important, while my mom doesn't quite understand. Because of this, I avoid discussing the details of my social life with her." Hailey naturally identified with her father, particularly in her aspirations for social success. Despite both parents being professionals, Hailey seemed to unconsciously assign higher value to her father's career and achievements compared to her mother's, reflecting a widespread perception among children that professional careers are more closely associated with men than women. She also noted a subtle distinction in her parents' education: Her father started his studies abroad as an undergraduate, while her mother began hers in graduate school. This distinction, she believed, forged a unique bond between her and her father, prompting her to confide more about her life abroad with him than with her mother.

James, a graduate of a U.S. boarding school, was another child who deeply valued his father's emotional support throughout his extensive education abroad. Yearning for a closer bond with his parents, he cherished his father's efforts to foster a strong father-son relationship:

> While I'm in Korea [during school breaks], my father cancels most of his appointments to spend the night with me. At dinner, he discusses what he hopes to teach me as a father and is eager to hear about my life at school [in the United States]. If I were attending college in Korea, he could support me directly, but since I'm in the United States, he can't be there. That's why he makes an effort to spend as much time as possible with me when I'm in Korea.

As James matured, he came to recognize and deeply appreciate his father's consistent efforts to strengthen their relationship. Contrary to the stereotype of elite men being consumed by their careers, his father prioritized allocating time for meaningful father-son bonding, which James valued.

Moreover, James internalized his father's high expectations for his academic performance and future career achievements: "My father wants me to surpass his own successes. He graduated from the top college in Korea and worked tirelessly to achieve everything he has. I am incredibly proud of him. He is a remarkable man, but he encourages me to achieve even more than he has." James emphasized that his father's approach was not about pushing him but rather setting high expectations, which became a motivating factor that spurred James in his academic studies. "I want to live up to his expectations," he happily remarked.

James also reflected on the evolving dynamics between himself and his parents: "From the midpoint of high school [abroad], I began focusing on my mom's emotional well-being. She was once the one who took care of me, but now I feel that I support her emotionally more than she supports me. As I get older, I also find myself having more meaningful conversations with my dad, such as sharing a beer and reminiscing about the past when I'm home in Korea." Here, James drew a dichotomy between his mother, whom he perceived as becoming more dependent, akin to a child, and his father, an independent adult with whom he could have an equal relationship, like a friend.

However, not every child shared such positive views of their fathers. A significant number of sons, more so than daughters, revealed the complexities in their relationships with their fathers. They underwent negotiation processes with their fathers (more so than with their mothers), particularly regarding major decisions or career choices. Despite not always agreeing with their fathers, few outright rebelled. Instead, they sought to understand the reasoning behind their fathers' advice. While most children followed their fathers' recommendations, some mentioned persuading them and advocating for specific schools or majors. Overall, children generally saw father-child conflicts as both resolvable and a natural part of contemporary family dynamics.

For example, Jack, a computer science major who frequently praised his father's career at a Korean conglomerate, discreetly revealed a significant conflict he had with his father. When Jack expressed his desire to take a year off from college to start a company, his father, who had initially been supportive, unexpectedly became angry: "I never knew my dad could say no so firmly. His response was a definite no. He rarely said no to me before, so it was a big shock. He wanted me to finish college as quickly as possible and didn't understand why I wanted to take a break to start a company, even in Korea. He believed I should start my career in the United States." Jack remained resolute in his choice to temporarily halt his college education abroad in order to join a start-up company in Korea. Nevertheless, he continued to feel remorseful about disagreeing with his highly admired father and earnestly sought to understand his perspective, seeing his father's long tenure at a major corporation as proof of his cleverness.

A few daughters expressed similar mixed feelings, noting that their fathers' intense involvement in their adult lives could sometimes feel overwhelming. Miranda, who completed her education in three different countries, described her father's expectations of her as "too much," which occasionally created a sense of distance between them: "The high expectations from people around me, including my dad's, sometimes weighed heavily on me. Everyone seemed to assume I would be accepted into one of the best colleges in the world, which was an enormous pressure. While my mom advised me not to worry too much, my dad was different. He had a specific college in mind that he wanted me to attend." She recalled the day she received acceptance to her first-choice Ivy League school, though it wasn't the same as her father's preference:

> Due to the time difference, the result [of my college application] came out at 5:00 a.m. [in the South Asian country where my family lived]. I was so scared of not being accepted. I didn't want to see the result first thing in the morning, because I thought it would ruin the whole day. However, my dad woke me up at 5:00 a.m. and asked me to check the outcome as soon as it was released. I showed my reluctance, but he insisted and begged me to view the result immediately.

While Miranda appreciated her father's multifaceted support, she admitted that his expectations could sometimes feel suffocating. Despite this, she aimed not to overly criticize his enthusiasm for her education, reflecting, "That was the only time my dad truly frustrated me."

Henry, an aspiring entrepreneur, also spoke of a conflict with his father over his career aspirations. His father, an engineering professor, wanted him to follow in his footsteps and pursue a career as a college professor: "My dad wants me to earn money while teaching at a college, just as he does, by collaborating with companies while teaching. He believes I can follow the same path. However, I honestly don't see the point in teaching if I'm not particularly interested in it. I'm more passionate about business than about teaching or researching." This anecdote stood out because it contrasted with the rest of his narratives, which consistently reflected his deep respect and appreciation for his father. Although he did not mention any overt conflicts, he acknowledged that his father's detailed expectations sometimes did not align with his own goals.

Despite occasional father-child conflicts in later years, children continued to highly value their father's significant involvement. Few questioned the influential role their fathers played in their upbringing. Instead, they acknowledged its value and sought to perceive it as largely beneficial, especially within their elite transnational context. They appreciated that such profound paternal involvement and investment in their successful life abroad was rare and highly valuable.

Children's Rosy Views of Their Families

During their upbringing, the children in this chapter encountered extended periods of geographical separation from family members while pursuing education abroad. Many, particularly those from highly transnational backgrounds, discovered that their bond with their families grew stronger rather than weaker. Rachel, who left Korea at age fifteen for a U.S. boarding school, emphasized the profound importance of "family" in her life and in the lives of her family members: "I've always been taught that family is the most important thing in the world. We [my family] still discuss our family a lot."

Yoana regarded her family as a "sanctuary" where she believed she "could be forgiven for anything." She attributed her parents' kindness to the infrequency of their face-to-face meetings, stating, "Because we cannot meet often, they are typically gentle and caring toward me. They always show their concern." Her story exemplifies how many children tend to depict their transnational families as supportive and positive, contrasting with society's pathological view.

Sam, who also underscored the importance of family in his life, praised not only his own efforts but also those of his parents in preserving family connections. He admired their dedication and thoughtful approach to nurturing family bonds: "Whenever I have time, I make an effort to visit my parents in Korea. When I'm home, my mom and dad always do their best to have dinner with me unless they have a serious appointment. I also enjoy these dinners, so while I'm there, I try to limit my dinners with friends to less than once a week."

The effort toward family bonding was notable in other children's stories as well. While they took pride in this dedication, they didn't find it unusual; instead, it was considered a norm within their community. Sean noticed that many of his friends who studied abroad shared similar values centered around family: "My friends from [U.S. boarding] high schools also place a high value on their families, perhaps because they've been away from their parents for so long. Many of them are eager to start their own families sooner rather than later, and I'm no exception. Even though I'm only twenty-three, I want to get married within the next three years."

Aware of the public's concerns about geographically separated families, children strived to challenge these perceptions by normalizing their own loving family dynamics and assuming that others also experience similar closeness. William represents this optimistic view widely shared among the children in this chapter: "My family has always had a wonderful relationship. I was very close to my mom until I finished middle school, and after I came to the United States [for high school], I had many opportunities to bond with my father. Everything has worked so harmoniously! I feel incredibly lucky for that."

With few exceptions, usually from less affluent or transnational backgrounds, the narratives of children in this chapter collectively paint a homogeneous picture of elite Korean transnational families—perceived as rational, efficient, and harmonious. Any differences or inequalities within these families were frequently minimized or omitted in their narratives, reflecting their (perhaps elites' in general)—tendency to view achieving familial bliss as a primary goal in life.

Children's Dichotomy of Public Fathering and Private Mothering

Children in this chapter expressed gratitude for their parents' deep involvement, portraying it as crucial and supportive. Within their circle of high-achieving Korean children abroad, substantial parental support seemed to be the norm. However, they clearly differentiated between their mothers' and fathers' roles, expressing gratitude to each for distinct reasons. These perspectives were heavily influenced by gender norms that assigned specific roles to women and men in Korean families.

Across genders, children perceived their mothers as managers of their early education and family well-being. While acknowledging their mothers' significant role in their early education, they tended to downplay the work by characterizing it as a collaborative effort, perpetuating the stereotype of "Korean manager moms." Instead, they more enthusiastically credited their mothers for maternal support—for providing nourishing meals, attentive listening, and being supportive cheerleaders. These forms of support are perceived as gendered attributes associated with women's roles, both by the children and society as a whole, often resulting in their contributions being undervalued compared to the work of men.

In contrast, children held a more understanding and appreciative view of their elite fathers' involvement, acknowledging its rarity and excellence. They expressed gratitude and placed special value on their fathers' deep engagement in their upbringing, despite demanding careers. Children's profound appreciation for this should be understood within a highly class-conscious context, considering their fathers' extensive educational and professional experiences abroad—pathways the children themselves have embraced. In such cases, children tended to accord greater recognition to their fathers' engagement, even if they did not always agree with their fathers' suggestions regarding academic majors or career paths.

While scholars have noted the connection between elite men's classed resources, such as global finance careers, and their active fathering,[18] there has been limited exploration of their children's class-specific respect and appreciation for this involvement. The narratives of children in this chapter prompt an intriguing discussion on how social class either enables or constrains the capacity of fathers to foster bonds with their children and earn their respect through engaged fatherhood.

Most children's optimistic views of their elite transnational families did not explicitly acknowledge or challenge the gendered division of parenting they perceived. Instead, they reinforced normative roles and expectations of women as caregivers and men as decision-makers, both within and outside the home. In their narratives, diligent and successful fathers often assumed roles linked to the public sphere, such as advising on college choices, career paths, and imparting social rules. Conversely, mothers, regardless of their educational or professional backgrounds, were predominantly depicted in the private sphere as homemakers and nurturers. This dynamic reinforces the idea that the public sphere is inherently masculine, while the private sphere is associated with femininity.[19] Despite the children's genuine gratitude toward their mothers, their narratives positioned their fathers—the eldest and most successful men in their nuclear families—at the apex of authority, thereby amplifying inequalities between couples within elite Korean transnational families.

2

Who Learns to Become Cosmopolitan Better?

Elite Western colleges, especially those in the United States, have consistently been high in world university rankings. This may help explain why they have become a magnet for international study abroad programs. Today, Korean students make up a significant share of the international student population at many U.S. colleges.[1] Given the familial and societal expectations surrounding the "Asian Global"[2] phenomenon, many high-achieving Korean students have sought and acquired education in the United States. To describe this well-known phenomenon between the West and the East in education, some have adopted the term *transnational student migration*.[3]

Academic studies on such student migrants have been limited. By adopting "culture shock theories,"[4] many scholars have explored the psychological effects of the foreign environment on Asian students' academic performances. Similarly, so-called adjustment studies have tracked the progress of Asian international students, whether linear or not, in terms of their adaptation to the host environment.[5] However, the processes by which students acquire transnational mobility, as well as the varying ways they experience and interpret this migration, remain underexplored.

Gender differences warrant special attention, as gender significantly shapes education. For instance, it influences how students assess themselves, with students across genders often perceiving men as more employable than women.[6] This impact persists and even intensifies in transnational contexts, where gender interacts with race and migration statuses to shape students' utilization of education. In one study, migrant men in U.K. schools who experienced trauma redefined themselves as having potential by utilizing the concept of diaspora,[7] while in another, the voices of women of color were frequently silenced, and their work as students was often undervalued in the context of U.S. graduate education.[8]

Despite these inequalities, women now outnumber men in higher education in many societies. The elite diaspora is becoming increasingly feminized, with more women engaging in cross-continental migration to pursue their achievements.[9] Asian women are no exception: About 80 percent of Japanese students abroad are women,[10] as are roughly 60 percent of Korean students[11] and nearly half of Chinese students.[12] In contrast to the traditional preference for sons in Asian societies, contemporary Korean and other East Asian parents, particularly those with resources, are now eager to support higher education for their daughters.[13] While social class is often emphasized as the primary factor driving the demand for education abroad, the influence of gender remains underexplored.

Drawing on students' narratives about their job and family aspirations, this chapter illustrates how gender, intersecting with class, creates differences between daughters and sons with similar levels of education abroad. To theorize these gender differences, I incorporate some theoretical frameworks about identities and the construction of the self in postmodern societies—Beck's "normal/choice biography"[14] and Gidden's "reflexive project of the self,"[15] which are "simultaneously organized around the modalities of marriage and family."[16] According to Beck, "normal biographies," typically observed among the working class, follow traditional trajectories dictated by gender and socioeconomic status. This entails men fulfilling the role of primary breadwinner, while women assume the responsibility of being the main caregivers for their families. In contrast, "choice biographies," often associated with the middle-to-upper class, afford individuals the freedom to determine their aspirations and actions. This leads to the development of a "reflective self-project," where individuals construct a narrative about themselves and grapple with essential questions such as what they should do, how they should behave, and who they should become.[17]

This chapter also embraces the concept of "agency for becoming," including Tran and Vu's four unique forms of "agency in mobility" that mirror the lived experiences of international students.[18] Here, *agency* denotes "an individual or collective capacity to act with intentionality in line with rational choices and in response to a given circumstance."[19] These frameworks serve to portray the students in this chapter as active agents capable of intentional action, with the potential to not only transform their own lives but also influence the world around them.

Sons' Classed Practices of "Agency for Becoming"

Strong Resistance to the "Broken" Korean Education

Majoring in subjects like biology, mathematics, economics, and engineering, almost all sons sought and believed they would achieve lucrative careers as CEOs, engineers, investment bankers, professors, or politicians. Their "dream jobs" reflect the tendency among Asian migrants to define a "good" education as one that leads to a few coveted, high-salaried, high-status professions, which represent the pinnacle of success in this frame.[20] However, men from more affluent and transnational families did not frame the ultimate goal of their education abroad solely in terms of acquiring a prestigious college degree and professional job. More than anything, they valued the opportunity to learn about and adapt to the competitive yet prosperous global world.

Many sons, especially those who started studying abroad early, considered their departure from Korea a crucial moment in their growth into a whole person. They believed Western schools were superior to Korean schools for various reasons. They perceived the competitive and authoritative culture of Korean schools as undesirable. For example, Aaron, who left Korea in his mid-teens to attend a Canadian high school, expressed sympathy toward his friends who completed all their schooling in Korea. He particularly appreciated that he did not attend multiple *hagwons* (private cram schools) while in Canada.

Drawing a stark contrast between students in Korea and himself, Aaron described his friends in Korea as "squirrels going round and round on a tread-mill": "The [Korean education] system puts students through a lot, and I'm not fond of it. [. . .] From my own experience and what I heard from my middle school teachers [in Korea], students attend school and *hagwon* without clear visions or purposes, except for a very few." Aaron tried to frame his negative educational experience in Korea as a structural problem of Korean society rather than an individual one. He particularly blamed the Suneung exam (the College Scholastic Ability Test for applying to Korean universities)[21] and the steep hierarchy among colleges as the core of the problem in Korean education. Seeing the Canadian school he attended as the opposite of those in Korea, he was thankful for the opportunity to "escape."

David was another son who strongly criticized the Korean education system based on his own experience. As a transfer student from a Korean university to an Ivy League college—a rare case—he remained in the Korean school system longer than any other student in this book. Having attended a Korean college for one semester, he could recount his senior year at a Korean high school, which he remembered as the most stressful period of his life: "While studying for the Suneung exam, I questioned myself daily—'Why am I doing this?' I still feel sorry for the twelfth graders in Korea who dedicate their entire senior year solely to preparing for the exam. They sacrifice all their high school years for this one test!" David found the exam almost meaningless. "I still don't know if the exam means anything important. […] I think [Korean] students waste their high school years because of the exam," he added. Having gone through the standardized college entrance system in Korea, he felt he had ample reasons to criticize it.

Similarly, Ethan, another U.S. boarding school graduate, elaborated on the "tough time" he experienced in Korea during childhood. He described Korean education as outdated and shortsighted, primarily due to its competitive and hierarchical nature, which he believed contributed to the low life satisfaction of Korean people. Praising the liberal culture of the selective U.S. boarding school he graduated from, he insisted on the necessity of educational reform in his home country. "Korean schools need to think about how to raise global citizens," he remarked.

Sons tended to frame their criticisms as constructively as possible, viewing the issues they encountered in Korean schools as societal rather than personal. Some contrasted the philosophy and curriculum of Korean education with that of elite Western education. Luke, a graduate of a selective Korean high school, discussed the qualitative differences between his applications to U.S. colleges and those to Korean colleges. "It was challenging to integrate the values of diversity and creativity into my portfolio [for U.S. college applications] with the activities I engaged in at a Korean school," he explained. Despite the support offered by Korean teachers in his "special class" for U.S. college applicants at his selective school, Luke felt that his application process could have been more effective and meaningful if he had attended a U.S. boarding school. He felt that elite U.S. schools offered a more humanitarian and well-rounded education, which included instruction in English, something he considered valuable for anyone.

Sons who had experienced long-term education abroad often portrayed Western schooling as a utopia. William described his time at a prestigious U.S. boarding school by highlighting it as a fun-filled experience with diverse nonacademic activities that he believed were impossible to replicate in Korea. "I loved my school. […] What I loved most was that I could play soccer for two hours every day," he said. A comparison between his experience in Korea and the United States highlights the differences William observed in school culture between the two countries: "I completed one semester at a Korean high school [before moving to a U.S. boarding school]. At the Korean school, I had to stay late every day to study after regular classes. In the United States, I finished my studies around 3:00 p.m., studying only half as much as I did in Korea but still more than most of my friends. Additionally, I participated in multiple extracurricular activities after classes." Generalizing his "suffocating" experience at a Korean school to Korea as a whole, he believed that a "free and fun" educational environment was only attainable outside his home country. "That's what made me cherish my days at a [U.S.] boarding school," he remarked.

Ethan shared similar memories, praising the diverse extracurricular activities he engaged in at a U.S. boarding school. "I had to manage my time effectively to participate in many activities, but it was all enjoyable. I had a wonderful time with my friends," he recounted. Ethan believed that compared to the monotonously test-oriented approach of Korean high schools, the curriculum at his boarding school was well balanced.

Ethan believed that the "well-roundedness" of the U.S. school's curriculum created a positive synergy with himself: "I'm quite good at multitasking, so managing my time wasn't a problem. I thrive in environments where I have to juggle multiple tasks rather than just focus on exam preparation. Engaging in sports and leadership activities provided me with a well-rounded growth experience. I believe these activities made me stronger. [. . .] That's why U.S. schooling fit me better than Korean schooling." Through diverse—and expensive—extracurricular activities, which were not yet common in Korean schools, graduates of U.S. boarding schools learned to embody privilege.[22]

Desire to Explore the "Wider World"

The enthusiastic reviews from sons who received an elite education abroad reflected a deep admiration for Western societies, where they spent their adolescence and early adulthood. In many of their narratives, the Western countries where they studied represented the "wider world" compared to their home country. They considered their education abroad valuable not only because they earned degrees from prestigious schools but also because the experience "broadened [their] horizons." They felt they had a unique opportunity to learn about a society that was relatively more diverse and expressive in terms of culture, race, and sexual orientation.

George began studying abroad in his mid-teens but recalled his time attending a Korean elementary school, describing the school's swimming club as the most "unjust" group he had ever encountered:

> We were all so young and just kids in the swimming club, but senior members regularly disciplined the juniors. My mom always insisted that I should never swear, no matter the situation. But one day after returning from the club, I swore badly, and my mom overheard. I can't even repeat what I said. [*Laughs.*] She was shocked to hear me swear, especially since I was only in first grade. She also got angry when she saw me bowing at a ninety-degree angle to second- and third-graders in the club, who were only one or two years older than me!

The swimming experience gave him a glimpse of Korean society's authoritative and hierarchical culture, which he found unbearable. This experience ultimately motivated him to insist on leaving Korea early.

Herbert shared a similar perspective on the cultural difference between Korean and U.S. schools. "I was always jealous of my friends who started living in the United States early," he said. "Schools abroad offer students much more freedom, and I envied that. [. . .] I think if I had started my education abroad earlier, I could have been much more cheerful. Even though it's been a while, I still remember the challenging time I had in high school [in Korea]." Herbert attributed his less-than-happy adolescence to Korea's rigid and competitive school culture, believing that cultural differences significantly shape individuals' characteristics. His narrative conveyed a sense of relief as he seized the opportunity to study abroad, albeit not as early as many of his peers.

Sons who began studying abroad early often believed they developed into "better people" through the curriculum of Western schools. In their narratives, being a "better" person typically involved embracing values and ethics such as creativity, diversity, and humanitarianism. Josh, whose family relocated to the United States for his and his siblings' education, mentioned that his parents deliberately chose California for its liberal environment. "[My parents] really wanted to raise liberal children," he explained. He particularly enjoyed his time at an alternative school in California where he not only studied academic subjects but also engaged in farming, tree planting, and gardening. Embracing his parents' educational philosophy, he valued the worldview this instilled in him, which he believed was more open-minded and value-oriented compared to that of students educated solely in Korea.

Jax also fondly recalled his days in a U.S. high school and appreciated the "free" atmosphere of the classroom. "I could ask as many questions as I wanted," he said. Jax remembered feeling apprehensive about asking questions in a Korean school, fearing being ignored or rejected. He attributed his cheerful character and leadership skills to the U.S. education he received, which he took great pride in.

Sean, who began studying abroad in high school, developed a deep affection for the city where he attended college—New York, which he considered the world's most diverse and cosmopolitan city. He elaborated on how his perspective evolved during his college years in the city: "[In New York,] I see gay couples on the street or at coffee shops every day. I've come to understand that their love is no different from my love for my girlfriend. [. . .] I've also met and gotten to know many Black friends on campus. [. . .] These interactions have broadened my perspective, I believe." Sean believed that studying at a college in New York helped him develop a tolerance for differences. He felt that he wouldn't have grown as much if he hadn't studied abroad. However, neither Sean nor other sons who studied abroad long-term mentioned what factors beyond academic efforts enabled them to thrive and develop in their "ideal" environment. The exclusiveness of such an environment remained a topic that was rarely discussed.

The contrasting views of these sons regarding educational opportunities at home versus abroad underscored a significant hierarchy between the West and their native country. Stephan, who started studying in the United States in middle school, believed that his long-term education abroad provided him with a broader—almost righteous—perspective on social issues, including climate change and racial justice. He attributed his social awareness to interactions with diverse people in a liberal environment abroad, which he felt was lacking in Korea.

In his narratives, Korea was portrayed as the antithesis of the broader world he experienced—narrow-minded and superficial, cultivating misguided perspectives about achievement and success. Criticizing the lack of diversity in people's aspirations in Korea, Stephan said, "Everyone [in Korea] thinks being a doctor is the best job, and that perspective never changes." At the time of his interview, he had secured an engineering job at a major IT company that would be the envy of many people. However, he harbored aspirations beyond just working for a renowned company: "My dream is to start a tech hardware company. [...] I believe people form relationships with the things they use, just as they do with other people. [...] By creating beautiful machines that people use every day, I aim to transform how people live." He saw making "meaningful changes to society" as a criterion for making life decisions, including career choices. Stephan expressed pride in distinguishing himself from many other Koreans, whom he believed prioritized wealth and success exclusively. He attributed his identity to his transnational upbringing, shaped by the elite U.S. education he received.

The strong preference and admiration for elite Western schools led some sons to dream of establishing similar institutions in Korea later in life. They saw this as a unique way to contribute to their home country. William was among them; he specifically mentioned his alma mater as a model for the school he envisioned building. "I saw a huge difference between the Korean and U.S. schools I attended. I loved my experience at my [U.S. boarding] school and wish there were more schools like that in Korea as well," he remarked.

Some of these aspirations seemed particularly viable, especially since, in certain instances, parents were already engaged in establishing schools, not only in Korea but also in underdeveloped countries in Central and South Asia. Sean, whose parents were involved in the education sector, had a definite vision of the type of school he aimed to establish in the future, ideally with the backing of his parents: "I want to offer a highly customized and high-quality education. My goal is to staff my school with excellent mentors, not just teachers. [...] I plan to emphasize English and other foreign languages in the curriculum and provide students with numerous opportunities to study abroad and experience other schools." William's and Sean's time in U.S. boarding schools bolstered their philanthropic aspirations, which intensified as they drew stark comparisons between U.S. and Korean schools. Additionally, their prestigious family backgrounds provided the support necessary to pursue their ambitious dreams.

Zeal for Transnational Career and Family

Legal status as a U.S. citizen or permanent resident significantly boosted children's ambitions for transnational mobility. Sons who were U.S. citizens or permanent residents (fifteen out of thirty-five) reported facing relatively fewer obstacles when applying for scholarships, jobs, and other opportunities while attending college in the United States. Holding a foreign nationality or residency status other than Korean acted as a significant class marker, even among wealthier families, creating its own level of disparity. These inequalities originated from familial backgrounds; in most cases, sons gained U.S. citizenship by birth during their parents'—primarily fathers'—study or work abroad.

Parents' occupations played a major role in determining their children's acquisition of U.S. permanent residency—wealthy professional parents, for example, could obtain this for their children via business investment programs. With minimal legal, cultural, and language barriers, these sons and daughters enjoyed the flexibility of choosing the location of their future careers and families. This tendency was particularly notable among sons.

Sam became a U.S. permanent resident through his CEO father's investment in the medical industry of the United States. "This country [the United States] is gathering competent people in the medical industry, so my dad was able to get U.S. permanent residency for my whole family," he recalled. At the time of his interview, Sam had received an offer from a major investment bank on Wall Street. He admitted that his legal status, paired with his Ivy League degree, gave him an edge in searching for jobs in the U.S. business field, which he found highly competitive: "Most of my male friends aim to work in investment banking or related fields, as they majored in economics or business. However, I'm the only one who secured a job during senior year, even among those who graduated from [U.S.] boarding schools. It's that difficult." Being a Korean citizen with U.S. permanent residency encouraged Sam to pursue a highly transnational career track. He aimed to gain work experience in investment banking in New York and other global cities—if possible, before eventually creating his own investment funds in Korea. Sam believed that such international work experience would provide him with a significant advantage when establishing a business in his home country.

Sam was not the only son who aimed to maximize his mobility throughout life based on an elite education abroad. Many sons aspired to begin their careers in the United States and then explore diverse opportunities in other cosmopolitan cities. For these sons, holding multiple nationalities and residencies seemed almost essential for envisioning their lives across countries and continents, considering the legal barriers foreigners face in the job market abroad.

Ethan, a senior with permanent U.S. residency and a job offer from a major bank in New York, described himself as "nimble" in choosing the location of his career and family. He refused to limit his future residence to one country, aspiring instead for a truly transnational and cosmopolitan life: "I'm uncertain about where I'll be in the next few years. [...] The only certainty is that I don't want to stay with one company for my entire life. Eventually, I plan to start my own business, though I'm not sure where it will be." He did not want to retire as a banker. His ultimate goal was to establish his own business in the United States, where he had studied since high school. When asked about a role model, he named his father, a CEO of a multinational company who was constantly "here" and "there" across continents for business—a common signifier of the cosmopolitan, transnational elite class in Korea. Ethan aspired to embody that way of life as well.

Sons with foreign or dual citizenship quickly gained their parents' support for a transnational life. Mark, a U.S.-born son who renounced his Korean citizenship and became a U.S. citizen primarily for the sake of his job search in the United States, discussed his parents' supportive attitude toward his nomadic lifestyle. He described their approach as "cool," emphasizing their flexibility regarding his residency. "My parents don't have any strong preference [about my residency], but my dad seems to want me to stay in the United States because he thinks working in Korea is too exhausting," Mark explained. He expressed gratitude toward his father for sharing similar concerns about Korean working culture and for allowing him the freedom to choose where to work and live. When deciding on his next destination, Mark did not seriously consider family-related issues, such as proximity to his parents for caregiving purposes.

Herbert shared similar stories about his parents, who actively encouraged him to stay abroad and explore career and marriage opportunities outside of Korea: "My mom and dad advised me to stay in the United States [after graduation]. [...] As time goes on, they respect my choices more and more. [...] They believe life in Korea will become even tougher, so they prefer that I don't return." His remarks also illustrated his parents' ambition to foster mobility across multiple generations. "They don't want me to raise my [future] children in Korea," he said, laughing. Similarly, few other parents mentioned in this book seemed to desire their sons' transnational journeys to end upon college graduation. Both parents and the sons themselves believed that high-achieving sons abroad were not only eligible but also responsible, in some ways, to pursue a cosmopolitan life after college.

"Noblesse Oblige" of the Chosen

A significant number of sons expressed their aspiration for substantial social standing and public recognition. When asked about his life goals, Simon, a graduate of a prestigious Korean high school who pursued further studies abroad, articulated his desire to be "different than others." For Simon, being different did not simply mean acquiring wealth and fame; rather, he aimed to be acknowledged for his positive impact on society.

By establishing his own business, such as a unique venture capital firm, Simon aimed to create an example of a company with a liberal atmosphere. He believed this contrasted with the authoritative work culture prevalent in his home country. His motivation behind this aspiration reflected a deep-seated social consciousness, a quality he attributed to the influence and upbringing provided by his parents: "My parents often remind me of my high school days when I was passionate about social enterprises. Both they and I have continued to focus on such projects. Recently, they've been bringing up the topic more frequently. [. . .] In their view, being an excellent person means sharing one's resources and talents. They hope I will embody this by using my abilities and assets to make a difference." His ultimate life goal was to leave a lasting legacy in society. To achieve this, Simon believed he needed to not only achieve worldly success but also embrace social responsibility.

George shared a similar aspiration, articulating it akin to Simon's perspective. "It would be sad if I'm forgotten soon after I die. I don't want to lead an ordinary life that people will easily forget. To avoid that, I must leave something significant in this world," George remarked. He framed his ambition in altruistic terms, emphasizing his "social contribution." For him, this meant more than just engaging in individual volunteer work; he aimed to enact meaningful change on a larger scale within societal systems: "Most financial laws in Korea are outdated and too rigid. If I become a finance expert, I want to work on changing them. This way, I can make a more significant impact than simply donating a portion of my income." George added, "That will be my way to live a meaningful life. A meaningful life is more important to me than wealth." He did not hide his ambition to become a politician with expertise in his field.

Running businesses, a common career goal among sons, reflected their multifaceted ambition for wealth, social recognition, and respect from society. Jack, aspiring to become the CEO of an IT company, aimed to achieve purpose through his work rather than through traditional volunteering. "I've already been sharing open-source software code. I've been striving to benefit as many people as possible through that," he explained with pride. This commitment to open-source was integral to the "meaningful life" he aimed to lead, one dedicated to contributing to human progress beyond the well-being of himself and his family.

Owen shared a similar ambition, detailing how his vision to contribute to society developed over his young adult years spent abroad: "My perspective has shifted. I used to spend a lot of time volunteering, especially during high school. However, now I believe that volunteering alone isn't enough to fundamentally change the world. I'm now focused on finding ways to transform societal systems on a larger scale than just through volunteer work." He framed his ambition as a "more effective and direct way" to enact societal change compared to traditional volunteering: "If I were to assist people with disabilities, I would focus on developing new technologies to improve their mobility. This approach would be more impactful and enduring than simply volunteering at a disability services center." Given his privileged transnational upbringing, he believed he was capable and responsible for making the world a better place.

The tendency to view their desire for social recognition as part of their elite social responsibility was widely shared among sons. John, who started his education abroad in high school, noted having several like-minded friends in college: "My friends also want to give back what we've received throughout our lives. Not everyone shares this mindset. Some friends are only focused on landing lucrative jobs and maximizing their earnings. However, those who have taken many liberal arts courses often feel a sense of duty to contribute." He credited his long-term education in the United States for instilling in him a sense of social responsibility. "I believe I need to pay back what I've received. I got this perspective from the American style [education]," he added. John was among the individuals who highly valued the curricula of U.S. (and other Western) schools, which included volunteering activities. He mentioned learning about the social responsibilities associated with the choices one makes.

The emphasis of sons on social responsibility reflects their internalization of the idea of "noblesse oblige," referring to the unwritten moral obligation of the privileged, such as acting honorably and generously toward the less privileged. Although they dream of cosmopolitanism, their ambition often circles back to their home country.

James, a prospective entrepreneur, desired to "leave [his] mark," particularly in Korea, which he envisioned himself as helping to make more diverse and inclusive. Aiming to integrate social values into his future business, he considered changing Korea one of his responsibilities. "I've been extremely fortunate, so it would be too selfish if I only cared about myself. [. . .] [Through my work,] I wanted to improve women's and LGBTQ rights [in Korea]," he said.

The ambition of sons for social recognition was particularly notable among those from more affluent and transnational families. While elaborating on their plans to "improve Korea," some sons emphasized their identity and sense of belonging as Koreans. Aaron, who left Korea to study abroad at ten, hoped the destination of his career journey would be Korea. He said, "My brother and I have lived abroad for over a decade and may continue residing in the United States for several more years. However, we always feel that we should return to Korea eventually."

Aaron's motivation to return to Korea someday was not family-related. Acknowledging his privileged position, he felt he had "something to do" for Korea, the country he left early in life to study abroad. Sons with more extended experiences abroad often shared this sense of responsibility toward their homeland and fellow citizens. These patriotic aspirations sometimes fueled their ambition for a political career, with some explicitly expressing interest in becoming a politician or even president.

Sons of Less Affluent Families: Prioritizing Personal Happiness

Despite sharing similar ambitions for success and recognition, sons from less affluent backgrounds, who were often the first in their families to study abroad, held different perspectives from their more affluent counterparts. Kyle, who had not experienced life abroad before college, shared his challenges in the U.S. job market. He felt that his nationality and international student status overshadowed his achievement as an Ivy League graduate. He found himself receiving significantly fewer interviews with companies and institutions, presuming that they favored U.S. citizens or permanent residents. "Even if I manage to start my career here, I doubt it will last more than two years. I don't have any American dream I'm aiming to fulfill," he commented sarcastically. He seemed to encounter the "bamboo ceiling"[23]—a combination of individual, cultural, and organizational barriers encountered by many Asians in the professional world.

Altruistic or patriotic ambitions were less emphasized among sons from less affluent backgrounds, as they rarely discussed or boasted about them. Especially among those from migrant families, the priority tended to be the personal wealth and happiness of themselves and their immediate families. Eric, a son of migrants, exemplified this perspective. His parents, who had held elite professions in Korea, experienced a dramatic decline in social status after migrating to the United States for their children's education. He felt distinct from many of his college peers, whom he perceived to be more financially affluent and ambitious in their career aspirations. He attributed the disparity to class differences: "I don't understand people who prioritize helping others and giving back. My main goal is to provide for my family and loved ones.

Once I've achieved that, I might then consider focusing on helping others and contributing to society." The economic hardship that Eric and his family experienced appeared to profoundly influence his priorities and perspectives in life, which were more centered on himself and his family compared to other sons who emphasized prioritizing humanitarian goals.

Steve, whose family also underwent education-driven migration for the sake of their children, was another son among the few who did not overly emphasize humanitarian goals. Instead of focusing on a long-term career plan, he was occupied with balancing his studies and multiple on-campus jobs to pay tuition. He was one of the few students who openly discussed his and his family's financial struggles: "The tuition is around $60,000 per year, and my scholarship covers about $50,000, leaving me with a $10,000 gap to cover on my own. To make up for this, I work at the library and the IT support center. My experience running a computer repair club in high school has been incredibly helpful. I also work as a mentor for first-year international students, which I almost forgot to mention!" To enhance his applications for scholarships and job opportunities, Steve obtained U.S. citizenship after a lengthy waiting period as a migrant. His decision to naturalize as a U.S. citizen seemed unconventional; he noticed many of his U.S.-born Korean friends willingly fulfilled their military duties to maintain dual citizenship in Korea and the United States. However, Steve did not find a compelling reason to maintain his Korean citizenship at a significant personal cost, as he had no strong desire to return to his home country.

Steve compared himself to his friends who managed to maintain their citizenship and cultural identity as Koreans:

> Do they want to become politicians in Korea someday? [*Laughs.*] I don't think they understand Korean politics well enough. If they did, they might not want to return to Korea. [...] Even if I decide to work and live in Korea, I don't necessarily need Korean citizenship; I could work there as a U.S. citizen. [...] To be honest, spending two years in the military feels like a waste. I'd rather use that time to learn something new or earn money.

To Steve, his Ivy League education was solely his personal achievement, and he did not attribute much credit to his migrant parents who had experienced significant downward mobility upon moving to the United States. As a result, he did not feel a strong obligation to repay his family or contribute to his home country. Instead, Steve valued the U.S. education system, which offered support for underprivileged students' college applications, such as free consultations, editing services, and assistance with application fees. This less privileged history and trajectory in life distinguished him significantly from many other sons discussed in this chapter.

Daughters' Constrained Ambitions for Global Citizenship

Personalized Narratives About "Escaping" from Korea

Similar to their male counterparts, daughters who had highly transnational upbringings valued the opportunity to experience different societies from a young age. Yoana, who attended a Canadian elementary school for several years, felt that her childhood in Canada "opened [her] eyes" and offered her "more options in life." She believed that this upbringing shaped her values, particularly in fostering tolerance toward others. Yoana expressed a desire to pass on this privilege to future generations. "I want to give my [future] children a similar opportunity. I don't want them to be limited to Korea only," she remarked.

Despite sharing similar views toward elite education abroad as sons, daughters tended to personalize their motivations for leaving Korea to study abroad rather than framing those motivations as serving larger purposes. Rachel explained why she chose a U.S. boarding school over a Korean high school: Her older brother attended one of the most famous U.S. boarding schools, and she felt jealous of him. She explained, "High schoolers in Korea were always consumed with studying for exams, leaving little time for other activities. In contrast, my brother seemed much happier [at his U.S. boarding school], where he had the chance to play many sports." Her brother played a significant role in shaping her transnational upbringing, a sentiment echoed by many other daughters in similar circumstances. Despite her parents' desire to keep her, their only daughter, close to them in Korea, she chose to follow in her brother's footsteps. Rachel recalled, "My parents were hesitant about me studying abroad because I'm their youngest child and only daughter. [. . .] If my brother hadn't gone abroad first, I would likely still be in Korea."

Thanks to the boarding school's sibling policy, which reserved spots for the siblings of current students, Rachel felt that her admission went more smoothly. She recognized that her brother played a significant role in both her application process and her mental well-being while abroad. Their close relationship grew even stronger during that time. "I think we got even closer to each other after moving abroad," she said. "We talk a lot about our family while we're here."

Miranda, who spent her childhood and adolescence in Singapore while her father worked as an expatriate, reminisced about her "happy days" at an international school in Singapore. Like many others, she found the education she received outside Korea to be qualitatively different from her experience in Korea. Diverse extracurricular activities, such as swimming, filled her memories of those days: "In Singapore, nearly every apartment complex has a swimming pool, so I could swim whenever I wanted. This not only gave me more freedom but also helped me make many friends. Life there felt much freer compared to what I was used to before moving." She also mentioned the school's violence-free environment as a factor that contributed to her happy childhood: "My school in Singapore had no issues with bullying. Hard-working students formed their own circles, so they didn't have to worry about being bullied. However, my brief experience in a Korean elementary school was a culture shock." While reminiscing about the past, she emphasized her traumatic experiences rather than delving into a critical analysis of the Korean education system. "I knew I could not be happy in Korean schools," she added, refraining from extending her criticism to offer specific suggestions for addressing the problems in Korean schools.

Similar to Miranda, daughters with highly transnational upbringings tended to present their preference for education abroad as a personal choice rather than as a condemnation of Korean schooling, nor did they as often express grand ambitions for educational reform. Joy, who began her education abroad relatively early, elaborated on her stressful days in a Korean middle school, which eventually prompted her departure: "The atmosphere at the school was extremely competitive. Many of my friends studied almost all night, but I couldn't keep up because I needed my sleep. [. . .] There's no way I could have succeeded in a Korean high school under those conditions." She emphasized the "stressful" and "suffocating" school environment as a key reason for transferring to a U.S. middle school. While strongly criticizing the Korean school she attended, she did not share specific ideas about changing it for future generations. She framed the problem of the Korean school as her personal experience rather than a societal issue.

Despite their overall satisfaction with schools abroad, not all daughters described their transnational upbringing in overtly optimistic terms. This set them apart from sons, many of whom recognized their "in-between" identity as advantageous in various aspects of their lives. Unlike sons who tended to extol the virtues of being multicultural and bilingual, some daughters expressed feelings of personal confusion and ambiguity stemming from their transnational experiences.

Jennifer was one of those who found herself feeling "belonging to nowhere." She was among the more transnational children in this chapter: born in the United States, spent her childhood in Korea, and returned to the United States for high school and college. She appeared confused about her cultural identity, as her "mother tongue" was neither Korean nor American English. Laughing, she said, "Half of my friends are Korean, and the other half are American. My Korean friends tell me not to use English, and my American friends sometimes find my English broken!"

Jennifer admitted that her U.S. citizenship and fluent English immensely helped her apply for scholarships available only to U.S. citizens. However, beyond that, she did not find her "in-betweenness" particularly advantageous in her life. This contrasts sharply with highly transnational sons who often viewed their multilingualism and identity as "third-culture-kids,"[24] exposed to diverse cultural and educational influences, as a positive asset for their cosmopolitan lives.

"Success" in Daughters' Own Terms

Across various familial backgrounds, many daughters discussed their career aspirations or plans in vague terms and expressed uncertainty about their future trajectories. They were still in the process of determining how to leverage their education abroad for the rest of their lives. Particularly among first- and second-year students, there was a tendency to speak in generalities when describing their job aspirations, setting them apart from many sons who, regardless of their academic year, appeared more resolute about their life goals—or at least aimed to present themselves that way.

Yvonne, a first-year student at an Ivy League university who had grown up in multiple countries, seemed to still be figuring out which career path to pursue after college. "I don't know yet what I want to do for work. Nothing is certain about my future career," she said hesitantly. The only certainty for her was her desire to prioritize her personal satisfaction when choosing a career. "I just want to find something I can genuinely enjoy. I want to love my job," she added. For Yvonne, finding fulfillment and enjoyment in her work held more importance than pursuing fame or seeking social standing.

Unlike sons, daughters across various social classes rarely expressed a strong desire for altruistic social influence. Instead, many daughters defined success on their own terms, prioritizing personal fulfillment and happiness. In this context, some daughters even questioned or challenged conventional notions of worldly success. Mia was one of them; she elaborated on her vision of a "good life." "I have my dream job, but I don't see success as solely tied to my career. While many equate success with high income and a grand house, I've never been motivated by those things," she explained.

In this, Mia found herself diverging from those around her, including her brother, who had also graduated from an Ivy League college and was working in the United States at the time of her interview: "I don't often use the term *success*. That sets me apart from my brother. [. . .] He has grand ambitions and is driven by high income and numerous goals. While I'm not against making money, I believe living a happy life is more important." Acknowledging the gender difference, Mia added, "My brother and I have a lot in common, but we have different ambitions." She equated personal happiness with life satisfaction; to her, this was distinct from pursuing high achievement in an overly competitive manner. "My goal is to live a happy life," she asserted.

Mia's parents appeared to adhere to traditional gender stereotypes when guiding their children's career choices, encouraging Mia to pursue a field traditionally considered less masculine. She recalled a conversation with her father, who held a corporate executive position: "My brother works in finance consulting and earns a substantial income. However, my dad doesn't want me to follow that path. He's said, 'I'll introduce you to someone who works in a different field.'" Mia believed her father preferred that she avoid careers involving intense competition and stress, a burden she assumed her father understood well from his long-term corporate experience. "I initially wanted to work in marketing, but now I'm considering a job that's less business-oriented," she said. Pursuing a psychology major, she aimed to find work in design or fashion, fields traditionally more associated with women than finance. It appeared her father's advice on her career path had largely influenced her decision.

Juno echoed Mia's perspective on life priorities, elaborating on her reasons for not endorsing the conventional notion of success: "I don't think much about success, and I wouldn't want to achieve it if it means being self-centered. I dislike people who use dirty tricks and hurt others to advance themselves. My goal is to live a different way." She believed that success and wealth often involved fierce competition, dishonesty, and "tricks," things she sought to avoid whenever possible. Instead, Juno prioritized what she considered more important values in life: inner and outer health and good relationships with others. Her perspective contrasted sharply with the efforts of many sons, who aimed to uphold their values mostly through work achievements.

Maria, one of the few daughters majoring in STEM, found herself caught between others' expectations for her career and her own aspirations. She believed that her major in computer science heightened the expectations others had regarding her income and career achievements.

Mia rejected people's—or society's—definition of success based on objective and measurable indicators like grades, rankings, and income. She disagreed with the notion that occupational success would inevitably lead to happiness: "For me, leaving my mark on something isn't that important. But many people see social standing as necessary. So I'm looking for a balance. It would be ideal to achieve my personal goals while also meeting others' expectations." She decided to strike a "compromise" between her personal aspirations and the expectations placed upon her by others.

Actively defying this widespread belief, Mia aimed to forge her own path to happiness on her own terms. She acknowledged her talent in communication and supporting others, qualities often stereotypically associated with women. "Creating or developing something new is not my greatest talent," she remarked. This realization guided her aspiration to become a "bridge" between engineers and businesspeople, opting to work as an administrator with IT expertise rather than pursuing a career as an engineer herself. Her aspirations and self-assessment appeared gendered, as few men with similar majors sought roles "behind the scenes."

Daughters' preference for academic or research roles reflected their more modest aspirations and life goals compared to sons'. They perceived these positions as offering more autonomy and less competition than careers in fields like finance or engineering. Cognizant of potential gender discrimination and the "glass ceiling" in male-dominated elite professions such as consulting and banking, many daughters consciously or unconsciously opted not to pursue careers in these sectors. They believed that such roles might clash with their desired lifestyles and family commitments, or they express sentiments such as "I'm not suited for that role," possibly underestimating themselves.

Sue, a daughter who began her education abroad relatively late in college, chose a career path as an NGO worker or researcher. Unlike most sons who praised their "dream jobs," Sue downplayed the value of her chosen profession, describing it as "not that lucrative." Regarding her own ability to achieve this goal, she expressed uncertainty, saying, "I'm not sure if I can become one because I'm not good at persisting with goals." Such self-doubt was unusual among sons.

Constrained Career Aspirations of Daughters

Family, both present and future, profoundly influenced the life priorities of many daughters, even those with relatively clear career plans. Doubts about the feasibility of their goals were prevalent, with many daughters anticipating uncontrollable variables linked to their families. This stood in stark contrast to the experiences of sons, who rarely encountered concerns about future work-family conflicts.

As one of the few daughters majoring in STEM, Emily had a clear aspiration to become an architectural engineer. However, unlike many sons who often boasted about ambitions to achieve "something big" through their work, Emily prioritized happiness in daily life and job security over social status and recognition. Reflecting on her evolving perspective, she shared, "When I was young, I thought I was different and exceptional. I believed I would leave my mark on history. But now, I just want to live happily."

Her idea of happiness centered around family values rather than career achievements, and she seemed prepared to make sacrifices in her career to achieve the happiness she envisioned: "When people ask me what I plan to do after graduating, I always respond, 'It will depend on my future partner or children.' I don't want my husband and children to have to adjust their lives for me. I'm willing to make changes in my life for them. My family will always come first, no matter what." In her early twenties, she was already committed to the value of building a "good" family. She did not envision herself being unmarried or leading a work-centered life.

Rachel similarly envisioned her future largely revolving around her partner and children. She also demonstrated flexibility in altering her career trajectory to accommodate the needs of her future family, saying, "I don't think I can choose my path alone." She added, "Things could change dramatically. If I manage to get a work visa [in the United States], I'd like to work here for at least three years [before returning to Korea]. [. . .] But who knows? If my future partner decides to pursue graduate school in the United States, I would accompany him and stay here longer."

Both Rachel and Emily foresaw their career paths being influenced by their future significant others. Their heterosexual, nuclear-family-centered perspective aligns with societal expectations of women primarily as mothers and wives. These gendered expectations appeared to impact daughters more significantly than sons, as no son mentioned a determination to adjust or change their career for their spouses or children.

Jennifer was another daughter who prioritized family over personal achievements. When asked about her life values, she firmly responded, "[My] family." She perceived her ambition as "not that big" compared to others in her circle: "It would be wonderful if I could contribute to society, but that's not my ultimate goal. I don't have a grand dream. My main aim is to live happily, even if that means becoming a stay-at-home mother." Like Jennifer, other daughters also envisioned being a stay-at-home mother as a highly possible life path. This differentiation between daughters and sons emerged again, as no son mentioned the possibility of becoming a stay-at-home parent. The breadwinning role was largely reserved for sons.

Marriage was a significant theme in the narratives of many children, regardless of gender. With very few exceptions (one or two), all children considered heterosexual marriage essential and expressed a desire to find a partner with whom they could share similar interests, preferences, and goals. However, daughters tended to articulate more detailed and practical expectations and hopes about their future partners compared to sons. Daughters openly expressed a preference for like-minded and financially secure individuals as their life partners. For instance, Jennifer expressed a desire to "see the potential" in her prospective partner, defining "potential" in terms of career prospects and financial ability.

Miranda's narratives were detailed. As a student majoring in social science and an aspiring human rights lawyer and social activist, Miranda emphasized the importance of finding a partner with a stable and successful career, especially as a fallback in case she couldn't "earn enough" on her own. She jokingly remarked, "I sometimes tell people I want to marry a millionaire." However, her serious critique of a male-centered society underscored her genuine concerns: "It's hard to claim that men and women are truly equal in marriage and career. Women's lives often hinge on their husbands' careers, even today. So if my husband earns enough, it will give me more options and flexibility in my own life." Her remark suggested her and many other daughters' insecurity about job stability, work-life balance, and financial security in the future. This uncertainty led her to view financial stability as a critical criterion for an ideal spouse. Interestingly, no sons explicitly mentioned seeking high-income professional partners. This contrast in marriage expectations underscores gendered norms among the high-achieving children in this book, perpetuating the stereotype of men as primary breadwinners and household heads.

Gendered differences also emerged in how legal status was valued for daughters compared to sons. Yoana, a Korean citizen who came to the United States only for college, found that her status as a non-U.S. citizen woman limited her job search options on Wall Street. In response, her mother suggested a highly gendered solution. Laughing, Yoana candidly shared, "My mom tells me to marry a U.S. citizen. [. . .] That will be the fastest way to solve my problem. That's why I'll try to give my child U.S. citizenship no matter what."

While some Korean-citizen daughters, like Yoana, seriously considered marriage as a means to enhance their transnational mobility, no sons explicitly mentioned a desire to acquire U.S. citizenship through marriage. For men, "flexible citizenship," in both legal and cultural senses, was something they could or should attain by birth or career achievements. They were well aware of the significant advantage it provided them in the U.S. job market if they possessed it.

In contrast, even daughters with U.S. citizenship or permanent residency found their job prospects less attractive. Joy, a U.S. permanent resident who moved to the United States for middle school, discovered that her experience in the U.S. job market was "much rockier" than she had anticipated, especially compared to her men friends. Her ethnic identity as an Asian and her gender identity as a woman did not seem to aid her job search, despite her typically lucrative STEM major and Ivy League degree: "Originally, I planned to build my career in the United States and then return to Korea later. However, I'm now torn between continuing here and going back to Korea. [. . .] My mom keeps encouraging me to come back to Korea." Given the difficulties in her job search abroad and her parents' wishes, a return to Korea after graduation seemed to become a feasible—or realistically, the only possible—option for her. Other daughters confided that their parents explicitly wanted them to return to Korea, expecting a certain degree of emotional care. In contrast, no son mentioned his parents' specific desire for his residence and career in Korea.

Daughters' Filial Piety

Children's education abroad, and in some cases the consequent family migration, is always a high-cost family project, even for the relatively affluent families featured in this book. This led many daughters to become "debt-bound,"[25] growing up as disciplined and docile within familial structures of feelings and power. Their narratives often reflected the notion of debt as a filial obligation:

Many daughters felt a strong desire or obligation to repay their parents' investment in their costly education in any way possible.

Jennifer, who began studying abroad in middle school, felt the weight of being separated from her parents for an extended period. "My little sister and I have been apart from my parents for so long. It would be ungrateful to my parents if we continued living in the United States for the rest of our lives," she remarked. For her, being close to her parents meant more than fulfilling a filial duty; it was deeply personal. The long-term separation, a common outcome of studying abroad and education-driven migration, seemed to affect her emotionally more than it did for sons. "I haven't lived with my parents for a long time, so I don't have a complete view of family life. This doesn't mean my family is broken, but we've definitely been apart for quite a while." She added, "That experience has influenced my decision to focus on a family-centered life."

More daughters than sons expressed a strong yearning for closeness to home and family, which often fueled their desire to eventually return to Korea—or wherever their parents resided. Yvonne, who left Korea at the age of three due to her father's work abroad and subsequently lived in five different countries, did not identify any country as her home. She explained, "I don't feel at home in any country because I've lived in too many countries." Feeling rootless at times, Yvonne prioritized proximity to her parents when considering her future career. "I think I'll be fine as long as I'm with my parents," she said.

Daughters often strived to fulfill gendered expectations and roles—both those set by their families of origin and those they envisioned for their future families. Many daughters demonstrated considerable care and affection for extended family members, particularly grandparents, as well. Providing emotional support and care was a significant way for them to fulfill their roles as daughters, granddaughters, and sisters.

Sue, who began her education abroad relatively late, contemplated relocating to provide assistance to her parents. "There's one thing I'm worried about working in the United States. I'm concerned that I will not be able to be close to my parents when they are in an emergency," she remarked. Sue felt a deep emotional connection with her parents and wanted to fulfill her role as a filial daughter to demonstrate her love and care for them. "[If I get a job in the United States,] I'll visit my parents regularly as often as possible. I've already started worrying about what to do if my parents pass away," she added. Being the eldest daughter in her family, she believed she had a greater responsibility to care for her parents compared to her younger sister. In contrast, sons rarely articulated such a strong sense of filial obligation across birth orders.

Mia, a graduate of a U.S. boarding school, also displayed deep affection for her parents. To her, "home" unequivocally meant Seoul, where her parents resided. "There's no other city where I can feel more comfortable than Seoul," she emphasized. One of her regrets was not spending more "quality time" with her parents during her teenage years, feeling that she left home "too early" for boarding school in the United States. She expressed even greater yearning for her parents as she contemplated the timing of her marriage. "If I get married in my late 20s, I won't have much time to live with my parents from now on. So I really want some time to spend with my parents after college graduation," she said.

Hoping to marry shortly after college, Mia contemplated pursuing a job in her homeland. She had already completed internships in Seoul, which she saw as a valuable opportunity to spend time with her parents. Her career aspirations markedly diverged from those of her brother, who also had an extensive education abroad: "My brother keeps saying that he wants to live in the United States. [. . .] He's already secured his first job here and genuinely enjoys it, so there's little reason for him to change his career direction. He might consider returning to Korea later in life, but for now, he's committed to staying in the United States."

Yet for daughters who chose to return to Korea after graduation, working in Korean companies presented its own set of challenges. Many were uncertain of their ability to (re)assimilate into the culture of Korean companies and institutions, which they perceived or assumed to be masculine and authoritarian.[26] For instance, Hilary, who began studying abroad in her mid-teens, described her internship experience at a Korean company as "emotionally draining" and sometimes "unbearable." She disliked and even feared the male-dominated staff dinners and drinking sessions after work that she associated with Korean working culture.

When asked if her extensive experience living abroad influenced her perspective, Hilary responded, "Perhaps yes. I am not very familiar with corporate life in Korea. [. . .] I wouldn't even want to marry a man who enjoys such culture." Despite her desire to be close to her parents, she grappled with whether she could thrive—or even survive—in a male-dominated Korean company.

Daughters of Less Affluent Families: Navigating Insecurity

In this book, daughters who spent most of their upbringing in Korea and moved to the United States only for college were in the minority and faced multiple layers of challenges in adapting to and thriving at elite U.S. colleges. Their gender and familial backgrounds combined to create legal, cultural, and linguistic barriers, hindering them from finding like-minded friends, securing their "dream jobs," and developing a sense of belonging in the United States.

Heather, who went to the United States only for college, felt she drove her transnational life trajectory independently, motivated by the "American fever" prevalent in Korea. Her lack of experience abroad led her to identify as a native Korean—or, as she put it, a "Korean Korean"—within her social circle. She reflected on her adolescence in Korea: "Most kids [around me] were already familiar with American culture from their childhoods spent in the United States. However, a few of us, including myself, pursued studying abroad without a clear purpose. Our parents didn't pressure us. We simply yearned for the experience of living abroad." She described her motivation to study abroad as "too ambiguous" compared to other Korean students, whom she believed were deliberately raised transnationally by parents with experience studying abroad.

Heather attributed her struggles in college life in the United States to her parents, who did not guide or fully support her education abroad: "I had almost no idea what life in the United States would be like. I had no one who could share their experiences or offer guidance. And my parents lacked any studying abroad experience themselves. I felt unprepared. This lack of support made things particularly challenging for me [while attending an Ivy League college]." With a bitter laugh, she continued, "I didn't know [at first], but as time passed, I realized how differently I was raised compared to other Korean students abroad." Heather strongly felt the class gap between herself and her friends, whom she described as "having different resources." What surprised her the most was the language difference. "A friend of mine communicated in English at home," she said.

Heather recalled that life in the United States differed significantly from what she had imagined. Her challenges included managing her grades, exploring career paths, and networking with people from different cultures. Among these difficulties, a weakened sense of belonging was particularly notable. Identifying herself as a minority, Heather recalled, "I felt WASP [White Anglo-Saxon Protestant] students constituted a mainstream [among students]." The feeling of being excluded bothered her significantly—she said she "tried too much" to find her place among people on campus, which led to burnout:

> I pushed myself too hard. [...] I tried out numerous activities, from working at the media center and joining a frisbee club to pledging a sorority, but nothing seemed to work out. [...] I struggled with feeling like a minority and found it difficult not to dwell on my [subordinate] position. I wish I could have ignored those concerns and followed my own plan, but my intense desire to fit in with the mainstream ultimately led to a lot of stress.

Heather lacked confidence in her ability to thrive in elite circles abroad, so she initially desired to return to Korea after college graduation. Reflecting on her decision, she explained, "I didn't enjoy living in the United States much. I lacked connections and didn't quite fit into the culture." However, influenced by her then-boyfriend's strong desire to stay, she later changed her mind and accepted her first job at an IT company in New York. Despite this, she eventually resigned from the job and returned to Korea: "My boyfriend at the time was the only thing keeping me connected to the United States. [. . .] I relied on him too much, which led me to push myself in the wrong direction. [. . .] Learning the job was challenging, and adjusting to life in a large U.S. city was also tough. [. . .] I struggled to find any joy in my life there."

Heather was one of the rare children participants who frequently expressed feelings of regret. Despite acknowledging the "high-quality classes" she attended during college, she appeared dissatisfied with her overall experience in the United States, particularly grappling with the challenges of assimilating into the culture of transnational elites. Her race, gender, and familial background collectively posed a complex barrier that she endeavored to overcome throughout her life abroad but eventually felt defeated by. At the time of her interview, she was trying to figure out how to leverage the value of her Ivy League degree in Seoul, preparing herself to compete with local elites in Korea.

Jenna shared many similarities with Heather. Like Heather, Jenna completed all her schooling in Korea except for college. Her childhood experience abroad was limited to occasional visits to her uncle, who lived in California. Compared to most of her friends in the circle of Korean students abroad, she perceived herself as much less transnational and cosmopolitan. This difference complicated her friendships during college: "Some Korean students on my campus avoid interacting with other Koreans altogether. They make an effort not to engage with the Korean student community. [. . .] Sometimes, they even look down on me and question, 'Why do you only socialize with Koreans at a U.S. university? You're missing out!'" Such conflicts led her to withdraw from the Korean student community at her college. She recalled feeling lonely most of the time. For her, attending an Ivy League college as an Asian international student was a source of stress rather than an opportunity for multicultural and personal growth.

Winona, a first-generation study abroad student, observed class distinctions among Korean students both in the United States and during her high school days in Korea. She reflected on her experience in a selective Korean high school that provided specialized courses for college-abroad applicants: "I realized that my friends and I had very different starting points. They excelled at everything, including English, and came from influential families. It seemed like they had little experience with the hardships of life." To close the distance between herself and her high school friends, she "pushed [herself] to the limit," which had a negative impact on her mental health. Raised in the highly competitive atmosphere of elite students, she characterized herself as a workaholic, saying, "I'm constantly focused on survival within my social circle. I'm strict with myself, perhaps overly so. To stay competitive, I feel I need to work twice as hard as everyone else."

Winona's inclination to overwork intensified after she enrolled in an elite U.S. college. "Now, in college, I constantly compare myself with my Korean and American friends. I still feel like I don't quite fit into either group. I don't even feel confident in my English," she candidly expressed. These honest admissions distinguished her from many other children, particularly sons. Despite encountering more challenges, she did not shy away from acknowledging them, unlike some more privileged peers who might conceal their difficulties.

Winona's narratives illustrated the two different worlds she was navigating: When with her parents in Korea, who had never studied abroad, she felt estranged, attributing this to their lack of understanding of her situation. She also perceived a class difference when interacting with Korean friends who had similar educational backgrounds, particularly in terms of parental support. Among her American friends, she felt discomfort due to a cultural gap that proved difficult to bridge. The intersection of class, culture, ethnicity, and language differences made her education abroad psychologically challenging, despite her excellent academic performance.

Winona sought assistance but found few who could truly understand her situation, with one notable exception—an international professor at her college. "The professor herself is from Japan. She grew up there and came to the United States late, just like me. She knows exactly how I feel on this campus. Her advice is practical," Winona shared. As a Korean citizen without U.S. citizenship or permanent residence, Winona opted to pursue further education abroad at a U.S. graduate school, aiming to extend her student visa for a longer duration. For her, studying abroad became a solitary journey motivated by personal reasons rather than any grander purpose.

Gendered and Classed Aspirations of Elite Korean Students Abroad

The absence of longitudinal data on children's postcollege life trajectories may be seen as a limitation of my analysis in this chapter. Instead, I emphasize the exploration of children's visions for their future careers and families.[27] Aspirations and expectations play a crucial role in shaping individuals' behaviors and can arguably enhance their accomplishments.[28] Therefore, this chapter provides valuable insights into the influence of transnational education on young Korean elites.

The narratives presented in this chapter delineate the gendered context in which high-achieving Korean students abroad choose and potentially enact gender scripts, wherein women often have only a limited repertoire of behaviors from which they can choose. More sons than daughters attempted to exercise their "agency for becoming" based on the mobility gained through elite education abroad. Exercising such agency to the limit, many sons planned out "choice biographies" where their past, present, and future would progress in a linear fashion, pursuing positions for themselves as part of a skilled diaspora. Their eagerness for cosmopolitan life and familial support sometimes seemed to conceal any struggles or hardships they might have experienced during their life abroad as Asian men in the Western world, who are often seen as "perpetual foreigners."[29]

Few sons commented on their ethnic identities, possibly because they focused more on elaborating their ambitious life trajectories. Their endeavors shed light on the culture of elite schools,[30] which some daughters in this chapter found to be male-dominated or male-friendly. The "sense of entitlement"[31] seemed to be actively cultivated among the circle of men from privileged backgrounds. More sons than daughters constructed themselves as "new elites" who "think of themselves as far more individualized, supposing that their position is a product of what they have done."[32]

The attitude of such sons reflected their pursuit of hegemonic masculinity. These sons' career-oriented biographies reflect and reinforce gender stereotypes of (elite) men as successful breadwinners, achievers, and philanthropists. As transnational elite men, they depicted themselves as productive and prudent, and therefore morally worthy,[33] aligning well with the archetype of successful men in modern capitalist society. In striving to underscore the societal impact of their ambitious career goals, they naturally framed their class status as a moral virtue.[34] Consequently, they often failed to acknowledge their inherited privilege and overlooked their position as an ethnic minority in the Western world—except for a few sons from less privileged families. Despite pursuing similar ambitious goals, these sons with less familial support could not help but notice how their lack of class resources exacerbated their disadvantages as racial minorities within their elite circle.[35]

Daughters' tendency to follow "normal biographies"—centered around roles as mothers, wives, and daughters—shows how elite education abroad maintains gender differences and inequality within the circle of Korean students. They often seemed to lose their ambitions while proactively worrying about work-family conflicts in their future career trajectories. Women's insecurity about their lives abroad underscores two significant gender-related implications. Firstly, gender and racial discrimination prevalent in both the U.S. and Korean job markets have dissuaded numerous high-achieving Korean women, including those with ample resources, from pursuing a career-oriented, cosmopolitan lifestyle abroad. Secondly, gender norms pertaining to Asian daughters have played a pivotal role in shaping women's envisioned life trajectories, as they have often felt compelled to prioritize their roles as daughters by ensuring accessibility to care for their parents. In this ethnicized and gendered framework, women from less privileged backgrounds find themselves particularly challenged, feeling trapped between two worlds—the cosmopolitan realm of transnational elites and the family-centric local society—often lacking the agency to fully leverage their qualifications for careers abroad.

My findings support and expand upon existing studies of Asian women navigating Western society. Many daughters in this chapter negotiated "competing pressures,"[36] balancing their aspirations for professional cosmopolitanism with social and familial expectations that often steer them toward marriage and family. Their narratives highlight the unevenness of the transnational landscape, challenging the normative ideal of cosmopolitanism that assumes homogeneity among the skilled diaspora. Gender, intersected with class, determines who can more readily embrace and achieve the "utopian and automatic cosmopolitan vision."[37]

3

When Class Trumps
Gender: Korean
Parents' Views

Over the past thirty years, the socioeconomic shifts driven by globalization have made studying abroad a key strategy for boosting employability and competitiveness in the Korean job market. As Korea's economy has transitioned to a postindustrial, knowledge-based, global landscape, English proficiency has become a vital asset. Today, most Korean companies require TOEIC (Test of English for International Communication) and other English proficiency exam scores during the hiring process, making English communication skills essential for the majority of office workers in the country.

When financially feasible, Korean parents strive to expose their children to an immersive English-speaking environment as frequently as possible. In some cases, this begins at an early age, with affluent parents enrolling their young children in English-speaking kindergartens, which incur tuition costs that are nearly double the average fees of domestic universities.[1] These substantial efforts continue as children grow older, with participation in a thriving market of student exchange programs and summer camps in Western schools. Additionally, private agencies (*yuhagwŏn*) providing personalized support to students applying to schools abroad add to the wide array of resources available for pursuing foreign credentials.[2]

But for some parents and families, sending children to study abroad is about much more than just teaching them English. They view it as a way to escape the perceived intense competitiveness of the Korean educational system. Through overseas education, they seek to expose their children not only to elite language proficiency but also to Western (elite) culture, despite the high costs, which they are generally willing to pay. Their primary goal is for their children to join the network of cosmopolitan Korean elites. From their viewpoint, elite Western high schools and colleges are the places where these "positional goods"—beyond mere English skills—are cultivated, shared, and instilled. In particular, those who attended these prestigious schools abroad themselves aim to educate their children in a similar environment to perpetuate such class privilege.

This chapter highlights the varying levels of enthusiasm for educating children abroad, addressing whether all parents find costly transnational parenthood worthwhile. It also investigates whether parents of high-achieving Korean students abroad share the same purposes, motivations, and expectations for their children's education. What exactly do they expect from their children's education abroad? What factors underlie the differences—or inequalities—that exist among these parents?

By comparing and contrasting parents' narratives, this chapter closely examines how class and gender simultaneously shape the motivations and strategies for elite transnational parenting, a privilege often inaccessible to most parents. I use the term *cosmopolitan* to refer to relatively more affluent parents with long-term experience abroad and international careers and *locally based* for parents without such experience or with relatively brief experience. Some locally based fathers did study or work abroad, but their occupations (at the time of their interviews) did not require frequent international travel anymore. Both terms are relative and do not necessarily reflect the amount of parental income or wealth. However, locally based parents, outnumbered by their cosmopolitan counterparts, often viewed themselves as less affluent and a minority among the group of high-achieving Korean students studying abroad.

Cosmopolitan Parents' Well-Planned Transnational Parenthood

Among the thirty-four parents I interviewed, nearly half—eight fathers and seven mothers—were leading highly transnational and cosmopolitan lives at the time of their interviews. Their elite professions as CEOs/businesspersons, college professors, medical doctors, or researchers at private institutions spoke volumes about their life trajectories: They had studied in the United States or other foreign countries for their graduate (and sometimes undergraduate) degrees. Some had also worked abroad as expatriates or visiting staff. Appreciating their experiences abroad and believing in the academic and cultural values associated with elite Western education, they sought to provide similar opportunities for their children.

Cosmopolitan Fathers

Fathers who earned degrees abroad were particularly positive when talking about their children's education overseas and the elite transnational parenthood associated with it. They regarded U.S. education as superior to Korean education for both academic and cultural reasons, genuinely valuing their children's opportunity to learn in the United States.

For instance, Jenna's father, a U.S. doctoral degree holder and the CEO of a trading company, framed his motivation for sending his daughter to a U.S. college as a globally minded aspiration and explained why he thought it was necessary to "learn globally": "These days, it's really important to understand how connected the world is. Everything and everyone is linked, and countries feel much closer than they used to. Young people need to get that. [. . .] My daughter can't just stick around Korea for her whole life [regardless of her major]. She needs to think globally and be open to experiences beyond our borders." He unconsciously equated the term *global* with *Western*. His understanding of "being global" sharply contrasted with "being local," even in a post-industrial, relatively wealthy country like Korea. Jenna's father expressed that throughout his career in the trading field, he had strongly felt the importance of having a "global mindset." He hoped his daughter would cultivate a high degree of mobility, believing it would empower her to excel in a world shaped by the movement of people and cultural influences across international boundaries.

Sending Jenna to a U.S. college was his strategy to offer her maximum mobility and, consequently, a wide range of life choices. With evident pride, he remarked, "[After college graduation,] she will be able to move to another country [other than the United States] and work there if she wants." He believed that this possibility justified the costs of their transnational family arrangement, both financially and emotionally.

Owen's father, a CEO who completed an MBA program in the United States, described his decision to send his two children to U.S. boarding schools and college as a form of "protest" against the Korean education system. He expressed feeling "desperate" when he reviewed the textbooks his children were using in Korea: "It was frustrating to see my children studying the same outdated material I learned ages ago. The world has globalized and evolved so much, but they were still focused solely on tests and exams in Korea. It seemed like such a waste!" He mentioned a conversation in Los Angeles where a Korean friend explained why his son loved his boarding school in that area. This inspired him to send his child there as well. Often, fathers with ample resources, like Owen's father, used their international connections to establish what they deemed an optimal educational setting for their children.

Highly motivated, Owen's father meticulously planned his children's education abroad, carefully detailing his criteria for selecting schools, which he considered more rational than those of many other Korean parents:

> I didn't focus much on school rankings. What mattered more was finding a school near an airport so my kids could travel there easily within an hour. It might be hard to prioritize that when choosing a college, but it was important for me that they could come home for winter and summer breaks and that my wife and I could visit frequently. I also preferred a school with around one hundred students per grade. I wasn't keen on schools with fewer than fifty [students] because they often don't offer enough AP [Advanced Placement] classes.

Owen's father believed that the selective boarding school he chose provided an ideal environment for fostering values of diversity and inclusion, which he saw as crucial components of a cosmopolitan education. He remarked, "I really appreciated the codes of conduct at my children's schools. They emphasize teaching students to care for others, which I love. It's been great to see how my kids have grown and changed since attending these schools." He was convinced that this learning environment significantly benefited his children's mental health during their teenage years. This conviction underscored a clear hierarchical difference between elite U.S. education and Korean education, reinforcing his decision to invest in their schooling abroad: "You're probably aware of how stressed out Korean students are. Kids who excel academically are under immense pressure, and those who struggle face their own stress. Some deal with bullying, while others contend with intense peer pressure. It seems like every student in Korean schools is dealing with some form of victimization!" He proudly stated, "My kids were able to experience the value of diversity in high school. If I hadn't sent them to the United States, we would have missed out on a significant opportunity."

Owen's father wanted his children to acquire intangible values during their studies abroad, such as empathy, an open and generous mindset, and confidence. He believed these qualities could be ingrained in his children while in the United States, a country he admired for its greater racial diversity and superior human capital compared to Korea: "I always remind my kids, 'You're studying in a far better environment with top-notch professors compared to Korea.' The faculty, culture, and facilities [at elite U.S. colleges] are definitely superior. I just want my kids to experience an outstanding learning environment." He took pride in appreciating the culture of learning and the overall environment in U.S. colleges rather than placing emphasis solely on the prestige of their degrees.

In fact, Owen's father's approach to parenting was quite idealistic. During his interview, he made a point of steering clear of an overemphasis on the market value of his children's degrees. "I don't want to focus on material things," he said. "What really matters is inner strength—the ability to face any irrationality or injustice." He extended this perspective to his hopes for his children's careers, expressing a flexible stance on their future paths and where they will choose to live. "I have no particular preference for their future," he noted, possibly to ensure he wasn't seen as materialistic, elitist, or snobbish: "My daughter's [Owen's older sister's] major is definitely not about chasing social success or a high income. She's studying art history, which isn't exactly known for its lucrative prospects. [*Laughs.*] I always tell her, 'Please don't sell your soul for a career or a big company. I don't want you working for someone else's corporation for the rest of your life.'" He believed that offering such pep talks distinguished him from other parents of students studying abroad, whom he assumed to be more concerned with their children's career achievements. "Perhaps I'm the only parent who expresses these sentiments," he remarked, proud of his liberal parenting philosophy.

For cosmopolitan fathers, sending their children abroad for higher education represented a pivotal step in orienting their family life toward a society outside Korea. Nicole's father was among those highly satisfied with his daughter's education abroad. Anticipating that his daughter would eventually settle outside Korea, he felt his transnational fatherhood aligned well with his vision for his family's future. His frequent travels abroad for work, attending conferences and undertaking projects that sometimes kept him overseas for months, reinforced his preference for an international lifestyle. "I'm accustomed to living abroad," he explained, reflecting on his experiences.

Having previously worked in the United States as an expatriate, Nicole's father proudly stated that none of his family members had any concerns about this lifestyle: "My kids and my wife really love living abroad. They enjoy their schools overseas, get along well with their friends, and appreciate the overall environment and facilities. They seem to enjoy it much more than I do." Time abroad provided him with a respite from the pressures of life in Korea, where he felt compelled to work hard and compete intensely. "I enjoy [that time as a way of] taking a breath and looking back on my life," Nicole's father explained. He believed such a break was only possible while abroad, and for that reason, he welcomed any opportunity to stay overseas, whether with his family or alone. He hoped that Nicole's education abroad would serve as a crucial form of momentum, making his entire family more mobile and cosmopolitan—and even more humane.

Owen's father was another parent who was open to maintaining transnational family arrangements after his children's college graduation. He anticipated that his children would naturally lead cosmopolitan lives abroad in the long-term, thereby fulfilling his investment in transnational parenthood. "Both [of my children] were born in Korea and educated mostly in the United

States, so I expect they will work and live in either country, maybe even both," he said. Rather than envisioning a reunion with his children in Korea, Owen's father imagined himself moving around the world to accommodate their cosmopolitan lives. "I have no reluctance to live abroad," he remarked.

Owen's father's long-term transnational fatherhood aligned seamlessly with his aspirations for his own future life: "I actually enjoy living in different countries, like splitting my time between Korea and Hawaii. [. . .] My wife and I are even thinking about selling some of our properties [in Korea] to buy homes in a few cities outside the country." Building a "residence system across national borders," as he put it, was his wish, not only for the sake of his children but also for himself and his wife, both accustomed to life abroad. If this scenario unfolds, it will solidify his view of successful transnational parenthood. He affirmed, "Sending [my children] to the United States was unquestionably the right decision, and my wife agrees."

Though not explicitly stated, Owen's father's wealth enabled him to envision this highly transnational family life. His resources, such as fluent English and familiarity with Western culture, bolstered his confidence in the success of a long-term transnational family arrangement, such as maintaining multiple homes in multiple countries. He envisioned collective happiness through such a family arrangement, characterized by freedom, adaptability, and the pursuit of diverse global experiences by each family member. This optimistic outlook underscored the value he placed on his transnational fatherhood.

Cosmopolitan Mothers

Mothers who had studied abroad themselves shared a similar perspective as fathers who had done so. These mothers exerted considerable effort to provide their children with what they deemed a creative and less competitive learning environment. A common strategy among them was sending their children to summer camps or student exchange programs in English-speaking Western countries before the formal commencement of their overseas education.

Sam's mother, who acquired her undergraduate and graduate degrees in the United States, had a clear vision of the ideal learning environment for her son. She believed such an environment was unattainable in Korea, citing a significant lack of diversity and creativity in Korean education. She adamantly stated, "Korea was too small [for Sam's growth]." To support her beliefs, she ensured that Sam participated in multiple educational programs abroad during his childhood: "After returning from a summer program [in the United States] when he was in third grade, Sam decided to attend school abroad. Spending those four weeks made him realize how important it was to meet people from diverse backgrounds." She observed that her son was "always curious about everything." To nurture his curiosity, she made deliberate efforts to expose him to a diverse range of experiences both within and outside Korea. However, she felt that Korean schools did not fully nurture her son's potential. She remarked, "Korean teachers do not appreciate students who ask many questions in class."

Hailey's mother, also a graduate of a U.S. college, held similar views regarding Korean education and its cultural limitations. Initially, she had reservations about sending Hailey abroad for education. "I didn't want to send her anywhere in the world for education. She's my only child, my only daughter. I wanted to keep her close to me," she recalled. However, her perspective shifted when Hailey expressed a strong desire to study outside Korea. "If she hadn't been so determined to study abroad, I would never have sent her so far away," she emphasized.

Hailey's mother recalled a particular incident that she felt influenced her daughter's decision to study abroad. She vividly remembered why the Korean public middle school education system didn't fit her daughter's needs:

> Hailey had a physical education test where she had to kick a ball into the center of a goal to score full points. If the ball missed the center, she'd lose one or two points. She really hated it. She didn't understand the point of the test and thought it was unfair. I wasn't a fan of it either, but her reaction was more intense than I anticipated. I remember her asking, "Mom, wouldn't it be more beautiful if my ball hit the post and bounced in?"

She agreed with her daughter's view on the "unfair" evaluation standards, seeing it as a fundamental flaw in Korean education overall. She recalled, "Hailey couldn't tolerate anything she perceived as unfair. Even though she got good grades and had many friends at her Korean middle school, she constantly expressed a desire to study somewhere else."

Hailey's mother aimed to differentiate her daughter from the majority of other Korean students abroad, whom she saw as going overseas to "escape." She clarified, "Initially, I thought Hailey simply wanted to escape from Korean schools, but she persistently presented me with serious reasons." To emphasize that her daughter's decision to study abroad held deeper significance, Hailey's mother elaborated on another incident that solidified their decision to choose a school outside Korea: "Hailey was placed in a TOEFL [Test of English as a Foreign Language] class because the institution grouped all their top students together. Since she hadn't attended many English *hagwons* [private cram schools] before, she struggled to adjust to the competitive environment. The class required her to memorize nearly one hundred English words each day!" She remarked, "I didn't think their system fit my daughter," echoing her daughter's discontent with the English learning experience in Korea. Alongside her dissatisfaction with English education in Korea, her husband's confidence in the value of a U.S. college education further solidified their decision to educate their daughter abroad.

Hailey's mother relied on her husband, who had studied abroad as both an undergraduate and graduate student, to guide their daughter's education at an Ivy League institution: "Since he had studied in the United States himself from an early age, my husband was well aware of the benefits of American higher education. He believed it would be ideal for Hailey to start studying abroad as early as high school so she could get accustomed to the U.S. education system from the outset." Despite having less experience with U.S. colleges than her husband, she still relied on her own firsthand experience studying abroad to guide her daughter's education: "I started studying abroad in graduate school, so I didn't fully understand why U.S. undergraduate programs were considered superior to Korean ones. Even now, I can feel the gap between U.S. and Korean academia. What I learned in my U.S. graduate program is still not taught in Korea. At the time, I didn't realize just how advanced the graduate program was." Her narrative exemplifies how mothers who have studied abroad actively participate in their children's education, often with strong support from similarly educated husbands. In fact, couples in which both parents had studied abroad displayed the highest preference for and trust in an overseas education.

Sam's mother's narrative illustrates how such couples often worked as a team in overseeing and supporting their children's education abroad. She detailed her husband's active role in Sam's education, both in the early stages and later on—a commitment she deemed equivalent to her own. Sam's journey into education abroad began during their initial residence in the United States, which was prompted by his father's business. Following their return to Korea and before Sam's enrollment in a U.S. boarding school, he attended an international school in Seoul. While Sam adjusted to the international school, his mother took on the role of a private teacher, noting that she and her husband identified areas for improvement in the school's curriculum. She proudly shared, "We taught him from the beginning. [. . .] The three of us spent most of the night studying."

While framing her maternal support as natural and expected, she notably praised her husband's academic involvement, which she deemed uncommon and highly valuable in Korean society: "[At work] Sam's father didn't have lunch with his colleagues for three years [while Sam was at an international school in Seoul], so he could use lunchtime to study Sam's school materials. I prepared sandwiches for him every day during that period! [*Laughs.*] He would read Sam's notes, create his own summaries, and fill in any gaps. He practically made a custom book just for Sam." She believed her husband's rigorous educational efforts were all aimed at preparing their son for his eventual "return" to the United States, firmly viewing Sam's schooling in Korea as a temporary phase.

Their intensive support and management continued even after Sam began his second phase of studying abroad at a prestigious boarding school. Daily family calls became the norm, a detail she happily recalled: "We always keep in touch through [international] calls. That's what keeps us connected as a family. When Sam was in boarding school, he'd call us every day to talk about each class: science, writing, and all the other subjects. [. . .] We'd update him on our business, sharing what was going well and what challenges we were facing." Even after Sam entered college, these family calls persisted—a source of pride for Sam's mother. "A few weeks ago, Sam talked so much about his finals [in college] that we knew what the questions of his exams were!" she exclaimed. She boasted that her husband continued to stay involved in Sam's college education, reading Sam's textbooks and brainstorming ideas for his essays. Her pride in her husband's engagement reflects the classed aspect of their parenting: She acknowledged that not many Korean fathers were capable of being as involved in their children's education as he was.

Sam's mother believed that the deep involvement of both parents, particularly the significant paternal engagement, made her son's upbringing and the bonding within their family particularly special. Moreover, she found it enjoyable for both herself and her husband. "[Helping Sam] is one of our hobbies. We love catching up with what Sam is learning. It's really fun," she remarked. Sharing a similar experience of studying abroad in the United States seemed to be the foundation of her family's bonding, a connection that Sam's mother believed was stronger than that of other families.

Affluent stay-at-home mothers with extensive experience overseas (often due to their husbands' education or work) shared similar accounts, praising education abroad and the resulting transnational family arrangements. Unlike the (small number of) mothers without much experience abroad, these mothers were well acquainted with schools outside Korea and their potential benefits. Their decision to send their children to schools abroad was not arbitrary; while their husbands often initiated the transnational family project, these mothers had their own reasons for supporting their children's education overseas—reasons that often aligned closely with those of their husbands.

Mark's mother was among the few former wild geese mothers I spoke with, having raised her children in the United States alone for ten years while her husband returned to Korea after completing his overseas work assignment.[3] Instead of sending their children to boarding schools, she opted to care for them herself. She asserted that her experience of parenting alone abroad was worthwhile, believing that her children benefited significantly from their U.S. education and the ideal environment she created for them by staying to support them.

Mark's mother perceived the educational environment in the United States as more liberal and student-centered compared to that in Korea, which she saw as providing students with ample emotional benefits: "U.S. schools helped my kids become emotionally stable. It wasn't easy raising two kids on my own without my husband, but I know it was the right choice for them. [. . .] In Korea, students are overwhelmed with busy schedules. So many of them are sad." Like many parents who experienced studying abroad themselves, both mothers and fathers, she highly valued U.S. education, considering it qualitatively superior to education in Korea: "We took advantage of a great opportunity. Some kids can thrive in Korean schools without too much stress, but my children didn't seem suited for that environment. Some people have very sensitive natures, and I didn't want [my children] to be hardened or made selfish through the intense competition in Korean schools. If they had gone to Korean schools, they would have had to toughen up to survive."

Mark's mother emphasized that it was her husband, not she, who initiated their children's education abroad. She credited him for seizing an opportunity to work in his company's U.S. branch for their children's education. "Mark's dad chose a neighborhood without Koreans so our children could learn English as accurately as possible. [. . .] Mark was the only Asian student in his class," she said. She solidified her role as a caregiver and "emotion expert," while praising her husband's role as a planner and decision-maker: "My husband is very meticulous and doesn't let things slide. He wanted our children to explore the world beyond just studying all day. [. . .] I'm thankful we shared that vision. [. . .] I didn't do much for their education beyond the basics: I drove them to and from school, cooked for them, and quietly watched TV while they studied in their rooms at night. That was pretty much it."

To ensure her children could "learn happily," Mark's mother made significant sacrifices during what she called her "golden age" between the ages of forty-two and fifty-two. Reflecting on her relatives' visits to their home in the United States during this period of intense motherhood abroad, she felt a mix of pride and regret. She was proud of the dedication she gave to her children but also felt sorry for the younger version of herself who had devoted most of her time to them. She said, "When one of my uncles visited us in the United States, he asked, 'Why are you living in exile?' I understood why he said that. I did feel like I was living in exile for those ten years."

Describing the transnational family setup where she single-handedly raised her children amid significant responsibilities, Mark's mother recalled, "My children and I lived in a small, predominantly white town where we were the only Koreans. I had to drive over five miles to buy groceries." Despite the isolation, she fondly reminisced about that period: "I used to drop Mark off at school around 7:30 in the morning. The drive took about an hour, but I cherished those moments. We had deep conversations on our way to school."

Those ten years of wild goose motherhood marked an intense chapter in Mark's mother's life on multiple fronts. She shouldered a heavy responsibility for raising her children "properly," yet she also found the intense mothering abroad deeply fulfilling, giving her a profound sense of pride and accomplishment. Despite this ambivalence, she emphasized that her sacrifices were worthwhile, believing her children became capable of pursuing their aspirations and "emotionally stable." "If I had prioritized myself, I wouldn't have supported them so diligently," she reflected. Above all, her children's remarkable achievements validated her prolonged motherhood abroad. With her daughter employed in New York and her son earning an Ivy League college degree, she felt reassured and viewed her motherhood journey positively.

Mark's mother expressed gratitude for her husband's extended stay in Korea, acknowledging it as a significant sacrifice for the sake of their children. In doing so, she aimed to portray their family as maintaining intimacy despite the prolonged separation:[4] "My husband made a significant sacrifice by living apart from our children for ten years. He made sure to visit us multiple times a year, including during summer breaks, Thanksgiving, and New Year's. When he came, he would stay with us for almost a week each time." She actively challenged the stereotypical view of transnational families by emphasizing her husband's strenuous efforts throughout his wild goose fatherhood rather than her own: "People often assume that wild geese families are broken and predict that such couples will divorce soon. [*Laughs.*] But my husband worked hard to stay connected with our children. I worried that he might become too distant. [. . .] Whenever he visited us in the United States, he made a point to take our children to many different places." Fighting against the pathologizing view of wild geese families seemed important to her. While emphasizing her husband's efforts for family bonding, she also sought to normalize the phenomenon of growing distance between fathers and children, which she framed as common across diverse family arrangements. She asked, "Isn't it true that even when parents and children live together under one roof, fathers easily grow distant as children get older?"

Kyla's mother, another stay-at-home mom who used to work as a school teacher, resided in the United States for nearly ten years while her husband pursued his doctoral education. Unlike Mark's mother, she and her husband jointly raised their children abroad. They viewed their extended stay in the United States as a deliberate and strategic choice, describing it as a multifaceted arrangement for their family. She recalled appreciating the opportunity to raise her children in a different country, one she perceived as more developed than Korea. "I thought that bringing up children in a broader world would be wonderful. I didn't hesitate or feel any fear when we decided to move to the United States," she reflected.

The cost of private education in Korea, which was quite high even for affluent families like hers, further justified her decision to educate her children abroad. Reflecting on the days she raised her children in Korea, she said, "Educating three children as much as I wanted to in Korea cost quite a lot." Her husband's pursuit of a doctoral degree in the United States therefore presented a significant opportunity for an ambitious mother like her, who sought an English-speaking environment and liberal education for her children.

Kyla's mother admitted that moving to the United States with her family, particularly her husband, brought her significant peace of mind. "If I were a wild goose mother, I would have felt so afraid going out [of Korea]. But with Kyla's dad by my side, I felt relieved," she said. All three of her children excelled in U.S. schools and were admitted to prestigious universities, with Kyla attending an Ivy League college. She felt that her ten years of motherhood abroad were more than worthwhile, equating her children's academic success with her own as a mother, viewing it as evidence of her effective parenting.

Kyla's mother believed that living in the United States provided ample opportunities for her family and herself, ensuring a high quality of life. By the time of her interview, she had spent about a year back in Korea after returning with her husband. She found it challenging to readjust to life in Korea, particularly noting the difference in the pace of life between the United States and her home country: "My husband and I moved back to Korea a year ago after our children went to college [in the United States]. [. . .] When we first returned, everything felt exciting! [*Laughs.*] But now, I'm feeling overwhelmed. There's so much to manage and take care of! [. . .] Korea is like a fun kind of chaos, you know what I mean?"

Unlike Mark's mother, who practiced intensive mothering abroad alone, Kyla's mother did not find her role to be emotionally taxing. This was primarily because she lived with her children and husband throughout their education in the United States: "I was always with my family, so I never felt lonely [in the United States]. We'd visit our family and friends in Korea every two years during the summer, staying for about one or two months. It was always so much fun and really helped relieve my stress." Envisioning a sustained physical separation among family members due to the children's settlement in the United States, she was prepared to travel across continents as often as possible to maintain a healthy family bond. She saw remigrating to the United States, near her children, as a viable option for her after her husband's retirement from his college faculty job in Korea. Having such an option was a source of joy rather than stress, as she found life abroad personally more comfortable than life in Korea.

Recalling her days in the United States, she felt a strong sense of nostalgia, saying, "I missed those days." She remembered her time there as relaxed and easygoing, though sometimes "too quiet." During that period, she felt less constrained by the gendered duties of a daughter-in-law: "My mom always said, 'Just stay there [in the United States] and enjoy your life fully.' She knew how involved I was with my in-laws, since my husband is their oldest son. While she wanted me close so she could see me often, ultimately, she wanted me to settle in the United States for my own sake." Given the disproportionate workload placed on women for family gatherings and other ancestral rites in Korea, wild geese and other types of mothers often appreciate their time abroad as periods when they can be less bound by their duties as wives and daughters-in-law.[5] For Korean mothers, educating children abroad, particularly when accompanying them, can serve as a way to live in a society with fewer gendered responsibilities.

Locally Based Parents' Accidental Transnational Parenthood

The six parents in this book who had only limited temporal experience abroad tended to describe their transnational parenthood as entirely incidental. For them, sending their children to prestigious and expensive universities abroad was a matter of "letting [the children] do what they wanted." None believed they initiated or significantly influenced their children's decisions to pursue higher education abroad. This contrasted sharply with their cosmopolitan counterparts, who had meticulously planned and purposefully embraced transnational parenthood.

Locally Based Fathers

Natalie's father, a college professor and former government worker, explained that it was neither his plan nor desire to send Natalie to the United States at an early age. "I thought it would be great if she could study abroad for her graduate degree. But I didn't imagine her going to the United States for a high school or college diploma," he said. He seemed to believe that obtaining a graduate degree from a U.S. college would be sufficient for living as an elite in Korea, just as he had done.

Downplaying his influence, Natalie's father stated, "My daughter initiated her education track on her own." He pointed to a work-abroad program during his government employment, which allowed him to bring his entire family to the United States for one year, as an event he believed sparked his daughter's eagerness to study abroad: "During my time in government service, I had a chance to work and study in the United States. I applied and was accepted, but my primary goal was to advance my career, not to use it as an opportunity to educate my children there." Natalie's father adopted a defensive tone as he sought to distinguish himself from fathers who actively used their careers as a pathway to transnational parenthood: "I hesitated to bring Natalie to the United States because I worried it would be difficult for her to readjust to a

Korean school after we returned. [At that time,] I was considering quitting my government job and pursuing a faculty position after the [work-abroad] program, so the move to the United States was mainly for my career. Natalie's education abroad wasn't a major focus for me at that point." Unlike the cosmopolitan fathers highlighted in this chapter, who openly acknowledged their intentional planning of their children's early education abroad, Natalie's father expressed reluctance to fully embrace the philosophy or environment of elite Western education, questioning the benefit of sending young children to schools abroad. His stance aimed to portray himself as less assertive about his children's educational choices, positioning himself as distant and passive in the decision-making process.

Sue's father, a teacher at a large *hagwon* (private cram school), presented a unique case among parents who had experience with higher education abroad. His journey began with a doctoral program at a U.S. university, which led to their family relocating with him. Both of his daughters were born in the United States during his graduate school years. However, their time abroad came to an abrupt end when he withdrew from his doctoral program. "When your dissertation advisor suddenly dies, you lose your way, not knowing what to do," he recalled.

Sue's family became split across two locations. "My wife chose to stay in the United States with the kids [for their education], so I returned to Korea alone," Sue's father explained. Reluctantly, he became a wild goose father for the sake of his children: "We lived apart for nearly four years. If my wife had secured a stable job there, she might have preferred to stay longer with the kids. However, she grew tired of managing part-time work and raising the children alone [in the United States], so she eventually decided to return to Korea." He did not regret the wild geese family arrangement, as his older daughter Sue thoroughly enjoyed studying in the United States: "Sue excelled at her U.S. elementary school. [. . .] I remember reading her report card and seeing the teacher's note: 'I've never seen such a smart child.' Sue even skipped a couple of grades! Sometimes I wonder what might have happened if she had stayed and continued her studies there. I can't help but feel a bit sorry for making her return to Korea."

Despite appreciating his daughter's early experience in a U.S. school, Sue's father explicitly stated that it was his daughter, not he or his wife, who initiated her return to the United States for college: "Sue was determined to attend a foreign language high school in Korea, which had a special preparation course for colleges abroad. She felt much more comfortable studying in English than in Korean. [. . .] Studying abroad had been her longtime wish." Downplaying his daughter's aspiration to study abroad, Sue's father added, "Until she reached tenth grade, Sue was unsure if she wanted to attend a U.S. college specifically. She just seemed to want to study in English." Nonetheless, based on her early schooling experience in the country, he believed sending her to a U.S. college would be the best option.

Throughout the interview, Sue's father consistently emphasized his passive role. "All I did was not strongly oppose what Sue wanted to do," he said. Unlike cosmopolitan fathers who had specific "dream schools" abroad for their children, Sue's father said he had no strong wishes or expectations about his daughter's college, as long as he could afford it.

Reflecting on the family discussion about his daughter's college choice, Sue's father admitted that he was initially unaware of U.S. liberal arts colleges: "I didn't really get the hype around liberal arts colleges until Sue got accepted into a few. Even though I had attended a U.S. graduate school, I hadn't paid much attention to liberal arts colleges before. After researching more about them, I called a family meeting and said, 'All right, I'll cover the tuition by selling the house or my car. Sue, just focus on doing your best there.'" Laughing, he added, "I think I sighed after saying so."

Sue's father exhibited an inner struggle over the high tuition of the U.S. liberal arts college his daughter was accepted into. Recalling the day he learned about Sue's desire to attend such a college, he said, "I had to mull over the tuition for a while. I thought to myself, 'Oh my, I need to tighten my belt so hard for four years.'"

Sue's father believed his financial situation influenced his daughter's college choice, and he felt apologetic about it. "I found out that the college Sue chose offered needs-based scholarships. There were not many schools like that.[6] I felt relieved [after learning about that]," he said. This honest confession about financial hardship set him apart from cosmopolitan fathers, who willingly and comfortably invested a great deal of money in their children's elite education abroad.

Natalie's father also found that his financial situation complicated his involvement in and support for his daughter's education overseas. In her senior year of high school, Natalie was not accepted into an Ivy League college, which had been a goal for both of them. After attending a selective private college outside the Ivy League for one year, she transferred to an Ivy League college with his strong encouragement. He felt compelled to push her to transfer, given the high tuition at Natalie's initial college, which was nearly as expensive as that of most Ivy League schools.

During his daughter's first year at college, Natalie's father wanted to closely monitor her to ensure that the expenses were justified. He proposed a promise, which his daughter agreed to before her departure to the United States: "You could say it was a sort of contract. [*Laughs.*] Since Natalie was about to live alone abroad, I had faith she'd do well, but I felt a bit of pressure was needed. So I wrote things like, 'Maintain a certain GPA' and 'Don't overspend' [on the contract]." He laughed awkwardly, saying, "We made a kind of agreement."

The contract reflected his feelings about the outcome of Natalie's college applications, though he tried to downplay them. "I'm not saying I was disappointed because she didn't get into a particular college. I just couldn't say for sure that she did her utmost best," he added. Attributing this to a perceived lack of effort on his daughter's part, Natalie's father attempted to justify his close supervision of her college life abroad: "I just wanted her to do her best wherever she was. [. . .] She got straight A's in her first year at [her first] college, which was a huge relief. She seemed to be doing really well, and that made me happy. I think she liked that college a lot."

Despite his daughter's satisfaction with her first college, a well-known U.S. private university, Natalie's father strongly advised her to transfer to another institution. His reasons appeared multifaceted: He was concerned about the high cost of the school, the unavailability of financial aid, and the relatively lower prestige of the institution compared to similarly expensive Ivy League colleges. However, he emphasized the diverse scholarship opportunities at Ivy League schools in particular, possibly to downplay his strong preference for prestigious institutions: "School names were important, but more than anything, I wanted her to secure financial aid. Her first school was just too expensive. One day, I said to her, 'Do you really need to graduate from that school, spending so much money? You're getting great grades, so you could transfer to another excellent school that's more affordable.'" He seemed to want to avoid the impression of being solely focused on "big-name schools." To present himself as less authoritarian, he added, "I believe Natalie was already contemplating a transfer."

Ultimately, Natalie's successful transfer to an Ivy League college brought him a sense of relief and satisfaction. Even after his daughter became an Ivy League student, Natalie's father continued to ensure that his investment in her expensive education was worthwhile. He endeavored to persuade his daughter to pursue a career path he deemed "lucrative enough." He openly acknowledged that he strongly recommended Natalie to pursue a graduate program while abroad: "I didn't give her any special career advice, but I did explain why getting a doctoral degree could be the ultimate achievement. I told Natalie that a bachelor's degree in sociology alone wouldn't lead to significant status attainment." To him, his daughter's academic achievements were significant benchmarks of his transnational fatherhood, the results of what he considered to be a substantial investment. Unlike cosmopolitan fathers, who emphasize their parental investment in terms of their children's personal growth and development, Natalie's father couldn't help but emphasize his ambition for his daughter's tangible accomplishments.

Heather's father, also locally based, was uncertain and concerned about the value of his daughter's education abroad. He sought to validate his considerable financial investment in her education by ensuring her success in the job market. As a parent who did not study abroad himself, he harbored doubts about the value of a degree from an elite U.S. university and cautioned about the potential challenges of his daughter's return to Korea. He believed that the culture of Korean companies might not always align with what Heather learned during her time at an Ivy League college: "As a manager, I've met many young employees from top colleges who don't perform well at work. Sometimes, the name of the school doesn't matter much once you're on the job. [. . .] I advise Heather to forget about her Ivy League background. If she works in Korea, thinking she's special just because of her school could cause problems. Her colleagues and bosses might not appreciate that attitude."

Heather's father was particularly concerned about his daughter's lack of local connections in Korea, which he believed were crucial for her career success in the country. At the time of his interview, his daughter had decided to return to Korea because she was unable to secure stable and lucrative employment in the United States. This decision intensified his regret about sending her to a U.S. college, despite the prestige associated with her Ivy League education: "Communities are vital in Korea, especially for career development. It might have been more beneficial for Heather to graduate from a Korean college before pursuing graduate studies abroad. By starting in Korea, she could have built stronger local connections, which would help her career advancement later." He did not view Heather's struggle to find a job in the United States as unfair or incomprehensible. Instead, he saw her decision to return to Korea as an inevitable or predicted outcome. This pessimism prompted him to reevaluate the value of his daughter's education abroad and, consequently, to question the worth of his substantial investment in it.

Locally based fathers tended to apply more pragmatic standards to evaluate their parenthood and transnational family arrangements, while their cosmopolitan counterparts often romanticized their children's education abroad and the resulting transnational parental role. For instance, Natalie's father struggled to provide a definitive assessment when asked about his transnational fatherhood, as he did not fully embrace the cultural values associated with early education abroad. "I cannot make a fair evaluation [of Natalie's education] because we never know what would have happened if Natalie had gone to a Korean college," he expressed ambivalently.

Natalie's father approached his daughter's education abroad from a cost-effectiveness perspective and ended up feeling some, though not strong, regret. He recognized the significance of degrees obtained abroad as prestigious credentials for Koreans. However, he did not believe that studying abroad for high school or undergraduate degrees was necessary: "I initially planned for Natalie to complete her undergraduate education in Korea before going to the United States for graduate school. This way, she could have secured a full scholarship and financial aid, which is a common path for many Koreans.

But Natalie was adamant about attending a U.S. college for her undergraduate degree, and it was difficult for me to deny her request." For him, the primary goal of studying abroad was gaining a competitive advantage in the Korean job market rather than fostering a sense of global citizenship. Therefore, he leaned toward advocating for pursuing graduate degrees abroad as it seemed to be more cost-effective.

Sue's father also felt ambivalent about his daughter's education abroad. Since Sue had attended a prestigious Korean college for one semester before transferring to a U.S. liberal arts college,[7] he could easily imagine what might have happened if she had stayed in Korea and graduated from an elite Korean institution: "If Sue hadn't been admitted to a U.S. college, she could have completed her degree in Seoul, and it might have been just as valuable as studying in the United States. Because of this, I'm not entirely sure whether sending her to the United States was the right decision or not." He did not attribute special credit or admiration to his daughter's education at the elite U.S. college, despite her excellent performance there. Instead, he genuinely worried about her physical and mental well-being during her study abroad.

Sue's father recalled, in an emotional tone, helping his daughter move into her college dorm: "I went with Sue to college when she was just starting out. After helping her set up her dorm room, I had to head back to Korea alone. When we said goodbye, I told her to take care, and she cried. Seeing her like that broke my heart. [*Long pause.*] She had a tough time in her first semester, facing everything alone in the United States, and I felt deeply sorry for her." He added, "She's petite and physically not that strong, so I'm always worried about her." This concern made him feel more aligned with mothers in this chapter, especially locally based mothers, than with other fathers who tended to boast about how well their children would "fit in" at elite U.S. schools.

Sue's father felt that his transnational fatherhood was incomplete and even inadequate compared to other fathers. "I guess fathers with many resources might want to control their children's future. But I'm not like them. [. . .] I'm not as competent as those fathers," he said with an awkward laugh. The sense of helplessness imposed quite an emotional toll on him. He assumed his daughter wanted to start her career in the United States, a prospect seemingly beyond his control. Reflecting on the prolonged separation from Sue, he said, "I'll keep worrying about her and feeling apologetic, just like I did on her first day at college."

Moving abroad to live near his child was not a feasible option for Sue's father. "Sue is visiting us every summer now, but if she gets a job there, she won't visit us often. Then we'll try to visit her [abroad] from time to time," Sue's father explained. He believed Sue's college education and potential career abroad wouldn't offer another chance for his family to leave Korea. He perceived his daughter as independently starting her cosmopolitan life, physically and emotionally distant from other family members.

Locally Based Mothers

Locally based mothers, constituting a small minority, also shared narratives of accidental transnational parenthood. For instance, David's mother, a stay-at-home mom who had never visited the United States at the time of her interview, described her son's education abroad as a "total coincidence." Her son's decision to study abroad came as an abrupt surprise to her; she tried to see it as a result of his hard work. "David was always an ambitious kid. Even when he was a small child, he seemed to prefer the idea of living and working abroad," she recalled.

While acknowledging her son's cosmopolitan ambitions, David's mother had never imagined educating him abroad, due to a lack of financial resources. She vividly recalled the moment her son announced his plan to transfer to a U.S. college from his Korean college. "My husband and I tried to persuade David to go to the United States after finishing college in Korea, but he didn't listen to us," she remembered.

The news of her son getting accepted into an Ivy League college was a cause for concern rather than celebration, at least for David's mother. "I couldn't sleep the night I heard he got into that school, thinking, 'How am I going to support him now?'" she recalled. She saw her son's education abroad as "out of [her] hands," believing that David had taken control of his ambitious life trajectory: "David once told me, 'Mom, if I work hard, I can definitely graduate from an elite U.S. college.' He was thrilled about the possibility of transferring and felt confident that his excellent transcripts [from his Korean college] would secure him a spot at his dream school. He was very sure of himself, but I wasn't entirely confident that I could support him through the process."

To do so, David's mother made significant financial sacrifices, including closing a savings account originally intended for David's marriage funds. Embracing the role of a devoted Korean parent,[8] she explained how she altered her plans to support her adult child: "David wanted to study in the United States so badly. How could I ignore that? I was even prepared to go into debt for him! Parents should support their children's dreams. Many parents take out loans for their children's weddings, so I figured I was just investing in David's future a bit earlier than usual. I told him, 'You should start saving for your wedding yourself, because I've already done enough to support you.'[9]"

To David's mother, David's study abroad was unexpected and unwanted in many ways, given its high financial cost. However, she made a concerted effort to see the bright side, embracing the cultural prestige associated with Ivy League degrees over Korean college degrees. She hoped that this prestige would translate into tangible advantages in the job market, enhancing her son's employability: "Sending David to an Ivy League college was the right decision. Many young people in Korea struggle with unemployment, and even those in their forties can face layoffs, even when they work for big corporations. I'm not a fan of the corporate culture in Korea at all." She hoped that David would realize his work potential in a more favorable, "developed" environment than Korea. Based on a stereotypical understanding of Western societies that reinforces the cultural hierarchy between them and Korea, she envisioned the society of her son's future residence as "developed" without specifying how: "Working abroad, whether in the United States or elsewhere, often seems much better than working in Korea. Korean society has room for improvement. It might be developed economically, but it still lags behind in political and cultural development."

David's mother was one of the rare parents who articulated her expectations for her child's education abroad in concrete, quantifiable terms. Her focus on the return on her investment underscored her particular socioeconomic status, distinguishing her from most other parents discussed in this chapter: "If David lands a job in the United States after graduating, it would be fantastic. He'd likely earn more than he would in Korea, and his Ivy League degree should give him an edge over most of his peers. I believe he'll be able to recoup the investment we [my husband and I] made in his education within just a couple of years." While she did not expect her son to repay her with money, nevertheless, she anticipated that he would acknowledge and reciprocate her and her husband's investment in some form: "It's not that we're pressuring him to repay us. We don't want our children to feel like they owe us anything. But realistically, we'll be quite old by the time David is in his career prime. At that point, he might need to support us in some way."

While cosmopolitan parents often hoped for their children to achieve social standing and global recognition, David's mother had different expectations, emphasizing measurable achievements such as a high income. "High status does not guarantee happiness. Climbing the ladder requires a lot of sacrifice," she remarked. Prioritizing financial stability over social status, she believed that a solid financial foundation would provide her son with a more comfortable, "ordinary" life. This perspective set her apart from the cosmopolitan parents who shared their children's grand ambitions for social acclaim and humanitarian goals.

David's mother was willing to endure the long-term geographical separation from her son as long as he could gain numerous rewards from his work abroad. What set her apart from more affluent, cosmopolitan mothers was her candid acknowledgment of the emotional toll this separation took on her: "I'll miss him a lot. Once he settles abroad, he should be able to visit us in Korea at least once a year. If he can't make it, we'll try to visit him instead.

Even if he ends up working in Korea, it won't be easy to see him as often as I'd like. So having him abroad might not be so bad. It'll just mean we'll have to spend a bit on travel." As a rare parent who had never visited her child in the United States, David's mother did not have any specific plans or desires to be geographically closer to her son through family migration or other means. Her narratives often implied how isolated her son was in terms of managing and navigating his transnational mobility.

Joy's mother—another less affluent, locally based parent—offered a distinct perspective on sending her two daughters abroad. Her dislike for the intense competition and fierce academic rivalries typical of schools and *hagwons* in Gangnam (the most affluent district in Seoul) drove her decision to enroll her children in a school near family in the United States: "One day, I asked Joy, 'Would you prefer to study in Gangnam or go to the United States and live with Grandma?' She replied, 'Mom, I heard all the kids in Gangnam are so smart. They seem intimidating.' That's when I decided to send Joy and her sister to live with my mom in the United States." With her parents and brother residing in the United States, sending her children there for their education was a feasible and economical choice. She framed her transnational parenthood as also financially motivated rather than educationally purposeful, stating, "If my parents and brother were not living in the United States, I wouldn't have sent my kids there for school. [. . .] We saved a considerable amount of money [that would have been spent on English *hagwons*], thanks to my family."

With two daughters studying in the United States for more than five years, Joy's mother wanted to view their education abroad primarily as an opportunity for them to experience life outside of Korea rather than as a stepping stone to cosmopolitan careers. She envisioned overseas education as liberal, flexible, and culturally diverse—qualities she imagined rather than had firsthand experience with: "Looking back, I believe sending Joy to the United States was the right choice. She's such a creative and insightful kid, with a sharp perspective on things. Although I didn't fully realize it at the time, her teachers have consistently highlighted these qualities. Studying in the United States has been really beneficial for her."

Joy's mother credited her husband for their daughters' successful education abroad, seeing him as more enthusiastic and knowledgeable about their schooling. This distinction set her apart from mothers with extensive experience abroad, who often framed their children's education abroad as a family decision: "My husband was the one who chose the United States [for our children's education]. Maybe he saw something I didn't, given that he majored in engineering while I majored in music. [*Laughs.*] To be honest, I'm not really that interested in education in general. I just prefer to live life as it comes and follow some basic guidelines. But my husband wanted to give our kids the chance to experience a broader world." She attributed her husband's educational fervor to his upbringing, which she believed had been more privileged than her own: "My husband grew up in Gangnam, where many of his friends studied hard from a young age [at expensive *hagwons*]. But his own parents weren't as well-off as those of his friends, so he often had to study on his own. I think he's motivated to support our kids in ways he wished his parents could have supported him." She added, "Thanks to my husband, our daughters speak perfect English. If we had raised them only in Korea, they wouldn't speak English as fluently as they do now." Her emphasis on English proficiency and exposure to another culture, rather than global citizenship or cosmopolitan life, aligned her more closely with many local Korean parents, distinct from those of elite students studying abroad and their parents.

Throughout her interview, Joy's mother highlighted the differences in parenting styles and philosophies between herself and other mothers of Korean students abroad. She found these other mothers to be "qualitatively different," describing them as hyperdiligent, intensely passionate, and nearly obsessed with their children's education: "I don't worry about [my children's] grades [at U.S. schools]. Other mothers track their children's grades online, but I don't bother. One day, Joy asked, 'Mom, why don't you check my grades? Other moms always check their kids' grades.' I just told her, 'I trust you completely!'"

Despite her children's outstanding academic achievements—such as her older daughter, Joy, attending an Ivy League college—Joy's mother consistently downplayed her expectations and hopes for their education abroad: "Joy often tells me, 'Mom, everyone at my Ivy League college is so brilliant.' I always reply, 'Don't stress, Joy. Just enjoy the experience and take advantage of the opportunities that come your way.' I truly mean it! I'm just thrilled that she's having such a fantastic college experience. It will benefit her in so many ways." Her satisfaction with her daughter's education was rooted in her idealistic view of Ivy League institutions. She appreciated the prestige of the Ivy League more than the specifics, making no mention of the curriculum, faculty, student activities, or networking opportunities. She focused on the exclusivity of the education rather than the other ways it benefited her child.

Despite her happiness about her daughter's Ivy League degree, Joy's mother also wrestled with concerns about the potential drawbacks of a competitive, high-achieving life. In this regard, she shared a perspective similar to David's mother, who, like her, had never studied abroad: "I wasn't entirely relieved when Joy got accepted to an Ivy League college. I worried she might face extreme stress. I've heard that some students even commit suicide under such pressure. That's something I can't tolerate. If the stress gets to that point, I'd rather my daughters not push themselves so hard." While entrusting her children's education abroad to their own efforts, she held her own distinct hopes for their future. "I don't think it's right to push children too hard. I don't believe academic achievement should be the ultimate goal in life," she said.

Joy's mother's vision of success contrasted sharply with that of many other parents discussed in this chapter: "I believe that surpassing others isn't true success. What's important is learning to get along with people beyond just family. I value living a modest, ordinary life. Even exceptionally talented individuals need to stay humble and avoid showing off. My daughters will become parents someday too. They'll need to connect with everyday people and navigate those relationships." With both her children being daughters, her vision of a "good" life was deeply influenced by a gendered perspective. "Joy will get married and become a mother someday. Pursuing a high goal is great, but raising a happy, beloved child is more important," she remarked. Her modest expectations for her daughters abroad appeared to influence Joy's aspirations and future plans, as Joy was one of the few who chose to return to Korea for her first job.

Joy's decision to return to Korea was influenced not only by the challenges of securing a desirable position in the United States but also by her desire to be closer to her family. Joy's mother expressed contentment regarding her older daughter's return. She longed for the reunion of their family after the prolonged separation. "I keep telling my younger daughter [Joy's sister, who is in a U.S. high school,] to consider returning to Korea for college," she added.

Sending both of her daughters to the United States had left Joy's mother with a profound sense of grief, facing an early version of the "empty nest." She shared, "After my younger daughter left Korea, I felt extremely lonely and lethargic. [. . .] I'm always thinking about when I'll be able to live with them. Joy also wants to live near me." Her strong desire for an intact family drew her to Korea despite her U.S. permanent residency, sponsored by her brother and parents, who migrated there: "I ended up gaining U.S. permanent residency thanks to my brother's assistance, although I wasn't particularly focused on obtaining it. Even my elderly parents, who live with my brother, are now considering returning to Korea. I believe they'll make the move back once my younger daughter starts college." Given her legal status, she could have initiated her entire family's migration to the United States, a preferred option among more affluent and cosmopolitan parents. However, finding no personal benefit in living abroad, she strongly desired to stay in Korea. She viewed the U.S. residency her family achieved as beneficial primarily for her daughters' education rather than for the entire family's mobility.

Classed Parental Aspirations: Inequalities Among Parents of Korean Students Abroad

The impact of parents on their children's educational goals and subsequent achievements has been extensively researched. Highly educated and financially resourceful parents often have expectations and aspirations that positively influence their children's educational goals and achievements.[10] Parental encouragement is particularly significant, especially for high-achieving students from relatively affluent backgrounds, strongly impacting their college plans.[11] As a result, parental expectations have long been studied as a key factor in students' educational aspirations, which are frequently linked to the parents' level of education and involvement in academic pursuits. However, these high expectations can be moderated by parents' unfamiliarity with higher education and concerns about its affordability.[12]

Expanding on the existing discussion, the stories of parents in this chapter underscore the need for a more nuanced understanding of parents' socioeconomic statuses and educational backgrounds, particularly given the rising trend of education abroad. Parents' own firsthand experience with studying abroad creates notable differences among them, driving strong motivation to encourage and set high expectations for their children's education overseas. Those who had lived, studied, or worked abroad for extended periods—whom I refer to as *cosmopolitan parents*—tended to engage in well-planned transnational parenthood, articulating their rationale for pursuing a transnational education for their children with clarity. For these parents, sending their children abroad was a deliberate and familiar means of class reproduction. Their choice of schools and involvement in school events served as markers of social status, aiming to highlight their approach as distinct and superior compared to parents whom they perceive as less cosmopolitan.

When justifying their decision to educate their children abroad, these parents often glorified elite Western education, thereby reinforcing the global hierarchy of languages and cultures. They internalized Western hegemony, which benefited them within the uneven landscape of global education. Parents who had studied abroad were convinced that their foreign credentials had significantly advanced their careers and enriched their lives overall. They also attributed not only academic but moral value to the experience of studying abroad, reinforcing the dichotomy between the liberal Western world and authoritarian Korean society. By passing down the experience of studying abroad, cosmopolitan parents utilized their children's education overseas as a "positional good"[13]—a prestigious experience and lifestyle accessible only to select groups of people. For many of them, it also could serve as an important way of gaining momentum to make their family dynamics more transnational.

Although few, the parents I spoke with who had limited experience living abroad—whom I refer to as *locally based*—had different rationales and approaches to their children's education abroad compared to their more transnational counterparts. For them, their children's studying abroad was a rare individual event, with their children typically being the only family members with foreign degrees and cosmopolitan aspirations. Their more accidental transnational parenthood brought numerous concerns and occasional regrets about whether their investment in their children's education abroad was worthwhile. Many of them remained uncertain about the tangible value of an elite education overseas, reserving judgment on its overall impact.

Locally based parents had a grounded and realistic view of success. Consequently, they evaluated the value of education abroad primarily in terms of job prospects. Their goal was not to raise "Asian globals"[14] but to secure foreign credentials for their children, particularly from Ivy League institutions, to give them a significant edge in the Korean job market, with the expectation that they would return to Korea eventually. Their pragmatic view sometimes led to anxiety, as they worried that their children might become too accustomed to Western culture, given the significant perceived cultural gap between Western society and most Korean local companies. Some of them also worried that their children might "burn out" in the competitive elite circles, a concern not commonly shared by cosmopolitan parents.

Gender had less impact than class on parental expectations and aspirations. Mothers who had studied abroad shared similar views with fathers who had also done so. Conversely, fathers and mothers without long-term experience overseas had much in common. This suggests that studying or working abroad is a crucial class marker among Korean parents who send their children to schools outside of the country. The narratives of locally educated mothers who accompanied their husbands' or children's extended study abroad illustrate this well: Their rationale for educating their children had much in common with that of mothers and fathers who had studied abroad. This highlights the significant impact of extended periods of living abroad on the motivations and expectations behind children's elite education overseas.

While the impact of class was powerful, gender still created interesting differences in how parents evaluated their involvement and envisioned their families' futures. Fathers tended to highlight their abundance or lack of financial and cultural resources for parenting, implying their internalization of the breadwinner norm.[15] On the other hand, mothers, especially those based locally, emphasized their supportive roles, such as encouraging their children's pursuit of foreign credentials, while being candid about the emotional toll of transnational parenthood. However, a small number of employed mothers who had studied abroad mirrored fathers in this regard, exhibiting decisiveness, confidence, optimism, and stoicism when discussing their transnational motherhood. This indicates that gender, closely intertwined with class, created nuanced within-group differences among Korean parents who sent their children to elite U.S. colleges.

4

What Makes for a Perfect Transnational Mother?

The formation of transnational families challenges established norms and practices related to parenting and parenthood.[1] Sometimes, it reinforces the existing gendered division of care within the family, while at other times, it transforms or subverts it.[2] Studies of working-class transnational families, where migrant mothers often work in developed countries while fathers and children remain in their home countries, have found that mothers gain earning power and perform breadwinner roles while simultaneously providing remote emotional care through telecommunication technologies.[3] When fathers migrate, mothers take on most of the caregiving responsibilities, while fathers financially support the family but remain physically and emotionally distant from their children.[4] However, recent studies suggest that middle-to-upper-class fathers tend to face fewer challenges in connecting with their children, fully utilizing advanced communication technologies.[5] This implies that parental class background, particularly in terms of income and education, is a major factor in transforming or reinforcing gendered roles and responsibilities in transnational families.

The stories of the parents in this book offer a unique opportunity to examine how an elite context shapes the division of parenting and the parents' understanding of their parenthood within transnational family arrangements. Most families featured in this book are led by parents with high incomes and prestigious occupations, with elite fathers typically maintaining absolutely their status as the primary breadwinners. Few of these families experienced long-term separation, as parents often chose to send their children to boarding schools abroad at early ages, frequently traveling back and forth between their children abroad and their families in Korea. This high-cost arrangement sets these families apart from most Korean transnational families, including wild geese families—the most common yet controversial arrangement among this demographic, characterized by the extended separation of fathers in Korea from mothers and children abroad.

Examining such privileged transnational families calls for keen attention to the following questions: Do elite parents with ample resources experience dramatic changes in their parenting and parenthood upon their children's departure to schools abroad? Are the power dynamics within elite transnational couples similar to or different from those in their less affluent, less educated counterparts? What challenges do they face in transnational parenting, if any? Do they find transnational parenthood rewarding and worthwhile, or do they find it taxing? These questions might matter more to mothers than to fathers, as parenthood typically changes women's lives more dramatically than men's, especially when it comes to their careers.

This chapter explores the narratives of twenty-four Korean mothers who have experienced transnational motherhood due to their children's elite education abroad. Turning to the stories these mothers tell, this chapter delves into their ideals of transnational motherhood and how they pursued them, depending on their employment statuses and educational backgrounds. In contrast to most studies on education-driven transnational families, which often concentrate on discussions of full-time motherhood, this chapter sheds light on the differences between full-time mothers and employed mothers within elite Korean transnational family circles.

For comparison, I categorize the mothers in this chapter into two groups: stay-at-home mothers, who value their undivided provision of traditional maternal care, and employed mothers, who engage in what I term *all-around motherhood*. This comparison examines what makes each group find motherhood fulfilling or not, based on their ideals of transnational motherhood. The analysis prompts a discussion on whether and how an elite class background enhances intensive mothering within a transnational context. It also underscores the need for greater attention to the significance of elite transnational motherhood to the mothers themselves.

Stay-at-Home Mothers' Undivided Motherhood

Traditional Norms for "Good" Mothering

Stay-at-home mothers in this chapter were highly educated, with all but one holding at least a bachelor's degree and four having postgraduate degrees from Korean or U.S. institutions. Their life trajectories closely resemble those of other highly educated Korean mothers, whose careers are often interrupted.[6] Despite their qualifications and professional experience, they chose to leave white-collar professions—such as translator, schoolteacher, or classical music instructor—to become full-time mothers. Their narratives provide insight into the concept of "good" motherhood and the work-family challenges faced by highly educated Korean women.

None of the women in this chapter expressed regret about their decision to become stay-at-home mothers, likely to avoid being perceived as "pushed-out mothers."[7] Instead, they framed full-time motherhood as a deliberate choice made for their children and also for their busy husbands with prestigious careers. They adhered to the belief that mothers should be the primary caregivers.

For instance, Sarah's mother, who had previously worked at a foreign embassy in Korea, viewed her decision to leave the workforce as typical for women of her generation. Reflecting on her late twenties, when she decided to marry, she recalled that the notion of a working mother was both rare and less desirable. "Back then, not many mothers of young children worked outside the home," she noted. Although working at a foreign embassy was a significant part of her life, she ultimately chose to leave the job for the sake of her children.

Sarah's mother viewed full-time motherhood as a class privilege. She remarked, "[While working at the embassy,] I was jealous of my friends who could focus on their kids at home. [...] Like them, I wanted to dedicate myself to raising my children well." She internalized the ideal of intensive mothering,[8] which demands a significant investment of time and energy. When she sought employment after Sarah turned five, she struggled to find a job that allowed her sufficient time for childcare. While she did not want her college diploma from a prestigious Korean institution and her career record to go to waste, she believed that prioritizing motherhood was the right decision. She aimed to be fully committed to and informed about "raising children right."

Like Sarah's mother, other stay-at-home mothers in this chapter actively embraced the concept of intensive motherhood, viewing it as incompatible with full-time employment. They saw providing 24-7 support—their undivided attention and energy—as central to being a "good" mother, even if it came at the expense of their professional careers. To them, fulfilling the traditional maternal role meant preparing nutritious and delicious meals, maintaining a clean and peaceful home, and providing substantial emotional support—elements that all reinforced the concept of motherly care.

This belief was even more pronounced in their transnational context. Despite being physically distant from their children, they made concerted efforts to ensure their well-being and uphold high standards of care. When separated, they prioritized ensuring their children were well fed and well cared for in a healthy environment. Stay-at-home mothers remained dedicated to providing the best possible motherly care, regardless of their physical location in relation to their children.

Mark's mother, a former classical music tutor, was a stay-at-home mother who experienced wild goose motherhood for the longest duration among the women in this book. She lived in the United States with her children for about ten years, while her husband remained in Korea to continue his career as an executive at a broadcasting company. Although her husband's career was what had initially brought the family to the United States, he returned to Korea alone after two years of his overseas assignment, while Mark's mother stayed in the United States with their children until they graduated from high school. Her extended stay abroad and wild goose motherhood were driven primarily by her desire to provide her children with an American education.

Reflecting on her time as a solo parent abroad, Mark's mother emphasized her efforts to create an ideal home environment for her children during her husband's absence, particularly by focusing on her role as a "good cook": "I stayed in the United States solely for my kids. I had only one responsibility: to take good care of them. [. . .] I focused on preparing nutritious, authentic Korean meals nearly every day. I never served them instant food as a main course, although they did occasionally have ramen as a snack. Even when I wasn't up for cooking, I made sure they had home-cooked meals rather than resorting to convenience foods." Her remark underscores how she viewed feeding as central to "good" mothering. In Korean culture, preparing meals for the family is considered a crucial aspect of the maternal role, providing mothers with a sense of satisfaction and pride.[9] For migrant or transnational mothers, this act takes on additional significance; ethnic food becomes more than just sustenance—it serves as a means to reinforce cultural identity and offer emotional stability. Mothers abroad use food and its preparation to connect their children with their heritage and maintain a sense of home.[10] Mark's mother exemplified this approach by using Korean cuisine to help her children feel grounded and at home in the United States.

Mark's mother believed that her devoted support, including meticulous cooking, served both emotional and practical purposes. She considered creating a homelike environment essential for enhancing her children's academic performance. She took pride in how she had designed their U.S. home to resemble Korea, believing that this familiar atmosphere contributed to her children's happiness and productivity. "At home, children stay emotionally stable," she remarked with a sense of satisfaction. She saw this as her most effective means of supporting their education abroad.

"Emotional stability" was commonly used among stay-at-home mothers to emphasize the benefits of their care, which they felt was often lacking in the care provided by their employed counterparts. Stay-at-home mothers firmly believed that true emotional stability in children could only be achieved through their mothers' undivided attention and care, a belief deeply rooted in traditional gender roles. Mark's mother, for example, deeply valued her decade of predominantly solo parenting in the United States. "I was well-known as one of the most devoted mothers in the neighborhood," she said proudly.

Mark's mother's deep commitment to her motherhood duties, including extensive homemaking and cooking, led her to attribute some, if not all, of her children's academic successes to her efforts. Although she initially considered pursuing a part-time job in the United States for personal fulfillment rather than financial necessity, she ultimately chose to dedicate all her time and energy to supporting her children. She expressed no regret about this decision, feeling that her children's academic accomplishments validated her choice.

Mark's mother's pride in her dedicated approach to motherhood led her to undervalue and, at times, criticize employed mothers, whom she believed lacked the time and energy to properly care for their children. Her ideal of a "good" mother, who consistently provides ample and nutritious meals, was evident in her statements questioning how "such busy women" could manage to prepare "warm, fresh dinners every night." Her concept of the "family devotion schema"[11] centered exclusively on the children, often at the expense of acknowledging the needs of other family members; she even regarded her role as a wife as secondary to her role as a mother.

While Mark's mother did not neglect her husband, who had been a wild goose father for a decade, her narratives revealed that she prioritized her role as a mother over her role as a wife. Her ideal of motherhood emphasized a child-centered perspective and intensive mothering, which she expected future generations to embrace. She expressed a desire for a daughter-in-law who would adhere to a similar family devotion schema, one that encompasses caring for all family members, not just children.[12] "I prefer a daughter-in-law who can provide Mark with peace of mind. I don't want someone who prioritizes her career above everything else," she said. By championing undivided motherhood as the domain of stay-at-home mothers, she aimed to perpetuate a neo-traditional family model similar to her own "opt-out mother"[13] trajectory, hoping to instill this ideal in future generations within her family.

Early Educational Support: The Role of Mothers' Groups

Many stay-at-home mothers recounted vivid memories of their children's early education, often echoing their children's own recollections but with more detail and positive framing. These narratives were frequently infused with a sense of self-pride, as the mothers viewed themselves as exemplary educators during their children's formative years. Jay's mother's accounts illustrated how highly educated stay-at-home mothers offered direct educational support to their children, both in Korea and abroad. She vividly recalled being a diligent teacher for Jay while raising him in London and Paris during her husband's overseas assignments.

Jay's mother spoke highly of the American school her son attended in Paris, praising its emphasis on humanitarian values and its less competitive atmosphere compared to most Korean schools. Despite this, she felt compelled to play a more direct role in Jay's educational development, especially in a foreign setting. Drawing on her experience as a high school math teacher, she actively applied her educational expertise to support Jay's learning. She believed this background set her apart from other stay-at-home mothers, considering herself to be in a "much better position" to assume a teaching role.

Jay's mother also reflected positively on her time as a voluntary supplementary teacher at the American school in Paris:

> I have taught at school myself, so I understand how things operate in that environment. [...] Shortly after we arrived in Paris, I visited the school and offered to volunteer, although my English was less than perfect. [...] They welcomed my help and allowed me to assist in my son's class as a supplementary teacher. My duties included making sure every student had their books, pencils, and other supplies and helping students get to the bathroom when needed.

Concerned about her son's adaptation to the new school environment, Jay's mother took it upon herself to closely monitor his academic performance. She took pride in her ability and "courage" to fulfill this role in a foreign setting.

Jay's mother's involvement extended beyond mere oversight. She meticulously crafted a "library-like environment" in their Paris home to support her children's reading and homework, aiming to minimize stress and create a conducive learning atmosphere: "During our stay in Europe, I purchased a large number of English books. Back in 1996 and 1997, when buying English books in Korea was quite challenging, the internet wasn't as accessible for this purpose. To find books for my kids at a reasonable price, I frequently visited flea markets." She proudly shared the methods she used to expose her children to the books she had acquired. "Kids don't take a book from a well-organized shelf. So I put books in random places—one on the sofa, one on the table, one on the floor, and so on," she explained. Her meticulously calculated efforts to tutor her children became a source of great pride. "With a little attention, I can easily find tips and tools to teach my kids well," she remarked.

Jay's mother credited her past work experience for her tutoring, believing it made her motherhood special. "I used to teach at a school, so I could be different from other mothers, at least in education," she said. Throughout her children's childhood, she chose to actively take on the role of their teacher, believing it was her duty as a highly educated mother. "Mothers should be active when teaching young kids. They should study with their kids. Even when I was tired, I taught my kids math at home. I felt I had to do so," she said.

While Jay's mother emphasized her individual efforts to teach her children early on, other mothers highlighted a more collective approach to supporting their children's education. Participation in mothers' groups emerged as an integral aspect of motherhood for many in this chapter. Such collective work, a common practice among middle-to-upper-class Korean mothers, was seen as one of the most efficient and effective ways to fulfill their role as "education managers."[14]

Mothers' groups exemplify the Korean maternal culture of "child management,"[15] which involves active oversight of school grades, daily schedules, and friendships to secure placements in prestigious schools. In fulfilling this managerial role, many mothers in this chapter often formed and joined groups with other mothers from similar class backgrounds, in which they collectively shared insider information about schools abroad, which many found practical and, to some extent, necessary due to the scarcity of such information. They also organized groups focused on volunteer work or performing ensembles to enhance their children's résumés. The U.S. college application process often involved SAT test results and AP (Advanced Placement) classes—requirements that were systematically different from those of Korean colleges, making mothers' groups particularly valuable. Together, they searched for and hired suitable tutors for their children, typically during summer breaks when the children returned to Korea from boarding schools abroad. These groups were often stratified, as the collective management of children's education is typically feasible only among individuals with similarly high cultural and financial resources.

Participation in such mothers' groups often held particular significance for stay-at-home mothers. They viewed their unemployment as an advantage, allowing them to engage fully as dedicated and diligent managers of their children's education. With the flexibility to set their own schedules and often outsourcing household chores, many of these mothers were able to invest considerable time and energy into the collective management of their children's education. Their focus on "having enough time" for their children underscored the value they placed on sacrificial motherhood. This sometimes led to frustration with their employed counterparts, who often struggled to attend meetings regularly due to time conflicts, as most meetings were scheduled during work or school hours.

Engaging in mothers' groups often went beyond mere "child management." Through their substantial investment in these groups, some stay-at-home mothers found personal benefits that sometimes outweighed those for their children. Emily's mother's comments highlighted that stay-at-home mothers, like herself, participated in mothers' groups for reasons beyond just parenting. "It's more like a social gathering," she said with a smile: "Kids handle most of their important decisions [regarding education] themselves, so there's not much for us to do directly. Trying to manage too many [practical] matters for them can disrupt family harmony. Instead, we support them from behind the scenes. We spend time together, have lunch, and occasionally discuss school, but that's about it." Emily's mother attempted to describe the meetings she attended as intimate, congenial, and centered on mothers rather than solely focused on children. While framing the teamwork of mothers as socializing, she simultaneously downplayed the institutional value of their collaborative management of their children's education, possibly concerned that others might view such activity as too exclusive.

This narrative seemed genuine to some extent, given the limited opportunities for stay-at-home mothers to interact with people outside their family circles. "If I don't meet other mothers, I don't think I would have any appointments outside my neighborhood," Emily's mother said with an awkward laugh. Her background as a highly educated transnational "opt-out mom," having grown up in Europe with a diplomat father and worked as a translator until childbirth, highlighted the context in which she found a rare joy in interacting with "people outside the home" during her life as a full-time mother.

The groups of mothers who sent their children to elite schools abroad often appeared highly class-exclusive. Mothers from less affluent backgrounds seemed to derive little enjoyment or benefit from participating in these groups. For example, Joy's mother, who had not studied or worked abroad, felt she was "not brainy enough" to fully engage in the mothers' groups. As a result, she found herself distanced from—and even uncomfortable with—most of the mothers of Joy's school friends: "I don't know many other mothers. [. . .] I haven't made an effort to join their group because I'm not well informed in education abroad. [. . .] To be honest, they are quite unique in many ways. They tend to share information exclusively among themselves. I'm not particularly close to any of them." To justify her exclusion, she disparaged both the mothers' groups and their culture of collective child management. She sarcastically questioned, "I heard they tend to selectively share information even within their groups. They're not always honest with each other. Why in the world are they like that?"

Joy's mother felt that her bachelor's degree in fine arts from a Korean college, coupled with the lack of any degrees from abroad, left her lacking the confidence to join any mothers' groups. She frequently compared herself to other mothers, describing herself as "not as savvy" as they were. Within the circle of privileged mothers, she appeared insecure about supporting her two daughters' education abroad. Justifying her distance from the mothers' groups, she said, "My kids are doing their best. They're doing well enough, and I'm happy with that. That's all I want." She sought to present herself as more generous and less anxious than the other mothers, adding, "In life, there are many things more important than education. Don't you think so?"

Children, reflecting the societal stigma against "intense" Korean mothers, often held ambivalent views toward their mothers' collective efforts. They tended to highlight their own work and independence, not wanting to be seen as beneficiaries of their mothers' networks. Bill was a case in point: He vehemently denied any substantial connection between his mother and those of several friends. He stressed that his mother was distant and different from the "intense mothers" of some of his friends, stating, "My mom rarely visited my school. She didn't even know who my teacher was." His tone conveyed his pride in his—and his mother's—shared independence, a trait he felt many of his friends and their mothers lacked.

However, the accounts from Bill's mother painted a picture inconsistent with her son's narrative. She admitted to participating in multiple mothers' groups, awkwardly smiling as she said, "I even had two planners, one for each of my kids, because I couldn't fit all the appointments [with other mothers] in one planner." She believed that this gendered teamwork had ultimately benefited Bill's college applications, viewing such participation as an essential aspect of her mothering—an acknowledgment that her son did not share.

While acknowledging the value of the work done by mothers' groups, Bill's mother did not fully embrace the culture of the groups in which she engaged. She recognized a division among the mothers based on the amount and type of resources they could contribute. Although her background as a public school teacher allowed her to connect with many members, she struggled to grasp the information about elite schools abroad circulated within the group, due to its exclusivity. For example, she felt that understanding such information required exceptional English proficiency and knowledge of the U.S. school system—traits she believed most of the mothers in her group possessed. To "keep up with" these mothers, she noted that she had to "work hard," making every effort to attend meetings as frequently as possible.

Despite varying views and experiences, mothers' groups appeared to have been an essential aspect of most mothers' approach to parenting in this chapter, particularly regarding tutoring and extracurricular activities. Fathers, however, rarely commented on their involvement in these efforts, suggesting a disproportionate division of labor in parenting within elite transnational families. In this gender-segregated context, mothers—especially stay-at-home mothers—felt a strong responsibility to collectively manage their children's education to maximize the impact of their support. Nevertheless, this does not imply that mothers solely led the family's educational endeavors abroad. Rather, they acted more as executors, implementing the family's educational plans on a daily basis.

Justifying Gender Divides in Elite Transnational Parenting

Stay-at-home mothers believed their responsibilities for their children were manifold, encompassing physical and academic growth as well as emotional health. This role consumed a significant amount of their time and energy, yet few of these mothers criticized or blamed the unequal distribution of this work compared to that of fathers. They often justified their husbands' minimal involvement in early parenting, accepting and understanding their work-oriented lives, which they saw as normal and successful, especially for men in Korean society.

Sunny's mother, who left her teaching job to focus on her daughter's education, willingly took on the role of her daughter's primary educator in the early years, much like many other stay-at-home mothers. She explained, "When we first got married, my husband and I didn't have much money, so I felt it was my responsibility to teach our daughter myself." Although she acknowledged that her husband was not very involved in their daughter's early education, she was careful not to portray him as indifferent or distant: "My husband and I discussed her education extensively, but he generally left the decisions to me. [...] That was his way of participating. He provided full emotional support by trusting my decisions, even though he wasn't directly involved in the decision-making process." Although Sunny's mother noted her husband's limited involvement in their daughter's early education, she sought to excuse his lack of engagement by framing it as a demonstration of his full trust in her abilities. She added, "I'm not the smartest mother in the world, but he showed how much he believed in my capacity to educate Sunny well." Embracing the belief that educating children is a maternal duty, she was able to be generous about her husband's minimal support in the intense management of their daughter's early education.

Sunny's mother was not the only stay-at-home mom who sought to downplay the disproportionate amount of work she invested in early parenting. Most stay-at-home mothers similarly praised their husbands' contributions, viewing them as architects who outlined their children's educational trajectories and made crucial decisions, such as school choices. This perspective was especially pronounced in their narratives about their husbands' involvement in their children's later education, particularly once their children began studying abroad.

Many stay-at-home mothers, lacking experience in studying or working abroad, felt less confident in managing their children's later education overseas. They often perceived their husbands—who typically had such experiences—as more knowledgeable in this area and consequently tended to highly estimate their husbands' involvement and guidance in their children's transnational experiences during and after college. For instance, Bill's mother, who had accompanied her husband on his sabbatical at a U.S. college, recounted how she deferred to her husband when their son was deciding whether to take a gap year. She said, "It's not my work [to guide him], so I just asked my husband to take care of it." This statement both consciously and unconsciously reinforced the gender divide in elite transnational parenting, drawing a distinct line between the responsibilities of a less-educated mother and those of a more-educated father. "I just tried to let my son know that I cared. That was all," she added.

The work that Bill's mother claimed as her responsibility reflected the gendered expectations of a mother's duties. "[While Bill was in Korea,] I helped him most by making him good food and giving rides, which every mother does. [. . .] Now I try to make him feel comfortable and relaxed," she said. While she strongly believed in the value of motherly support and took pride in being a devoted mother fulfilling her gender role, she also framed her contributions as ordinary and trivial. In doing so, she highlighted her husband's academic support for their son abroad and reinforced society's tendency to undervalue caregiving work.

Kyla's mother shared a similar perspective. Her family had moved to the United States primarily for her husband's doctoral studies and lived there for a decade, during which time her children completed most of their schooling. Before migrating, she had contributed to the family economy in various ways; after leaving her job as a high school teacher, she ran the family business with her husband for several years. However, after the move, she became a full-time "manager mother," dedicating all her time and energy to her children's—and her husband's—education abroad.

Kyla's mother recalled her time in the United States with fondness, taking pride in how she supported her children. During her stay, she felt compelled to broaden her efforts in managing their education. She described going the extra mile to gather school-related information in English, not just from the internet but also through connections with other Korean mothers in her neighborhood in Texas, showing how the collective management of children's education by Korean mothers thrived regardless of location. "I needed to join the network [of Korean mothers in my city in Texas] as soon as I arrived," she said.

Her network-based educational support continued for quite a long time, becoming even more important as her kids grew, given her lack of firsthand experience with the U.S. school system. For example, this network proved invaluable in supporting her oldest child's high school education and college applications, which she felt required additional parental involvement. "Kyla's younger brother and sister started learning in English [in the United States] at early ages, but Kyla had to adjust to a U.S. middle school quickly," Kyla's mother said. To provide Kyla with extensive help, her mother actively utilized a Korean mothers' group in her region, both online and offline. Much like in Korea, she found leveraging a mothers' network to be central to supporting her children academically: "I carefully listened to other [Korean] mothers and gathered valuable information. Meeting with them was very helpful, as they frequently discussed what extracurricular activities other kids were involved in and which tutors were the best. This made it easy to stay informed."

Her efforts extended beyond the circle of Korean mothers. Recognizing the need to adapt to the majority, which consisted of American parents, Kyla's mother pushed herself to step out of her "comfort zone." She made a concerted effort to integrate into the broader group of mothers by attending as many school events as possible, striving to connect with parents beyond her ethnicity: "American schools host so many events—concerts, parties, and more—almost every night! [*Laughs.*] I attended most of them, but my limited English made it hard to engage in much small talk with the teachers. You know what I mean, right? So I always brought my husband along to help." She recalled making efforts to stay connected with American mothers during the birthday parties of Kyla's friends: "I made an effort to socialize with American mothers while I was there. Although my English limited my ability to participate fully in conversations, I did my best to mingle. At parties, when most of the mothers were chatting outside, I felt a bit out of place on my own. Nevertheless, I tried to join in and engage as much as possible." She remembered the language barriers and cultural difficulties she faced and how she sometimes asked her husband for help. Despite such struggles, Kyla's mother continued to make efforts to avoid isolation, considering it essential to provide her child with as much academic support as possible.

Most of her efforts went unnoticed by her daughter, Kyla, who believed her mother did not—or could not—become very involved in her education in the United States due to her "not-that-good English." When asked about her mother's academic support during high school, Kyla responded, "I don't remember much. I don't think my mom met any of my teachers. [. . .] It was because she couldn't speak English well. [. . .] What could she do at my school?"

Kyla viewed her mother's socializing with other mothers, both in Korea and the United States, as mere recreation rather than something focused on her education. Laughing, she said, "[In the United States,] my mom spent most of her day just hanging out with other Korean mothers." However, Kyla gave her mother ample credit for the other support she provided, such as preparing good meals and giving rides during their time in the United States. This led Kyla to describe her mother as one of the most sacrificial mothers in her neighborhood, both in Korea and abroad.

Kyla's mother also did not view the academic management of her children's education as her primary responsibility. Instead, she consistently framed her support as nonacademic and private. This perspective reinforced a qualitative divide between her parenting and that of her husband. Proudly, Kyla's mother shared how she felt when witnessing her college professor husband and Kyla engaging in a "serious [academic] conversation" on their own without her: "My daughter's major happens to be the same subject that my husband teaches at college. They often discuss their research, and I find it heartwarming to watch them engage in these conversations. Even though I don't fully understand their talks about economic models or other topics, it's wonderful to see them sharing their passion." She felt that her husband saw her more as a spectator, offering emotional support rather than specialized guidance on their child's education. For example, she shared, "My daughter sometimes asks, 'Mom, aren't you bored just listening and not joining in?' When my husband overhears this, he says, 'Hey, your mom loves listening to us talk like this.'" She internalized the asymmetrical relationship between herself and her husband regarding the support given to their high-achieving daughter, adding, "I even tell my daughter, 'You should ask him more. You need to read more of his articles and see if you can do anything with him.'"

Costly Transnational Motherhood: Will It Pay Off?

Many stay-at-home mothers cherished the opportunity to educate their children abroad, seeing it as a way to secure their position within the transnational elite. Relatively affluent mothers viewed their children's education overseas as economically efficient. They believed that educating their children locally, particularly in the Seoul metropolitan area, would have required a similar or even greater expenditure of money and energy. This perspective was driven by their general dissatisfaction with the quality of Korean public schools and the intense competition among top-ranked students.

Sam's mother, who had studied abroad herself, expressed her dissatisfaction with Korean public education and its overall culture, feeling she "saved a great deal of [her] energy" by sending Sam to a U.S. boarding school. "I didn't like what Sam learned at school [in Seoul]. The school was too small, and the teachers were not that great. I could see how unprepared the teachers were," she explained.

Sam's mother was one of the few stay-at-home mothers who remained deeply involved in their children's education through the later stages. She described how she meticulously planned and guided Sam's preparation for studying abroad: "I carefully selected Sam's tutors who were familiar with U.S. textbooks, recruiting the best available in Korea and providing them with detailed guidelines on how to teach him. [. . .] It was a significant investment of both time and money." She framed her educational involvement as a collaborative effort, crediting her husband for accompanying her as an education manager. "[Before Sam's education abroad] my husband and I taught him at home every night. We just let him play at school during the daytime, and after he got home, we literally homeschooled him," she added.

This time- and cost-consuming educational involvement prompted her to transfer Sam from a selective Korean high school to a U.S. boarding school. For her, the U.S. boarding school they preferred was an economical choice considering the time, energy, and money she and her husband invested in supplementing Sam's education in Korea. Firmly believing in the superior quality of education her son received in the United States, she did not view the cost of his education abroad as excessively expensive.

Miranda's unemployed mother, who had lived in Singapore for over a decade while her husband worked as an expatriate, was generally satisfied with her transnational motherhood. She recalled investing most of her time and energy in her daughter's upbringing, whether in Korea or abroad. She believed her role still had a long way to go before yielding meaningful results, even though her daughter had already entered college. Concerning her daughter's future, she stated, "I want her to be able to do everything she wants." To support Miranda's ambitions, she felt she needed to remain a dedicated full-time mother indefinitely.

In line with the Korean cultural norm where grandmothers often take primary care of their grandchildren if their daughters work full-time,[16] Miranda's mother also felt pressured to assume this role for her high-achieving daughter's future children. "I already told Miranda that I won't help her raise her children," she said with a laugh, only half-joking. Nevertheless, she appeared ready to support her daughter as much as possible, particularly if her assistance was crucial for Miranda to accomplish her goals: "If Miranda struggles [to balance work and family], she'll reach out to me for help. How can I ignore that? If I were busy with my own job, I might be able to say no, but since I have some spare time, I don't think I can turn her down." Miranda's mother expressed satisfaction with her role, confident in her husband's ability to guide their daughter's career path toward becoming an international lawyer. She believed their transnational family project, centered on her husband's career and their daughter's education, had been executed nearly flawlessly. To perfect it, she was ready to temporarily relocate with her daughter to any country outside Korea if her daughter needed help balancing work and family. This commitment highlighted her sacrificial dedication to her role in transnational motherhood.

Conversely, stay-at-home mothers with limited financial resources, though a minority in this chapter, were uncertain about the value of investing in their children's education abroad. Their concerns went beyond the financial cost, questioning whether this investment genuinely enhanced their children's overall happiness and fulfillment. For example, Bill's mother, a former school-teacher with no experience studying abroad, shared that she and her husband had to budget carefully to afford sending both of their sons to a prestigious

Korean prep school that follows a curriculum designed for U.S. college applicants. Through her ambition and sacrifices, her son Bill gained acceptance to
an Ivy League college and was nearing graduation at the time of her interview.

While expressing gratitude for her son's achievement, Bill's mother also
felt ambivalent about the educational approach of the selective Korean school
that shaped him. Bill's mother recalled having empathy for Korean students,
including her son, who aspired to study abroad. She remarked, "I always felt
sorry for those kids [Bill and his friends]. They worked so hard, sometimes too
hard. It made me sad whenever I watched them."

Her ambivalence appeared to persist, even intensify, after her son entered
an Ivy League college. While Bill's mother wanted her son to join their ranks,
she seemed uncertain about the value of such a highly competitive and consequently exhausting life. She presumed that this lifestyle occasionally left her
son drained. She also worried that her son's success might unravel someday, a
possibility she considered likely: "Bill has accomplished a great deal, and I'm
grateful for that. However, I worry about whether he can handle hardships he
hasn't yet faced. I hope that someday he encounters a small challenge, rather
than a big one, so he can learn about the complexities of life." This concern
led her to question her maternal support, which focused on facilitating her
son's elite education abroad. She remarked, "I always worry that Bill works too
hard. He sometimes gets completely exhausted. When I see him like that, I ask
myself, 'Why did I send him to the United States for college?'"

At the time of her interview, her son Bill, who was in his senior year, had
already secured a job at one of the Asian branches of a large transnational corporation based in Singapore. Although she was grateful for this opportunity,
Bill's mother also felt a sense of sadness when imagining her son living abroad
for the rest of his life. When asked about any plans to move abroad to live with
or near her son, she adamantly rejected the possibility. Her brief experience
living in the United States, due to her husband's temporary overseas work,
did not instill in her a high value for living abroad. Awkwardly laughing, Bill's
mother said, "I don't like living in the United States. I love living in Korea. I
can't speak English well. More than anything else, I love watching Korean TV
shows. Moreover, all my friends are here, so . . ." This reluctance sets her apart
from more affluent mothers, who wished for their children to settle overseas
so they could move and be closer to them.

David's mother, who had never lived abroad and possessed the lowest
education level among all the mothers in this chapter, did not perceive her
motherhood as particularly transnational. She viewed transnational motherhood as something expensive, beyond her financial means, not only because
of Ivy League college tuition but also the cost of the international flights
she would need to take to provide on-site care for her son abroad. This

financial constraint likely contributed to her limited engagement in her son's life overseas compared to the more affluent mothers in the chapter. "[Paying the tuition] is the only help we can give our son," she said, implying that her husband, who also did not study abroad, did not engage much in their son's education other than financially supporting it.

The minimal parental involvement led David's mother to believe that her motherhood had nearly ended, wondering whether she and her husband could offer significant assistance throughout their son's adulthood. "What can we do for him besides that? Everything [our son does] is now connected to the United States or other countries. That's beyond our capacity," she said sadly. "Even when David gives his best effort in everything, he still needs a bit of luck. That's what my daily prayer is for," she added. Their son, David, a first-generation study abroad student, seemed likely to remain the only cosmopolitan individual in their family for a long time.

Employed Mothers' "All-Around" Motherhood

Juggling Career and Intensive Motherhood

Regardless of employment status, all mothers in this chapter adhered to the notion of intensive mothering as a normative standard and a "cultural script."[17] Employed mothers' narratives highlight how this norm was pursued and practiced intensively through their juggling of career and motherhood, often entailing sacrifices in their professional lives. Regardless of their work and academic paths, employed mothers structured their parenting practices around a highly gendered standard of devotion. Simultaneously, their education and careers defined their ideal of "good" mothering and motherhood, setting exceptionally high standards for maternal involvement.

The eight employed mothers showcased various ways of balancing intensive mothering with demanding careers, often through short or long transnational family arrangements. A few of them benefited from the relatively favorable family policies and job security available to public employees in Korea. For example, one mother, a vice-principal at a public school, mentioned that she could take long-term childcare leave without facing any penalties. However, many employed mothers frequently encountered conflicts between their elite professions and the demands of intensive motherhood. Besides the lack of institutional support, they felt inadequately supported by their family members, including their "always-busy" husbands. These mothers detailed the sacrifices they made in their careers while pursuing intensive motherhood, both before and after their children's education abroad.

Greg's mother, a professor at a Korean college, reflected on her son's early childhood, a period when she assumed most of the child-rearing responsibilities: "I struggled a lot [with balancing work and childcare], while my husband concentrated only on his job. Although he occasionally came home early, he didn't contribute much to childcare. It often felt like he prioritized his work over spending time with Greg, especially when he was a baby." Instead of solely blaming her husband for neglecting childcare responsibilities, Greg's mother internalized the role of the primary caregiver. She also generalized the unequal division of childcare duties, stating, "Maybe I'm not the only mother who did most of the child-rearing in my generation." Through these efforts, she tried to present her husband in a somewhat better light. However, she couldn't help but admit that her intensive motherhood had hindered her career.

Other employed mothers also tended to conform to—or even actively embrace—the traditional roles of mother and wife. They acknowledged the structural inequalities they faced while pursuing professional careers as intensive mothers. However, they sought to improve their circumstances personally, often by overworking both at home and in their professions, believing it was their only option. Herbert's mother, a successful pediatrician, spoke about the lack of support she received while advancing her medical career. "I was a top student at the leading medical school in Korea. If I had some support [for child-rearing], I could have become a medical professor at my alma mater," she said.

Despite her unfulfilled dream, Herbert's mother believed she made the "right decision" to prioritize motherhood over her career. She rationalized her choice to leave the graduate medical program and open her clinic at an early age: "Some of my [women] friends who have become medical school professors come home very late every day and are always busy. Since I work only from nine to six, I can go home relatively early and take care of my family." "I'm happy about it," she asserted strongly, perhaps to affirm that her decision was indeed the right one.

Her demanding career did not prevent Herbert's mother from fulfilling the role of an "education manager mother." Throughout her busy career as a pediatrician, she prioritized attending her son's school events and mothers' meetings as often as possible. For her, dedicating time to her son's education was an essential aspect of being a "good" mother, a sentiment shared by many Korean mothers regardless of their employment status. Living up to such high standards required career sacrifices for Herbert's mother, as it does for many employed mothers in Korea. She shared the details of her sacrifices, taking pride in them rather than expressing regret. "I never hesitated to close my clinic on their [her sons'] field days, picnics, or parents' days. Those events were my top priorities," she said. She did not frame her intense mothering as solely for her sons but emphasized how she, as a woman and mother, wanted it for herself and personally benefited from it. "I didn't want to miss those opportunities. Although I have my career, I am a mother above all else," she remarked.

What distinguished Herbert's mother from the stay-at-home mothers in this chapter was her determination to "do it all." She set very high standards for both her career and motherhood, striving to be the "perfect doctor/mother" who excelled in both roles. She took pride in not neglecting any of her responsibilities and highlighted her willingness to sacrifice her job for her children, a practice she viewed as natural. "Even animals like tigers and foxes have maternal instincts. It's not surprising at all," she said adamantly.

Despite her demanding career, Herbert's mother strove to provide care resembling that of stay-at-home mothers, viewing it as a duty for married women with children. Other employed mothers shared this mission, making similar efforts: preparing delicious meals, maintaining a clean house, and attending to their children's physical and mental well-being, either by themselves or with the assistance of paid housekeepers. Such "maternal practices"[18]—nurturing, protecting, and educating their children—were central to their identities, sometimes even more so than their careers.

Their relentless effort to "do it all" led employed mothers to establish a hierarchy among others in their circle. They believed they deserved to be ranked higher than stay-at-home mothers, whom they perceived as having only one straightforward duty—to be a devoted mother. Herbert's mother admitted that stay-at-home mothers could spend more time with their children compared to employed mothers like herself, but she did not consider this the most essential aspect of being a "good" mother. Instead, she valued the quality of engagement and the ability to balance professional success with sacrificial parenting. She sarcastically remarked: "They [stay-at-home mothers] often seem quite proud of how well they care for their children. I know they devote all their time and energy to being close to their kids and providing for them. I truly believe they do!"

While acknowledging the value of full-time childcare, Herbert's mother sought to challenge perceptions that questioned the dedication of employed mothers. By emphasizing her successful career and financial independence, she aimed to present an alternative—and potentially superior—approach to being a "good" mother, one that leveraged her professional status and resources to support her children. She illustrated this with an example from her involvement in a mothers' group dominated by stay-at-home mothers: She offered free health checkups and medicines to both mothers and their children in an effort to integrate with the majority. "They let me stay in the group because I was useful to them," she said, with a mix of sarcasm and pride.

Herbert's mother often expressed the tension she felt between employed mothers like herself and stay-at-home mothers. "I think they [stay-at-home mothers] sometimes get jealous of my career. If I attend any school event, they ask me, 'Why are you here now? Shouldn't you be working?'" she remarked. This tension highlighted the differing perceptions and challenges faced by mothers balancing professional and maternal roles. Despite this, Herbert's mother believed that her busy schedule was a testament to her ongoing effort to excel as both a successful doctor and an excellent mother—qualities she felt distinguished her from stay-at-home mothers.

Similarly, other employed mothers often sought joy rather than fatigue in their intensive—or extensive—mothering roles, even while managing demanding careers. With a positive outlook rather than a sense of sadness, Henry's mother, a vice-principal at a public school, fondly recalled her "second shift"[19] as she supported Henry through his Ivy League college admissions process in Korea: "I get tired quickly, so I usually take a short nap after returning from work. [During Henry's high school days,] after resting, I made dinner for Henry every day, using a variety of vegetables like tomatoes, lettuce, cabbage, and lean meats. Although it was sometimes challenging to wake up before he got home, I never missed a single day." Her tone reflected pride in her dedicated mothering efforts. Like many stay-at-home mothers, her primary focus was on providing nutritious meals and snacks rather than offering direct academic support, particularly after her son began preparing for college abroad. Henry's mother mentioned that any fatigue she felt was quickly forgotten when her son praised her cooking, noting, "It was the best thing I could do for him during those days. What could I do for him that would be better than that?"

Her career as an education expert also allowed her to actively participate in her son's early education. However, Henry's mother chose to emphasize the considerable time and energy she devoted to homemaking and cooking for her high-achieving son rather than focusing solely on academic support. She firmly believed that providing motherly care through nurturing and nutritious meals was the most significant contribution she could make. This underscores her alignment with the conventional ideal of a "good" mother, a sentiment shared among stay-at-home mothers in this chapter.

Greg's mother, a professor at a Korean college with experience studying abroad, was another employed mother navigating the challenge of balancing her professional and maternal duties. To justify her strong focus on mothering, she emphasized her dedication to her role, especially through cooking, frequently noting her "obsession with feeding [her son] well." Embracing her dual role of advancing her academic career while being a devoted mom, she managed to thrive rather than feel overwhelmed. With a tone of pride and accomplishment, she fondly reminisced about her daily routine during her son's high school years at an international school in Seoul: "Greg was always the center of my life, no matter how busy work made me. [. . .] When he started high school, we moved closer to my office so I could prepare dinner for him every day. My routine involved going home to make dinner, eating with

Greg, and then heading back to the office to finish my work until 11:00 p.m. That was how my days were spent during that time."

Her pride in the meticulous cooking she did for her son underscored how her concept of being a "good" mother aligned closely with that of stay-at-home moms. She sought to challenge the notion that working mothers are less devoted than those who stay at home by highlighting the quality of the meals she prepared for her child. "People think working mothers always feed their kids instant foods," she said with a laugh. By demonstrating that she could mother just as well as, if not better than, stay-at-home moms, she made feeding her son "right" a key measure of her success. "Feeding Greg was the hardest work," she reflected with a sense of accomplishment.

Greg's mother saw herself as superior to stay-at-home moms due to her ability to successfully juggle both a career and motherhood. She highlighted her strategies for making the most of "empty time," such as waiting for Greg to finish school or private lessons before picking him up. This efficient use of her time made her feel accomplished in her dual roles as both a "good" mother and a "good" professor: "I love working at a coffee shop, so it never felt like a big deal. I often invited my students or colleagues to join me there, and we got some work done together. It was almost like having my office hours in a more relaxed setting." She credited the flexibility and independence of her academic career as key factors that enabled her to engage in intensive motherhood: "As you know, with a laptop, we [academics] can work from anywhere, so I made the most of the time while waiting for him. I'd often do some grocery shopping as well, since I didn't usually have much time for that." In her view, employed mothers could be just as "good" as stay-at-home mothers, but it required a willingness to make sacrifices. By emphasizing her sacrifices, Greg's mother sought to elevate her motherhood above that of full-time moms, taking pride in her ability to embody the dual ideals of an exceptional career woman and a devoted parent.

The Pursuit of "All-Around" Motherhood

While prioritizing their maternal roles, employed mothers expanded the definition and value of intensive motherhood, particularly within the unique context of raising high-achieving children abroad. They argued that their careers allowed them to provide their children with multidimensional support, blending both maternal care and professional insights. They believed that this comprehensive support made their approach to motherhood distinctive, and potentially even superior to full-time motherhood.

Employed mothers highlighted the academic support they provided not only during their children's early years but also throughout adolescence and even into early adulthood. Many claimed that they "knew [their] children the best," believing their understanding surpassed that of their children's teachers and mentors. Mothers with education-related degrees and careers particularly valued their parenting rules and philosophies, asserting that these were grounded in expert-guided and professional insights for academic support.[20]

Hailey's mother, a vocational counselor with a master's degree from the United States, demonstrated an integrated approach by applying her career skills to her mothering. "I often apply the theories I use at work to [my conversations with] Hailey. I can't help but analyze my daughter," she said, laughing. She confessed that she naturally evaluated her daughter much like her clients at work, assessing her as a student. "In today's world, curiosity and perseverance are the most crucial elements of success, and Hailey has both of them," she said, echoing how she would evaluate one of her clients.

Hailey's mother described the effort she put into creating an environment where Hailey could fully develop her own "unique texture." To achieve this, she diligently researched a list of U.S. preparatory boarding schools: "Several factors influenced our choice. First was the school's size. I also wanted a school with a strong emphasis on writing. That's why we chose the school [Hailey graduated from]. I wanted her to focus on the humanities early on, rather than practical subjects, and I hoped she wouldn't choose applied sciences as her major in college from the start." Along with providing meticulous guidance on school and major choices, Hailey's mother endeavored to instill in her the parenting mottos: "Be unique," "Have fun," and "Persevere in everything." She believed these mottos aligned well with the curriculum of elite U.S. schools, in contrast to those in Korea.

Hailey's mother believed her experience studying in a U.S. graduate school greatly helped her understand and empathize with her daughter's life abroad, both academically and personally. She particularly enjoyed their overseas calls, during which Hailey would share details about her daily life, classes, and assignments. "We literally talked about everything on the phone," she proudly said.

Hailey's mother said that she could envision Hailey's day, week, or semester despite the geographical distance between them. "When I see the name of the class Hailey is taking, I can immediately picture what the class would be like," she explained. She believed her deep understanding of Hailey helped her build a close mother-daughter relationship. "[Knowing about Hailey's college life in the United States] makes our conversation more interesting and intimate," she added. She took special pride in the unique bond she believed she shared with her daughter abroad.

Due to her thorough familiarity with the language and culture of the United States, Hailey's mother noted that she was able to visit Hailey frequently while she was at a U.S. boarding school without any difficulty. She was also able to actively leverage her multicultural resources in her mothering during school-related events abroad:

The school invited all parents every October, and I never missed it. Hailey's father also attended with me. [...] The open classroom observations were particularly helpful because they gave us a genuine sense of what Hailey was learning. [...] We also had the opportunity to meet all her teachers. [...] In the school auditorium, we could greet each teacher and inquire about our daughter. In addition, the following day included a briefing and Q&A session for all attendees, which we attended without fail.

Her pride in her active participation suggested that not all mothers of Korean students abroad could engage as deeply as she did. Reflecting on the parents' weekends at Hailey's boarding school, she noted, "Not every Korean mom attended parents' weekends."

Hailey's mother continued to compare herself with other Korean mothers, assuming they were less transnational and multicultural than she was:

Some mothers attended, but they didn't meet all their children's teachers. But my husband and I participated in every program the school offered. That allowed me to vividly picture what Hailey was learning throughout the year, even from home in Korea. When Hailey talked about her math class, I could immediately recall what the math teacher had said during our visit. I had a clear image of the classroom, such as one with ten students, which helped me engage in more meaningful conversations with my daughter.

Unlike most stay-at-home mothers, who usually only talked about their husbands' visits to their children abroad, Hailey's mother vividly described how her own visits enabled her hands-on transnational mothering. She continued to visit her daughter even after Hailey entered college, firmly believing that these visits positively impacted her daughter's academic and emotional well-being.

Other employed mothers also took pride in the strong bond they shared with their children, attributing it to their firsthand transnational knowledge and high-status professional careers that their children admired. They found "serious" mother-child conversations particularly rewarding, believing these discussions contributed to a well-rounded approach to motherhood. For example, Herbert's mother, a pediatrician, was one of the few mothers who shared the role of career advisor with her husband. She genuinely enjoyed engaging in a wide range of conversations with her young adult son while he was abroad: "Herbert talks to me about everything in his life, including his classes, friends, and girlfriend. [...] The other day we talked about the gay parade in New York [her son attended] for multiple hours." She attributed her ability to have such meaningful mother-son conversations to her career and work experience at a U.S. university hospital. "It's because Herbert is a great kid, but also because I've been working for most of my life," she said. She believed she could offer guidance and support for her son's college education and career preparation just as effectively, if not more so, than her husband. This perspective gave her motherhood value, particularly when compared to that of stay-at-home mothers. "Most mothers of my generation are stay-at-home moms, and I believe I can provide my son with better answers than those mothers would give their children," she asserted with confidence.

Herbert's mother believed that her prestigious, high-income career served as a model for her son, alongside her husband's career as a medical school professor. This kind of self-evaluation was rare among the mothers discussed in this chapter. She recalled the day when her son expressed his admiration for her job in words: "Herbert once worked part-time at my clinic during a break. At that time, he expressed a desire to become a doctor like me, though he now has a different dream. He enjoyed seeing patients improve after receiving treatment from me. He could witness firsthand how rewarding my work was." She added, "I felt so good and appreciated. I joked with Herbert, 'Did you see the people [my patients] smile when they walked out of my office? It's funny because I'm so tough on them!'" Among the various forms of support she provided as a mother, she believed that her prestigious career deserved her son's respect the most.

Many children's narratives supported these views, as those with elite professional mothers often reported consulting both their fathers and their mothers about college and career-related matters. Thus, while this applied to only a few cases in this book due to the limited number of professional mothers, educational and career experiences were a core resource for elite transnational mothers, much like they were for fathers. For example, Herbert supported his mother's perspective by praising her dedication to her career, noting that it was widely respected by others: "I loved the fact that my mom was working just like my dad. I really appreciated it—it was a source of pride for me. Our neighbors were especially kind to me because I was the child of their children's pediatrician. Most of my friends were also my mom's patients. I felt very proud of her and her hard work."

Herbert's mother also noticed a rise in "serious" conversations between her husband and Herbert, particularly as Herbert began considering his career path. Many other mothers, especially those who were unemployed, shared similar observations. However, Herbert's mother felt included in these discussions as well. She happily noted, "Sometimes he talks to me before he goes to his dad."

Josh's mother, a college lecturer, considered herself a role model for her children too. While pursuing her postgraduate degrees as a mother abroad, with her husband running his business in California, she took special pride in her delayed but unwavering academic career: "My kids have grown up seeing me constantly writing at home. It's not that I pursued my PhD just to impress them, but they might have witnessed my dedication and hard work despite all the challenges." Josh's mother spoke of the difficulties she faced, including work-family conflicts during her intensive motherhood abroad, and desired acknowledgment from her children. Paradoxically, these challenges became a source of great pride and a testament to her competence and perseverance. She believed that her doctoral degree, earned while balancing motherhood abroad, held not only academic value but also moral significance. She hoped that these values would serve as a meaningful example for her children.

This sense of pride drove Josh's mother to set herself apart from full-time mothers, whom she believed deserved less credit for "just staying home" and "not achieving much." While placing significant moral value on her own hard work both inside and outside the home, she tended to undervalue the caregiving work of full-time mothers, viewing it as less productive for educational purposes. "If I were a stay-at-home mother, my kids might have seen me as lethargic and incompetent. That type of mother wouldn't serve as a good role model for her children, especially for grown-up ones," she added.

Alongside moral influence, the career-related resources of employed mothers, particularly their professional connections, were key benefits of the "all-around" motherhood they pursued. Some employed mothers were reported to leverage their connections to support their children's extracurricular activities or college applications. Although not widespread, many children of these mothers recognized and appreciated their efforts. For example, Greg acknowledged the advantages of his mother's professional connections, confessing that his professor mother "made [his] internship" possible at the NGO where she was involved as an external advisor.

Beyond tangible assistance, the social influence of his mother's professor career also inspired Greg to view her as one of his role models. "It felt natural for me to aspire to be a scholar. Because of my mom, I became interested in academia and decided to pursue an activist-scholar career like hers," he remarked. His admiration was significant, as few children named their mothers as role models. Typically, the term "role model" was reserved by most children for their elite fathers.

Successful Father, Successful Mother: Who Is a Better Example?

Employed mothers saw themselves as part of a team with their husbands, also elite professionals who often possessed higher levels of education or more experiences abroad. For example, Daniel's mother, a painter teaching at an international school in Korea, described how she and her professor husband collaborated on their son's college application, leveraging both of their study abroad experiences: "College applications need to be mistake-free. We discussed what Daniel should include in his statement, but neither my husband nor I edited it ourselves. We just assisted him in brainstorming ideas, and a professional editor took care of the final revisions. Even though the editor played a crucial role, we still needed to contribute during the earlier stages because we knew Daniel the best." Unlike most stay-at-home mothers who viewed the process of educating their children abroad as "father-led," Daniel's mother emphasized that her son's college application was a collaborative effort involving both her and her husband, along with their son. She used her judgment to suggest what she believed was best for Daniel, including decisions about his college and major. The choice to hire the best private editor for his applications was also part of their joint effort. She highlighted the rarity of her role, noting that few mothers had such authority and involvement in assisting their children's education abroad.

Only one employed mother clearly had more transnational resources than her husband, giving her greater influence in their children's education. Greg's mother, who had earned a PhD abroad and was married to a Korean college graduate, worked hard to persuade her husband—who had never studied abroad—not to pressure their son into applying solely to top-ranked "HYPS" (Harvard Yale Princeton Stanford) colleges. Sarcastically, she remarked, "I'm the one who makes all the fuss in our family," using the term "fuss" to describe her interventions in guiding her son's educational path.

Greg's mother's situation illustrates that educational and transnational resources, rather than gender alone, determine which parent has more influence in shaping their children's education abroad. With her extensive experience studying abroad, Greg's mother felt uniquely qualified to make significant educational decisions. She asserted, "Because I made most of the big [education-related] decisions, my husband tried to provide more emotional support to Greg."

Greg's mother's account highlights a reversal of the typical gender roles in elite transnational parenting presented in this book. Her advanced degree from abroad, which her husband lacked, positioned her as the primary guide for their son's higher education, while her husband's role was mainly to provide emotional support rather than concrete advice. Her narrative, notable even among employed mothers, parallels the deep engagement of many elite fathers in their children's later lives abroad. In this case, a woman with greater transnational resources became the more assertive parent, particularly in providing educational guidance. This suggests that within the context of elite parenting, education and transnational resources may outweigh traditional gender roles, indicating that gender, as a social construct, is often shaped by one's status and resources.

However, when it came to mentoring their son's career, Greg's mother still regarded her husband—a successful journalist—as the "better" mentor. She believed that his extensive experience in the media industry made him better equipped to offer valuable networking and career development advice, especially in a male-dominated field like media, where such resources are often more accessible among men: "My husband has a wide network of contacts from various backgrounds because of his work. [. . .] I often consult my husband if we need additional advice. He quickly finds someone who can offer valuable counsel. Sometimes, I ask him to meet with these advisors on my behalf, and he relays their recommendations to me afterward. This is the greatest support he provides for Greg." Despite her own efforts to support her son through her connections, such as introducing him to an NGO where she was involved, she still valued her husband's social relationships more. This preference reflects the perceived higher value of men's career-related resources in the labor force.

Like Greg's mother, many employed mothers deeply valued their husbands' support in the later stages of their children's lives, especially concerning career guidance. They particularly appreciated their husbands' connections with other professionals—often successful men—who could offer valuable advice on school, major, and career choices. Since mothers and fathers are typically (though not always) key figures in their children's social networks, the development of their children is often closely linked to the quantity and quality of the resources parents provide.

Herbert's mother, who takes immense pride in her career as a pediatrician, praised her husband's career as a medical school professor, viewing it as more successful and exemplary than her own. "Herbert aims to surpass his dad. My husband is like a towering figure for him. He has achieved so much success," she said. Despite earning a comfortable income from her pediatric clinic and being a respected figure in the neighborhood, she viewed her husband's prestigious career as the ideal her son aspired to.

At times, Herbert's mother seemed to envy his success, especially given her own decision to forgo pursuing a doctor of medicine with a doctor of philosophy degree (MD-PhD) in order to prioritize motherhood. Rather than lamenting the achievement gap, she regarded her husband's success as "well deserved." She felt it was "natural" for her to open her clinic while supporting her husband's graduate studies, especially since one of them needed to dedicate time to their children. Her decision was rooted in her belief that, as heads of households, men should pursue higher social status than women if sacrifices are necessary.

In addition to his career achievements, Herbert's mother considered her husband's character morally exemplary: "I have the utmost respect for him. Not many men earn such admiration from their wives. He is the person I hold in the highest regard in this world. He is generous to others but strict with himself. Our sons are fortunate to have him as their father, as they can learn so much from him. Just by living his life his way, my husband is educating our sons." She added, "Herbert often says he aspires to become an adult like his dad," underscoring her admiration for her husband as a role model—particularly as a male role model—for their sons. She believed that being close to one's children was not sufficient for good fatherhood; she saw her husband's perseverance, which she felt had driven his career success, as the key quality that made him an exceptional father and a true exemplar for their sons.

The descriptors Herbert's mother used for her husband—"hardworking," "enterprising," "reliable," "responsible," "respectable," and "family-centered"— were similarly used by many other mothers, whether employed or stay-at-home, to describe their husbands. These terms underscore the high moral value placed on the successful careers and breadwinning roles of elite fathers, even when mothers achieve comparable success outside the home. Within their elite transnational circles, being considered a great person often meant being an "all-around" individual—someone who not only excels in career and academics but also serves as a moral exemplar for others.

Idealized Views of Transnational Motherhood

Employed mothers, drawing from their own experiences studying or working abroad, tended to be more accepting and adaptable to transnational household arrangements compared to stay-at-home mothers. Many of them anticipated and were prepared for extended periods of separation from their children due to their children's careers abroad. For example, Herbert's mother expressed that she never felt sadness or anxiety about her son's likely long-term life abroad, as she believed he "fits in better with U.S. society." She added, "I'm completely fine with living far from him. [. . .] I've already begun to view him as an independent individual, not just as my son. His life is his own." She felt that the advantages her son would gain from living abroad would far outweigh any emotional cost of their physical separation.

Daniel's mother had a proactive approach to the anticipated long-term separation from her child. Embracing the prospect of living abroad, she planned to spend her retirement in the country where Daniel would eventually settle, if possible. "I feel even more comfortable outside Korea," she said. This suggests that the transnational resources of elite mothers—such as fluency in English, the financial means for frequent international travel, and a deep understanding of other cultures—help mitigate the emotional challenges of long-term transnational motherhood.

None of the employed mothers with experience abroad criticized transnational family arrangements as dysfunctional or problematic. None expressed concerns about weakening family bonds due to physical separation. Instead, they generally viewed these setups as serving specific purposes, and Greg's mother, who had lived abroad alone for her career, actively defended them. To her, living apart from family members was neither unusual nor negative.

She firmly rejected the conventional idea of a co-living family arrangement, actively justifying the costly transnational setup her family had chosen:

> People often believe that family members should live together or close by, but our family has experienced a different arrangement. I spent six years alone in the United States for my PhD degree while my baby son and husband stayed in Korea with my parents. Now my husband is in China for work, and my son is attending college in the United States. [...] I'm not suggesting that living with family is bad. What I'm emphasizing is that transnational families can be happy as well. Each of us has lived in various locations up to this point, so how could I now ask Greg to return to Korea and live with me?

As Greg was her only child, she admitted to missing him deeply during their time apart. However, she was willing to endure the emotional cost of transnational motherhood, viewing it as a sacrifice made for her child's benefit.

As an ex-international student, Greg's mother believed her son would benefit from a more extensive and immersive experience abroad. Reflecting on her own graduate school days, she remarked, "I always felt like an eternal stranger in the United States because I started studying abroad too late." Her past challenges as an international student motivated her to provide Greg with the opportunity for deeper transnational mobility. By sending him to the United States right after high school, she aimed to ensure he would have a smoother and more integrated experience abroad than she had: "I hope he can live anywhere in the world and make a global impact. I want him to overcome any language or cultural barriers he might face. If he can achieve that, it will be my greatest accomplishment." For her, the benefits of transnational motherhood outweighed its challenges, as she hoped it would enable her son to carve out a path of global success.

Greg's mother's case exemplifies how employed mothers positively embraced transnational family arrangements and a cosmopolitan lifestyle. They were willing to live apart, often on different continents, to support their children's global mobility. Believing that such mobility would enhance their children's career and marriage prospects, these mothers, equipped with substantial resources, emphasized the unintended benefits of transnational family arrangements while downplaying any potential drawbacks.

Extensive Transnational Motherhood: Varied Efforts and Approaches

The narratives of mothers in this chapter highlight how their class backgrounds have shaped their approach to extending and expanding *intensive mothering*—originally defined as "child-centered, expert-guided, emotionally absorbing, labor-intensive, and financially expensive."[21] The ideology of intensive mothering as a social and historical construct often serves as an ideal rather than a practical reality for many women.[22] It is not universally attainable but represents a hegemonic form of mothering influenced by class-based practices. The mothers featured in this chapter are those who, thanks to their socioeconomic status, were able to and chose to engage in this classed form of mothering to the extent they desired. For these mothers, such efforts were deeply meaningful and integral to their sense of identity, regardless of their employment status.

In Korean society, motherhood is frequently evaluated based on children's academic success.[23] Given this framework, the mothers in this chapter were well placed to view their own motherhood as commendable or exemplary. However, they placed greater emphasis on their personal efforts and work as mothers rather than solely focusing on their children's achievements. For these mothers, motherhood represented a significant, lifelong endeavor that they navigated individually. Their narratives underscore the essence of intensive, or extensive, motherhood, irrespective of their diverse educational and occupational backgrounds.[24]

What distinguishes the mothers in this chapter into two sometimes conflicting groups is their approach to transitioning from intensive to extensive mothering. Stay-at-home mothers portrayed their undivided motherhood as a deliberate choice, aligning more closely with "opt-out mothers" rather than "pushed-out mothers." These mothers emphasized their extraordinary efforts to provide comprehensive care for their children, even when physically separated from them. Whether within the same country or across continents, their maternal labor was dedicated to delivering care that they believed only mothers could provide. They highlighted their efforts to ensure their children were well fed, healthy, and emotionally supported, reflecting the traditional caregiving role of women within the home. By performing such pervasive motherly work, they considered their approach to motherhood extensive, taking great pride in it. Consciously or unconsciously, their approach to undivided motherhood adhered to traditional gender roles and the expectations of "neo-traditional families."[25]

Elite, employed mothers in this chapter adopted a distinct approach by evolving their intensive mothering into extensive mothering. They aimed for "all-around" motherhood, integrating a broad array of responsibilities and roles as accomplished worker-mothers. Their support was multifaceted, blending both maternal care and professional guidance. They believed that their careers and educational achievements enhanced, rather than undermined, their ability to provide high-quality support for their children, especially given the elevated expectations for "good" parental involvement in the context of high-achieving, cosmopolitan children.[26] By balancing both public and private realms of support, they perceived their motherhood as significantly more effective than that of their stay-at-home counterparts. This form of extensive mothering not only bolstered their self-esteem but also fostered a sense of entitlement to their children's respect.

While stay-at-home mothers adhered to the family devotion schema by emphasizing the importance of maternal care, employed mothers redefined the "career devotion schema"[27] in a way that was both family-friendly and self-sacrificial. By striving to achieve excellence in both motherhood and their careers, they leveraged their elite professional statuses to present themselves as "better" mothers than their unemployed counterparts. Employed mothers justified their extensive work—managing multiple responsibilities both at home and in their careers—raising the standard for what constitutes "good" mothering. They sought to downplay any stress associated with their multitasking,[28] focusing instead on their commitment to an "all-around" approach to motherhood.

Mothers' differing approaches to their ideal versions of motherhood, shaped by their education and employment status, frequently led to both overt and subtle conflicts, dividing them into two distinct groups. The narratives of many mothers in this chapter revealed a "mother war" that diverged from previous studies.[29] The "war" in this case centered on how far they should extend their support and involvement for their high-achieving children abroad. A key issue was whether maternal efforts should encompass academic and career guidance or remain focused on providing a safe and nurturing environment for their children.

With the exception of a few full-time mothers without much experience abroad, relatively affluent mothers across different employment statuses took great pride in their role and found significant value in it, despite their varying ideals of what constitutes "good" motherhood. However, their children sometimes undervalued or overlooked their efforts, particularly in the case of stay-at-home mothers. This reflects a societal tendency to take women's caregiving roles for granted, leading to the devaluation of careers focused on care work.

Few mothers attempted to challenge this undervaluation. Instead, many were prepared to extend their intensive mothering into their children's adulthood, often by assuming the role of self-sacrificing grandmothers.[30] Moreover, the career achievements of employed mothers did not overshadow those of their husbands. They frequently accepted or even embraced the gender achievement gap between themselves and their spouses, valuing their husbands' involvement in their children's higher education and careers abroad.

This acceptance of the growing influence of elite husbands in their children's lives likely stems from a recognition of the value of educational and transnational resources in guiding high-achieving children. Many mothers acquiesced to or even supported their husbands' increased roles because these proved so effective. The singular case of a mother who was more educated and transnational than her husband indicates that these resources, rather than parental gender itself, determine who becomes the "go-to parent" in elite transnational families. However, as long as the gender achievement gap persists, the hierarchy within Korean transnational elite circles is likely to remain unchanged: elite fathers with experience abroad at the top, similarly educated mothers in the middle, and parents without such experiences at the bottom.

5

Emerging Extensive
Transnational Fatherhood

Despite rising cultural expectations for increased paternal involvement in education, mothers, especially those from middle-to-upper-class backgrounds, are often still seen as the primary managers of their children's education across various cultures.[1] In a transnational context, the educational role of fathers is frequently overlooked, as is the broader concept of transnational fatherhood. To gain a more complete understanding of these families, it is essential to focus on fathers as key figures in their children's upbringing, rather than merely viewing them as financial providers.[2]

Wild geese fathers—the most well-known group of Korean transnational fathers—have traditionally focused heavily on financial support, such as sending remittances from Korea to mothers and children abroad. This highlights their role as the quintessential breadwinner.[3] However, recent academic research has begun to explore how nonfinancial paternal support is reshaping the concept of fatherhood. While the dominant image portrays fathers primarily as reliable providers, some transnational fathers are redefining and negotiating their roles, occasionally by embracing unconventional parenting practices.[4]

When men take on the roles of fathers, engage in fathering, and conceptualize fatherhood, they do so within broader social and cultural frameworks that intersect with systems of gender relations.[5] How does a transnational context influence elite Korean fatherhood? This chapter explores this question by examining the experiences of ten Korean fathers who sent their children to prestigious U.S. colleges. Except for two, the remaining eight fathers had significant transnational resources, including prestigious degrees, high-status occupations, and experiences abroad. These fathers, whom I term *highly transnational fathers*, provide insights into the ideal of transnational fatherhood and its implementation, utilizing their class-based and gendered resources—a phenomenon I describe as *extensive transnational fatherhood*. By contrasting highly transnational fathers with more traditional, locally based fathers—those without international study or work experiences—this chapter highlights the crucial role of transnational resources in facilitating generational mobility. Additionally, the analysis reveals how these fathers are reshaping masculinities within the Korean parenting sphere. Do their fathering efforts reinforce the ideal of "new age" fatherhood, or do they expand it in new ways?

Triangulating Narratives About Extensive Transnational Fatherhood

Daniel's Father's Story

Daniel's father, a college professor of engineering who earned his doctoral degree in the United States, exemplifies the elite transnational fathers discussed in this chapter. During our meeting in his office at his university in the Seoul metropolitan area, he openly shared his experiences and pride in his fatherhood. The interview, which lasted nearly three hours, was reflective of many interviews with fathers in this chapter. At its conclusion, he expressed genuine gratitude for the opportunity to discuss his role as a father and his relationship with his sons living abroad.

Daniel's father revealed that he was instrumental in encouraging both of his sons to pursue transnational education. Drawing from his own experience as a former student abroad, having completed his PhD in the United States, he felt well-justified in advocating for his sons to study there. To explain his motivation, he reflected on his own academic journey, starting from his days at a local Korean college before his move for postgraduate studies: "Few professors had studied abroad when I was at a local Korean college. I don't recall much of what I learned from the local professors. We were essentially self-taught. But in the United States, I had the chance to learn directly from the authors of some renowned textbooks. It was an incredible opportunity." He wished for his sons to benefit from the same enriching educational experiences he had, ideally starting from an early age. His admiration for U.S. higher education was evident, as both of his sons—Daniel and his younger brother—were attending U.S. colleges at the time of the interview.

His own life trajectory highlights the gendered dynamics involved in achieving transnational mobility. Reflecting on his time in a U.S. doctoral program, Daniel's father expressed regret for not contributing more to child-care. "My wife was also pursuing a master's degree at a nearby university, but I left her to care for the babies most of the time," he said, his tone tinged with apology.

Despite acknowledging his limited involvement in his sons' early years, Daniel's father believed that his engagement increased as his children grew and advanced in their education. He spoke with pride about his multifaceted support for their academic development. For instance, he recalled how he used his expertise as an engineering professor to teach Daniel math and science, particularly mathematical functions. Additionally, he facilitated Daniel's interest in neuroscience by connecting him with his colleagues who were experts in the field. His support paid off when Daniel chose neuroscience as his college major.

During his sons' childhood, Daniel's father viewed his sabbatical in the United States as a prestigious and exceptional opportunity for fathering. He devoted a substantial part of his interview to recounting this period. He said he meticulously arranged for his family to live in a neighborhood with excellent schools and a multicultural environment. He hoped that during their time in the United States, his sons would become fluent in English, as if it were their native language, by attending U.S. schools—an opportunity he had never had himself. Consequently, he extended his stay in the United States beyond his initial one-year tenure at the university, remaining with his family to fully capitalize on the benefits of this sabbatical. This strategy was similarly adopted by several other fathers in this chapter, who extended their stays abroad for the sake of their children's acquisition of English and cultural experiences.

Daniel's father reminisced about the sabbatical with great fondness, particularly valuing the time he spent sharing books with Daniel. He regarded these moments as some of the most intimate and meaningful experiences of his fatherhood. Reflecting nostalgically, he said, "I often took Daniel to a large pond in our neighborhood, where we talked about his future and discussed the books we read together. [. . .] Daniel read the books I recommended, and we talked about them after he finished." He felt that this period allowed him to forge a strong bond with his son through both academic involvement and daily interactions. Bolstering his positive self-assessment of his fatherhood, he added, "I spent a lot of time with my family. We traveled a lot. It was a wonderful year for our family. I wish we could have had more time like that. What made that year so special was the opportunity to talk and get close to each other. [. . .] During that one year, I think I was a decent father."

By blending academic and emotional support for his sons, Daniel's father felt he practiced fathering effectively during his sabbatical abroad. However, he did not rate himself highly beyond this. Despite his thoughtful and diligent efforts to assist his son both academically and emotionally, he still saw significant room for improvement in his parenting. Reflecting on the masculine ideals of "good" fathering, he mentioned, "I wish I could have played more sports and traveled with them more too." He felt that forging a closer connection with his son through physical activities was as crucial as providing academic support.

Daniel's father's remarks reflect his high expectations for himself as a father. Aspiring to be more than just engaged, he expressed a desire to be a "great" or "perfect" father. To achieve this, he believed he needed to provide substantial support for his children's growth, both academically and emotionally. Leveraging his career as an academic, he aimed to offer scholastic guidance while also building a strong father-son bond with both of his sons, hoping that these efforts would earn their sincere respect.

Daniel's Story

Daniel largely supported his father's accounts, indicating a genuine appreciation for the transnational upbringing he received. He acknowledged his father's direct involvement in his academic work, referring to him as his "best teacher" during his childhood, particularly while the family was in the United States during his father's sabbatical. Daniel reflected on the crucial support he received from his father as he navigated the challenges of adjusting to a U.S. middle school: "When I first arrived in the United States, I struggled with math problems in English. I couldn't grasp either the language or the subject. That's when my dad stepped in to help. He sat next to me and guided me through the math problems, providing one-on-one support." Expressing his gratitude, Daniel added, "The things I learned from him during that time still benefit me today."

Daniel noted that his father's academic support extended even into his college years and believed that the choice of his college major was a decision they made together: "When I got interested in psychology in high school, he gave me a lot of exciting books about psychology. Now that I'm considering studying neuroscience in graduate school, he's sending me some interesting journal articles. Whenever I become interested in a new topic, he starts exploring it as well so that we can discuss it together." Daniel did not question his father's direct influence on his interests and preferences. Rather than resisting, he seemed to try to embrace and appreciate his father's input into his choice of college major and future career. "That's how we communicate," he explained, acknowledging that such a father-son relationship is relatively uncommon, especially outside his social circle.

In many respects, Daniel viewed his father in a manner similar to how his father perceived himself. Both depicted Daniel's father as an engaged parent who consistently strived to be a "better" father—warm and competent, leveraging his resources to support his children. However, Daniel's narrative subtly revealed why his father might have placed such importance on a strong father-son bond. Despite acknowledging the support he received, Daniel admitted to feeling "awkward for a while" around his father, suggesting that their emotional connection had its complexities.

"I can't say I had no conflicts with my dad about my college major," Daniel said cautiously. "To be honest, I did not talk with him at all during my junior and senior years." He felt that his father strongly wished for him to attend medical school, a preference his father had not disclosed during the interview. For the first time, Daniel decided to diverge from his father's recommendations, opting instead for a graduate program in engineering at a prestigious U.S. university. "After I got accepted into graduate school recently, he and I started talking again," Daniel noted.

Perhaps in an effort to present himself as a supportive and amicable father, Daniel's father did not mention any conflicts between them. However, Daniel revealed to me that there was genuine discord regarding his career choice. He admitted feeling some dissatisfaction with their relationship, noting, "Sometimes, he just doesn't fully catch what I want to say. It sometimes makes it hard to talk with him."

Despite this, Daniel did not want to cast his father in a negative light. "My dad taught me so many things. I appreciate him for that," he emphasized. Even with the friction between them, Daniel genuinely valued—or at least wanted to value—his father's support. Daniel made an effort to show respect and appreciation for his father's hands-on support throughout his transnational journey. His positive view of his father seemed to be shaped by his mother's efforts in mediating their relationship. "My mom did a lot of reconciling work between me and my dad," Daniel noted.

Daniel's Mother's Story

Daniel's mother, an art teacher at an international school near Seoul, largely supported her husband's account. During her interview, she defended his limited involvement in early childcare, choosing not to criticize the unequal division of responsibilities. Instead, she accepted the imbalance as part of their respective roles, maintaining her own boundaries while acknowledging that her husband maintained his.

Daniel's mother credited her husband with significant contributions to their sons' education. She noted that he diverged from the typical image of Korean fathers, who are thought of as distant and uninvolved. "Sometimes he was even more engaged in our sons' education than I was," she remarked. Reflecting on their efforts to find the best *hagwons* (private cram schools) and tutors, she described her husband as a good collaborator. She proudly added, "We always make decisions together regarding our kids' education. [. . .] We visited schools and *hagwons* together to ensure they were a good fit for our children."

Daniel's mother genuinely valued her husband's dedication to their children's education. She highlighted his positive influence, particularly noting Daniel's interest in neuroscience, which eventually became his chosen major and career. However, she approached the topic of the father-son relationship with caution, acknowledging a conflict that Daniel had shared with her but not with his father. She admitted that Daniel often had more "honest" conversations with her about his stresses and concerns. "Daniel talks to me about what stresses him out," she revealed. This perspective supported Daniel's view of his mother as both a close confidante and an effective mediator within the family.

Daniel's mother aimed to downplay the father-son conflict she had mediated and sought to portray her husband as an overall "good" parent, a portrayal that Daniel also tried to maintain. "My husband sometimes expressed his ambitions quite openly regarding Daniel's education, which Daniel might have perceived as pressuring," she said, defending her husband. To frame this "pressure" in a more positive light, she explained, "[For example,] my husband merely wanted Daniel to achieve more recognition from his extracurricular activities rather than seeing them as mere hobbies. [. . .] For Daniel, such expectations could be stressful, because he always did his best [in everything]."

Whenever conflicts arose between her son and her husband, Daniel's mother viewed herself as a mediator, a role she described as "not a big deal" and one that often falls to women, particularly mothers. "I didn't take sides with either my husband or Daniel. The issues were mostly because of Daniel's stress about college applications. There was no major conflict we couldn't resolve," she said. "I just tried to clarify how their perspectives differed slightly, even though they both had the same goal," she added.

Triangulating the narratives of the three members of Daniel's family illustrates how elite fathers in this chapter assess their transnational fatherhood and how these assessments are corroborated or contradicted by their children and spouses. While most fathers in this chapter, being part of the privileged minority, appeared to find fatherhood both rewarding and fulfilling, examining the perspectives of fathers, mothers, and children revealed that achieving a harmonious understanding of extensive fatherhood was not always successful. Some families struggled to reconcile their differing views, and efforts by certain fathers to downplay or conceal family conflicts underscore the intense pressure and challenges associated with being perceived as a "good"—or even "great"—father within the elite Korean community.

Fathers' Academic Involvement

Highly Transnational Fathers

While most mothers in this book experienced interruptions in their careers or postcollege education due to motherhood, parenthood seldom impeded fathers from pursuing their education or employment abroad. Fathers often relied on the support of their wives and families to manage their professional and personal responsibilities. Few fathers reported conflicts between their careers and fatherhood, with many finding their roles in both areas to be complementary rather than conflicting.

The eight fathers who studied or worked abroad—referred to as *highly transnational*—were particularly successful in balancing their careers and fatherhood. These fathers initiated their transnational family arrangements, frequently during their time abroad, and took pride in relocating their families to the countries where they worked or studied, with the United States being the most common destination. Notably, only one of these fathers' spouses pursued and completed her education during their time abroad, highlighting that the seamless continuation of elite fathers' transnational careers was often supported by their families within a highly gendered context.

Highly transnational fathers often emphasized their significant involvement in their children's education throughout both the early and later stages of their upbringing. They felt that their elite status and resources uniquely positioned them to engage in intensive parenting. Jake's father, a CEO who successfully sent all three of his children to Ivy League colleges, believed his academic and professional background made him particularly well suited for guiding his children's education. Holding an MBA from an Ivy League institution and a degree from one of Korea's most prestigious universities, he felt his credentials gave him a distinct advantage over his wife. She, having graduated from the same Korean university, did not pursue further education after their marriage. He emphasized the critical role of elite fathers in educational support, stating, "Fathers should be attentive to their kids and assist them. [. . .] It's much more beneficial than relying solely on mothers for education."

When his children were preparing to study abroad to learn English, Jake's father actively sought ways to leverage his connections for their benefit: "One of my friends in Canada runs a language school and study abroad agency. He's very knowledgeable about the process, so I consulted him on which school would be best for my oldest son. His initial advice was not to send a young child alone, so I decided to send all three kids together."

Following his friend's advice, Jake's father sent his wife and children to a Canadian neighborhood with few Koreans, believing it would accelerate their English acquisition. During this time, Jake's father assumed the role of a wild goose father, temporarily separating from his family for a year. He took significant measures to navigate the challenges associated with this arrangement, underscoring his dedication to his children's education: "My wife managed the children's care in Canada for most of the time, but I made frequent trips back and forth between Korea and Canada. We wanted to evaluate how well the kids adapted abroad before deciding whether to send them to U.S. boarding schools. Given my numerous business trips to the United States at that time, it was relatively easy for me to visit them [in Canada] often." His engaged fatherhood in a transnational context was significantly bolstered by his occupational and educational resources, including his role as a company owner and his experience studying in the United States.

Jake's father stressed the importance of frequent conversations with his children's teachers—an advantage he could afford and enjoy due to his class-based resources, including fluency in English and flexible work schedule: "Whenever the school invited us to parents' weekends, we always accepted. The school would arrange individual meetings with teachers and staff. I firmly believe that parents must meet and discuss with teachers during these visits. Although attending parents' weekends was not always easy, I made sure never to miss any. I also made it a point to visit their schools and meet their teachers at the start of each school year."

Jake's father noted his advantages over other Korean parents, including his wife, who faced challenges in fully utilizing these visits. "I noticed some parents brought their other children along to translate between them and the teachers. For me, English wasn't much of a barrier compared to other parents. However, even my wife doesn't speak English that well," he explained. Embracing his role as the primary educational manager of his children, he took full advantage of his experience studying abroad. This background gave him both the authority and confidence to closely oversee his children's education.

Sophia's father, an engineer with a doctoral degree from the United States, noted that intensive fatherhood was quite prevalent among his peers. While recognizing his own commitment to his children's education, he sought to normalize it by pointing out that other fathers in his social circle were even more passionate and engaged than he was: "All fathers are passionate about their children's education; it's not just me. Most fathers in my circle are similar, especially if they've excelled academically themselves. Many choose to teach their children directly, and some even co-teach with other [similarly educated] fathers, based on their different areas of expertise. This sharing of knowledge is quite common." His high level of education afforded him, and his peers, both the capacity and legitimacy to oversee Sophia's education. Despite his wife also holding a doctoral degree, Sophia's father took on the primary responsibility for teaching his daughter, believing his own expertise provided a superior educational experience. By assuming this role, he willingly challenged the traditional gender divide in Korean parenting to ensure his daughter received what he considered the best education.

Some children distinctly remembered the early educational support they received from their fathers. Despite Jenna's father's impression that he "did not do much" for his daughter during her childhood, perhaps compared to other fathers in his social circle, Jenna recalled a different experience. She mentioned that her father had a significant impact, making her proficient in at least one foreign language other than English. Initially, she felt some pressure from his advice, but she ultimately came to value his influence and appreciated his role in making her multilingual: "Thanks to him, I was able to learn Japanese. My mom didn't like it because she thought learning Chinese would be more beneficial, but my dad was firm about me learning Japanese. I ended up loving it." Jenna believed her father had valid reasons for insisting she learn Japanese intensively, given his extensive transnational work experience: "My dad has good insights. [. . .] When he was younger, engineers needed to be fluent in Japanese for their business. He can also read Japanese a bit, which has helped him in his career. Initially, he pushed me to learn Japanese, but now I'm grateful for that." Fluent in Japanese, Jenna highlighted how it enhanced her studies in comparative literature and Asian history at an Ivy League college. She described her father as a "good advisor," adding with a laugh, "He gives me crucial advice once or twice a year."

Highly transnational fathers' international business trips or work-abroad opportunities—usually as expatriates or visiting scholars—played a crucial role in their active involvement in their children's education. Holding a strong belief in the superiority of Western education, they often relocated their families to English-speaking developed countries, with a preference for the United States, to provide their children with what they perceived as a better educational environment. This selective relocation, a privilege not available to all Korean fathers, was one of the contributions that many highly transnational fathers believed they made that benefited their children.

Some fathers recounted the meticulous preparations they made to ensure their children were well-prepared for life in an English-speaking country before their initial departure. Natalie's father, a college professor with a background in Korean government service, described his strategies for teaching his daughter English in preparation for their move to the United States for his university sabbatical: "I showed Natalie a lot of Disney movies without subtitles or dubbing. She loved watching them. Young kids enjoy television, so I made sure she saw as many programs and films in English as possible. I personally bought those Disney videotapes from a bookstore [in Korea]." He appeared very proud of his teaching strategy, convinced it yielded positive results. "I'm not an education expert, but I've heard that languages should be taught from an early age in a fun way," he added. His meticulous support continued even after they returned from his sabbatical. To re-create an environment akin to the United States, he selected a Korean private elementary school that offered a class specifically for "returnee children." He regarded his educational enthusiasm as "nothing unique," noting that many of his academic colleagues made similar efforts.

The educational involvement of elite Korean fathers intensified as their children grew older and opted to study abroad for extended periods. Many mothers and children noted that it was often the fathers who took the lead in orchestrating their children's education overseas. Fathers with personal experience studying abroad were especially proactive, strongly encouraging their children to pursue it, particularly at the college level. Some fathers admitted that sending their children abroad helped them "ease their minds," as they believed the benefits would significantly outweigh any potential drawbacks.

Sarah's father, a medical school professor and CEO of a medical start-up, was a strong advocate for education abroad. Embracing the "concerted cultivation"[6] parenting style, he asserted, "Parents should not allow children to do whatever they want." He emphasized that fathers, rather than mothers, should take a pivotal role in shaping the "Asian global"[7] through such experiences.

Reflecting on his early fatherhood, he considered certain "necessary interruptions" in his children's upbringing, such as relocating his family to California for his sabbatical, as crucial decisions. "It was a good opportunity to expose my kids to a larger country," he said, implying that Korea was too constrained for him to raise his children in the way he envisioned.

He elaborated on his parenting philosophy, which he felt deeply committed to:

> Learning English should be a top priority. To truly master it, children should attend elementary school in an English-speaking country. This is what parents should strive to do for their children, although not every parent can manage it, even the parents who are well-off. Of course, children need to be capable enough to thrive in this new environment. Parents can guide their children to a good pond, but it's up to the children to drink the water themselves.

In his narrative, the United States represented a "good pond" for raising children due to its liberal education system and the widespread use of English. This metaphor effectively captured the global hierarchy of education that many fathers, including Sarah's, had internalized.

Sarah affirmed the effectiveness of his parenting strategy. Like many other children in this book, she fondly remembered her time in a U.S. elementary school during her father's sabbatical, calling it one of the most precious periods of her life. She appreciated the chance to achieve near-native

English proficiency and enjoyed growing up in a more engaging and liberal environment.

For Sarah's father, raising the "Asian global" encompassed more than just imparting native-like English skills. He envisioned Sarah interacting with "pioneers" from various fields worldwide while attending an Ivy League college. "My goal [of sending my children to elite schools abroad] was to help my kids meet world-class scholars and leaders," Sarah's father said with evident enthusiasm. He lauded the exclusive networks linked with Ivy League institutions, believing that achieving his goal of raising his children to be ambitious and multicultural would have been impossible if his children had been raised solely in Korea.

His commitment to educational support extended beyond Sarah's entry into her desired U.S. college. Aware of the importance of staying informed about her academic progress, Sarah's father made an effort to understand the U.S. education system, especially the nuances of elite colleges: "I need to understand how elite U.S. schools operate. [. . .] I must stay informed about my children's lives [abroad]. Although I'm always busy with work, I make sure to read and study about their education. This preparation helps me to guide them effectively." Using online resources and his personal network, he meticulously gathered information about Sarah's college. At the time of the interview, his son, Sarah's younger brother, was also studying in the United States. As a father of two children studying abroad, he felt a deep responsibility to oversee their education and viewed himself as their primary coach.

His transnational fathering was notable for its depth, duration, and geographical scope. Far from being a burden, this extensive involvement was a source of joy and fulfillment for him. His commitment to his role as a father brought him immense satisfaction and pride, a sentiment reinforced by Sarah's outstanding achievements both academically and beyond. He even viewed his intense paternal academic support as an opportunity for personal growth, allowing him to become a more informed and engaged individual:

> Sarah's college sends a lot of letters to parents. By reading them, I gain insight into what she's learning. It's a way for me to acquire knowledge I didn't have before. While I can't return to being a student myself, her experiences allow me to learn something new at this stage in my life. This not only helps me ask her thoughtful questions but also makes her feel comfortable seeking my advice whenever she needs it.

Sarah's father saw the letters from her college as serving multiple purposes: They kept him informed about the school's state and fostered "interesting conversations" with his daughter. "Engaging in such deep conversations is truly enjoyable," he concluded.

Locally Based Fathers

Fathers who had not studied abroad often found themselves in the minority among the fathers of high-achieving Korean students studying overseas, recognizing their comparatively lower level of involvement. Heather's father, a manager at a multinational company who had only studied in Korea, openly rejected the idea of being a highly involved parent. He described both himself and his wife as "permissive," noting, "We didn't have many guidelines or rules. We just let Heather do whatever she wanted."

The term "permissive" requires some qualification, as his later narratives revealed a significant level of involvement in Heather's education prior to her departure for a U.S. college. He defensively noted, "I did not vigorously search for *hagwons* or tutors for Heather." However, his subsequent remarks illustrated his active support for his daughter's education while she was still in Korea: "I once introduced Heather to an academic institution that was more like a book club. They had an economics class for young kids, and I recommended she attend it for a while. And what else? [*Pause.*] Oh, I remember making her go to an English class too." Heather's father added, "That was all. Except for that, I did nothing." This understatement of his educational involvement made sense when compared to other fathers at Heather's school, whom he perceived as having significantly more resources for intensive parenting than he did.

Heather's perspective largely aligned with her father's. She found neither of her parents to be particularly intensive regarding her education. "I was the one who insisted on studying abroad. Their influence was minor," she remarked with a hint of cynicism, comparing her parents to others in her circle. However, if she had to identify one parent as having had more direct input, she would name her father, not her mother.

Reflecting on her adolescence, Heather recalled an instance of her father's hands-on support: a specific anecdote about an essay competition she participated in during high school: "I started by working as a student intern at my dad's company, even though the tasks I handled weren't particularly significant. Later, I wrote a minithesis based on what I learned during the internship. Initially, I struggled to come up with a topic because I didn't feel particularly smart." She continued with a shy laugh, perhaps hesitant to admit how directly her father had helped her, "One day, my dad noticed my struggle with writing, so he suggested a topic on B2B [business-to-business] marketing, which was his area of work. After reviewing some of his company's case studies, I followed his advice and wrote my thesis on that subject. I ended up winning an award, which was a great boost for my résumé." Heather recognized that her father occasionally leveraged his work experience to support her extracurricular activities. This sporadic involvement set him apart from her mother, who rarely assisted her directly with assignments or school applications. However, compared to the fathers of her school friends, Heather still felt that her father was relatively less engaged.

Despite Heather's clear recollection and appreciation of her father's hands-on support, Heather's father himself had little memory of it. "To be honest, I don't remember that much. Did Heather say I helped her a lot with the essay?" he laughed awkwardly. Instead of recalling the essay competition, he remembered another instance where he provided direct help: arranging an internship at his company for her. "I remember setting up that internship, but what else did I do for her?" he said, failing to recognize that arranging an internship might be seen as a form of intensive fathering by those outside the Korean transnational community.

This tendency to downplay his involvement persisted as he continued to reflect on his contributions: "Did I mention that I made Heather attend a children's financial academy? Since I work in marketing, I thought it would be beneficial for her to get an early start on that. But honestly, besides that, I don't really remember what else I did for her." Consistently defying the stereotype of an involved father, Heather's father emphasized his noneducational support. "I didn't do much beyond giving her rides wherever she needed to go. That's all," he said defensively. "[Besides giving rides,] what else could I do [for Heather]?" As a parent who had never studied abroad, he portrayed himself as playing a passive role in his daughter's college applications or education overseas. Despite his actual educational contributions, he emphasized his noneducational support, such as providing transportation, which other parents who hadn't studied abroad also considered a significant contribution.

Holly's father, a local Korean PhD and lecturer at a Korean college, ranked his academic involvement as the lowest among the parents presented in this book. He began his interview by asserting, "My daughter did everything on her own. I didn't assist her with her education at all." He insisted that neither he nor his wife were involved in their daughter's school choices. Regarding the selective Korean preparatory high school Holly attended, he cynically remarked, "To be honest, I didn't even know such a school existed." He added, "I didn't think the students at that school looked happy," expressing his critical view of selective schools and the intense competition surrounding them.

Throughout his interview, Holly's father emphasized his distinction from parents who aggressively seek prestigious educational institutions for their children, positioning himself as a fundamentally different type of parent. He perceived his family's approach to parenting as adhering to traditional gender roles, attributing his children's academic achievements primarily to his wife. When discussing the division of responsibilities regarding their children's education, he remarked, "My wife did a better job than me. [. . .] Managing their education was her role." He openly admitted to his limited involvement in his children's education, including Holly's, underscoring his self-identification as less engaged compared to other parents. "Thankfully, our kids listened well to their mother," he added. "I didn't need to contribute much more to their education because my wife handled it all."

His daughter, Holly, largely confirmed his account. Reflecting on her experiences, she remarked, "My dad . . . [*Pause.*] Well, he didn't do much for me [regarding education]." She clearly delineated the roles of her parents, noting, "My mom handles the finances in our family, so my dad had little influence over my education." Holly emphasized that her father did not prioritize private education and preferred a more hands-off approach, aiming to raise his children naturally without undue pressure. This led her to describe her father's approach as "laissez-faire," attributing the bulk of her academic success to her mother. "I should say my mom had a great deal of educational fervor. She wanted my sister and me to attend selective high schools, though only I was accepted," she noted.

Despite her mother's efforts to match the level of support provided by other parents in their academic social circle, Holly did not find either of her parents particularly helpful with her college applications, attributing this to their lack of transnational resources. Reflecting on her time in a selective Korean high school, which included a preparatory class for studying abroad, Holly noted, "Both of my parents don't speak English well, so I asked one of my friends to proofread my essays in English."

The limited involvement of her father, in contrast to other fathers who were deeply engaged in their children's education, stood out in her account. She remarked, "He occasionally gave me rides [to school and *hagwon*], that's all." Instead of highlighting any substantial academic support from her father, Holly described his easygoing attitude and liberal perspective toward education as his main contributions to her achievements. If she had to acknowledge any involvement, it would be his strong belief in her abilities. "He totally believes in me, especially my academic ability. He always says, 'Holly will do everything well because she's smart,'" she said.

According to Holly, her father hoped she would pursue a career in academia, a path he himself had chosen. This sentiment was common among many fathers in this chapter. However, her reaction to his aspiration further distinguished her from most other children. "He wants me to become a scholar and sometimes expresses this in front of me. But whenever I hear him say that, I lose interest in doing so," Holly said sarcastically. She felt that her father's support in terms of career guidance was lacking, which ultimately led her to lose faith in his advice. The only support she truly valued from him was his emotional backing, such as his "unconditional trust"—a quality more commonly associated with mothers in the experiences of many children.

While Holly didn't attribute much credit to her father for her academic achievements, her father did discuss some of the college assignments he and his wife had assisted her with: "After Holly began college, she occasionally sought our help with her papers. I don't recall if she asked for our assistance during high school, but [now], she discusses her papers with us from time to time, and we always strive to provide the best feedback." Unlike other fathers in this chapter who typically use terms like "I," "me," or "my" when discussing their academic support, Holly's father frequently used "we," "us," and "our" to describe his involvement. He also gave his daughter considerable credit, noting, "I don't need to explain much when giving feedback on her papers because she understands my points very quickly."

His humble—sometimes self-deprecating—tone persisted throughout the interview. Using the term "we," he admitted that neither he nor his wife were deeply involved in Holly's education, especially after she left Korea for college. "We were incapable of helping her, to be honest," he said. To him, and perhaps to his wife as well, assisting with Holly's essay was a rare opportunity to feel needed by and connected with their daughter abroad. Being able to substantially assist her seemed to bring him joy. Continuing to avoid the singular pronoun, he said, "We feel so happy when she asks for our help. It shows that she believes in and respects us."

While many fathers in this chapter emphasized their individual contributions in supporting their children, Holly's father did not consciously distinguish his support from his wife's. This may be because he did not see his involvement as surpassing that of his wife. Both of them, who held doctoral degrees from Korean universities and worked as local academics, had similar educational backgrounds. Despite their credibility in their fields, their local degrees and lack of international experience limited their ability to assist Holly effectively with her education abroad.

Holly's father felt that his lack of experience abroad made him less capable of deeply engaging with Holly's education at her highly selective U.S. liberal arts college. He expressed a sense of inadequacy, believing it was too late for him to acquire the necessary knowledge and experience to effectively guide her. This self-perception led him to feel deficient in his paternal role, noting a growing cultural gap between himself and Holly. He remarked, "She's the smartest person in our family," using "smartest" to signify not only intelligence but also a broader cosmopolitan experience and ambition. Unlike other fathers in this chapter, Holly's father appeared apologetic about Holly's independence, attributing it to his hands-off approach, which he tried to frame as a voluntary choice rather than a result of his limited paternal resources. This self-critique set him apart from the other fathers discussed.

Fathers' (Efforts for) Emotional Support

Highly Transnational Fathers

Given the rise of "new age" fatherhood,[8] providing emotional support is now seen as a fundamental aspect of being a "good" father across various social contexts.[9] Korean fathers are no exception; while in Confucian culture, fathers once epitomized authoritarian masculinity, contemporary society now expects them to be emotionally and educationally close to their children.[10] The concept of *nurturing* encompasses physical, emotional, intellectual, and spiritual care, all of which contribute to children's positive development.[11] Korean fathers are now expected to nurture in this broader sense, focusing on "the manner in which things are done, and their results for children."[12] To meet these expectations, they are encouraged to develop "emotional literacy."[13]

In this chapter, some fathers discussed their commitment to modern standards of nurturing and their efforts to practice it effectively. They highlighted their substantial attempts to maintain emotional closeness with their children and provide educational support. Compared to their perceptions of other Korean fathers, they viewed themselves as more approachable, friendly, and generous and less authoritative. They felt they offered their children comprehensive care on par with their wives. This self-assessment is notable, given that not many mothers and children detailed fathers' emotional nurturing efforts in their interviews.

Fathers with sons framed their emotional support in traditional masculine terms and acted accordingly. They emphasized spending significant time playing with their sons, particularly during their early years, believing that engaging in physical activities like sports helped strengthen their father-son bond. For example, Jake's father, who proudly boasts of his three Ivy League graduates, fondly reminisced about his children's childhood, saying, "I love kids, not just my own, but kids in general. I know many of my children's friends by name. [. . .] When my kids were young, I let them bring their friends over and played with all of them."

Jake's father embraced a traditional, masculine approach to active fatherhood, particularly in the early years. He valued "quality time" filled with masculine activities, especially sports, as central to his vision of ideal fatherhood. At times, he even prioritized this over academic support. He made a concerted effort to spend time with his children, whether on family trips or playing soccer, believing that engaging in such activities was the best way to stay close to his sons.

Even when his sons were at a U.S. boarding school, Jake's father was dedicated to maintaining their bond through sports. He stayed updated on their athletic activities at school and discussed them during international phone calls. This approach proved effective, especially since the school offered a range of sports including tennis, soccer, American football, and horse riding. Reflecting on the time his eldest son, Jake's older brother, was at the boarding school, he recalled, "Parents could see the soccer game scores on the school's website. I checked it almost daily so I could talk about the games with him on the phone." Although their conversations focused on sports, his intentions went beyond traditional masculine norms. He shared, "I felt these calls were important. Even though we were apart, I wanted to show my care as a parent. [. . .] I wanted my son to know that I genuinely cared about him."

Fathers often tailored their approaches to emotionally involved fatherhood based on their child's gender. For instance, Sarah's father employed a less traditionally masculine style of bonding with his daughter, focusing on being an attentive listener. When his wife took their son, Sarah's younger brother, to the United States for schooling, he recognized the need to offer additional emotional support to Sarah, who was a senior at a prestigious Korean boarding school at the time. Recognizing that Sarah needed a maternal presence for her emotional well-being in her mother's absence, he endeavored to fulfill both parental roles, dedicating extra time and attention to supporting his daughter's mental health. He saw the geographical distance between himself and Sarah, who was at boarding school, as an opportunity to strengthen their father-daughter bond, using this unique phase in their lives to foster growth and a deeper connection: "On weekends when Sarah came home from her high school dorm, I volunteered to pick her up, even though it meant driving over an hour each way. I also drove her back to school at the end of the weekend. During these drives, we had long conversations. She shared her conflicts with friends and teachers, and I listened attentively." He recalled, "It was so good to spend time and talk with my daughter." He expressed gratitude for the opportunity to be her "chauffeur," appreciating the precious one-on-one time it afforded him.

Fond memories strengthened his sense of accomplishment and paternal pride. In his wife's absence, Sarah's father saw solo parenting as a valuable opportunity, especially since Sarah, who was focused on her journey to Ivy League colleges, needed significant support and care. Viewing this period as a chance to embody his ideal of "all-around" fatherhood, Sarah's father committed himself to being fully engaged both academically and emotionally with his children. By taking on all responsibilities, he willingly assumed the role of primary parent, ensuring his children's well-being and success.

While deeply valuing his "all-around" fatherhood, Sarah's father seemed to downplay his wife's contributions to their children's development. "My wife mainly spends time with the kids, cheering them up when they're down. [. . .] That's pretty much it," he remarked. He viewed his responsibilities as more crucial and demanding than his wife's, occasionally taking on some of her tasks to ensure their children's well-being. Recognizing their unconventional division of parenting duties, he noted, "In most Korean families, mothers typically handle everything, right? But my wife breaks that mold entirely."

Avoiding the stereotypical label of Korean mothers as overbearing, Sarah's father referred to his wife as a "buffer," shielding their children from his occasionally overly meticulous approach. "Thanks to their mom, our kids are relaxed and independent," he noted. Rather than expecting his wife to adopt his method of "concerted cultivation," he recognized and valued her contrasting style. He believed their unique division of parenting responsibilities not only functioned effectively but surpassed his expectations, as demonstrated by their children's impressive academic achievements across continents.

Locally Based Fathers

The two fathers who primarily lived in Korea and had limited international experience also emphasized their commitment to providing emotional support, though their approach differed from that of their more globally oriented counterparts. For the fathers with experience studying or working abroad, emotional support was seen as the final aspect of their comprehensive "all-around" fatherhood through which they aimed to earn their children's sincere appreciation and respect. In contrast, the locally based fathers viewed emotional support as their main contribution to their adult children's development, especially after their children had left home for college.

Like many other fathers in this chapter, Heather's father highlighted his efforts to be approachable with his daughter. "I occasionally stopped by her [Korean boarding] school if I had a meeting nearby. [. . .] I would invite her out for lunch," he recalled. He also fondly reminisced about the drives between his home and Heather's boarding school outside Seoul. "She came home most weekends. I brought her back to school almost every time," he said with nostalgia. Holding a demanding position in a company, which offered less flexibility than the roles of business owners or professors, he emphasized the extra effort he made to prioritize these drives and their significance.

Heather's father viewed these drives as special opportunities to show his care for her. His emphasis on giving rides suggested he may not have considered himself particularly influential in guiding his daughter through her college education and job search in the United States. His perspective echoed the sentiments of many mothers who had never studied abroad. Unlike some highly transnational fathers who detailed their conversations with their children, Heather's father did not delve into the specifics of their discussions. Instead, he focused on the challenge of finding time for these drives, hoping that this effort would be recognized as a sign of his emotional support.

His daughter, Heather, did not mention her father's rides or "surprise visits" to her school during her three-hour interview. Instead, she emphasized his occasional assistance with her school assignments and college applications, suggesting that this type of support was what children in this book often valued most from their fathers. She recalled her father as a masculine figure who, although not as frequently involved as the fathers of her friends, provided some academic and career-related support. In doing so, Heather, like many others, unintentionally reinforced the gendered divide between public fathering and private mothering.

Holly's father, the least transnational father in this book, was unique in explicitly defining his parenting role as that of an "emotion expert," a term traditionally associated with maternal roles. Both he and his wife earned doctoral degrees from universities in Korea, which established an academic and professional parity between them. This equality in education and career enabled Holly's father to adopt a less traditionally masculine approach to parenting, in contrast to families where fathers were more educated and cosmopolitan and mothers were less so.

Throughout his interview, Holly's father emphasized his unfamiliarity with U.S. colleges and American culture, including Ivy League institutions. He admitted to being "unable to picture" what Holly's life would be like at an elite U.S. college. As their father-daughter conversations diminished over time, he began to feel the growing cultural distance between himself and Holly. During Holly's semesters at a selective liberal arts college, he noted that they rarely had phone calls, as he felt there was "not much [for him] to help with."

Although his daughter attended a U.S. liberal arts college he had "never heard the name of" before her acceptance, Holly's father made an effort to imagine the stresses she faced both on and off campus. He did his best to understand her situation and offer appropriate words of support. For him, Holly's summer break in Korea was nearly the only opportunity to be close to her. He sought to make the most of their time together by giving her as many rides as possible: "[While driving] I usually shared jokes with her to help relieve her stress. [...] I never brought up any serious issues, as I didn't want to add to her burdens. I believe our relationship improved during that time. I'm not sure how she feels about it, but that's what I believe." These drives were more than just transportation; for parents without study abroad experience, they symbolized a way to demonstrate their sacrifice and love for their children. In this way, Holly's father reinforced his identity as a dedicated caregiver, focusing on providing emotional support rather than acting as a social or moral guide or role model.

His narratives are similar to those of many stay-at-home mothers who willingly take on the role of an "emotion expert," especially as their children enter adulthood. Recounting a revealing moment that showcased his close bond with his daughter, Holly's father proudly said, "Holly sometimes tells me things she doesn't share with her mother. [. . .] I've noticed her hiding things from her mom but not from me." To him, this exclusivity in sharing secrets was a clear sign of the strong emotional bond he believed he had cultivated with Holly. It was meaningful to his sense of fatherhood.

His efforts in emotional care did not go unnoticed. Holly recognized her father's desire and efforts to connect with her. In her accounts, she observed how her father took a proactive role in fostering an emotional connection with his children. Holly admitted that she didn't call her parents as frequently during school semesters as she thought her friends did, which she believed disappointed her father more than her mother. "My mom doesn't mind the lack of international calls as much, but my dad does. He really wants me to call him more often," she said.

Despite this, Holly was grateful to her father for treating her as an independent "intellectual being" with whom he could engage in serious discussions. However, her view of her father was largely ambivalent. While she appreciated his efforts in emotional care, she also found him "sometimes not sensitive or mature enough" to fully safeguard her feelings. Unlike her father, who looked back on their drives with nostalgia and pride, Holly did not attribute much emotional significance to those experiences. She recalled, "[In my dad's car] we talked about our daily life, some trivial things. [. . .] He usually talked about his relationship with his brothers and how he spent the day, like who he met [at work] and so on."

When asked to describe her relationship with her father, Holly responded, "Our relationship is hard to define. We are close, but we don't love everything about each other." Despite acknowledging her father's efforts to be an "emotion expert," Holly didn't hold him in particularly high regard, which might reflect her disappointment in his performance as a less elite father with fewer valuable resources. Her perspective was notably different from those of many other daughters in this book; unlike daughters from more affluent backgrounds who often viewed their fathers as ideal models, Holly cynically stated, "I will never marry someone like my dad."

Holly's narratives underscore how children in this book frequently expected their fathers to fulfill traditionally masculine roles. They sought substantial support from their parents, often relying more on their fathers due to the gender gap in achievement between mothers and fathers. Although fathers made significant efforts to provide emotional care alongside academic support, children tended to value their fathers' contributions to their achievements more than their physical and emotional well-being. This dynamic continued to reinforce the gendered division of parenting within elite Korean families.

Reflections on Extensive Transnational Fathering

Highly Transnational Fathers

Despite varying levels of engagement and effort, all fathers in this chapter noted that significant involvement was standard among the fathers of high-achieving Korean students abroad. Jenna's father, who saw himself as quite engaged in her education, shared a story about attending an information fair for Jenna's U.S. college applications. He laughed as he recalled, "Almost half of the participants were fathers," downplaying his own involvement to avoid seeming unusual. He aimed to normalize this extensive level of fathering among Korean students abroad, anticipating that outsiders might view it as excessive.

Highly transnational fathers often evaluated their involvement and overall transnational fatherhood quite positively. Owen's father, a CEO of a design company with an Ivy League MBA, expressed pride in his decision, saying, "I'm happy that I sent all my children to the United States early on." By lauding his children's boarding schools and colleges, he naturally highlighted the significant financial, educational, and emotional support he provided, attributing considerable value to his parenting efforts: "I always joked [with my kids], 'I wish I had gone to the same school as you!' [. . .] Their [U.S.] boarding schools were small enough to foster close relationships between teachers and students. Plus, there were no serious issues like bullying or anything of that sort." He explained, "It's not material wealth that I aimed to pass down. I wanted to help them build inner strength, the strength that provides confidence and dignity in any situation." Instead of focusing on academic achievements, Owen's father emphasized the intangible values he believed his children gained from their transnational experiences: independence, self-motivation, and openness to diverse cultures. He viewed these attitudes and perspectives as the true successes of his extensive fathering efforts.

Fathers who viewed themselves as appropriately engaged often felt they deserved respect and appreciation from their children and spouses. Some were particularly confident in the respect they received from their children. For instance, Sarah's father, who believed he knew "everything" about his daughter, asserted with certainty that his entire family valued him for his thorough and involved fathering: "My wife occasionally teases our kids by saying things like, 'I wish I had a father like yours.' The kids understand why she says that. Just yesterday, she told my son, 'If I had a father like yours, I could have gotten into an Ivy League school too.'" This anecdote suggests that he, along with his wife and children, saw the most significant outcome of his extensive involvement as the notable success of his children's college admissions. While he contended that his focus was on helping Sarah become a well-rounded individual rather than just achieving academic success, it appears that both he and others primarily judged his fathering based on Sarah's educational achievements.

Despite taking great pride in his extensive fathering, Sarah's father occasionally struggled with the challenge of raising independent children. He questioned whether his hands-on support and methods of communication might come across as pushy or authoritarian to his daughter. This prompted him to critically reflect on how he interacted with Sarah. "Sometimes Sarah told me, 'Dad, you say I can do everything, but it's not true. There are some things that I just can't achieve.' Then I realized how pushy I was. I don't want to be pushy, so I try to tone [it] down," he said. He was concerned that his extensive support might sometimes be "too much" and potentially harmful to his children, admitting, "I become too nervous and cautious if my child has an application due soon. I must monitor every single step of the submission. [...] I worry that I might be raising my kids too cautiously."

While expressing these concerns, he was careful not to portray Sarah as overly dependent. He aimed to highlight her independence and self-reliance while defending the nature of their relationship: "Sarah always seeks my opinion after she has already made her decision. Sometimes she follows my advice, and sometimes she doesn't. She works hard to ensure she isn't overly influenced by me." This remark reveals his awareness of society's scrutiny regarding hands-on parenting, particularly within elite circles. Despite this, he chose to remain deeply involved in his children's lives. However, it also uncovered a rare anxiety about his level of involvement. As he strove to embody the ideal of an "all-around" father, he sometimes grappled with ambivalence and guilt, constantly concerned about how to balance his fathering to be both supportive and acceptable to others.

Daniel's father, another actively engaged transnational father, faced a similar challenge. Similar to Sarah's dad, he felt valued within his family and proudly remarked, "Both of my sons never disregarded my advice," believing he held a unique role in their lives. However, he also worried that his guidance might be perceived as overinvolvement or "spoon-feeding" by others, including his sons. He questioned whether his sons genuinely valued and appreciated his input. An anecdote about Daniel's career path highlights this concern:

> I introduced Daniel to a friend of mine, who is a well-known neuroscientist, because I strongly believed that neuroscience was a good fit for him. However, I'm unsure if Daniel and I were on the same page. I sometimes question whether I made the right decision. I might have rushed him into choosing a major without giving him enough time to consider other options. He sometimes asks me, "Dad, am I going the right way?"

Such concerns led Daniel's father to question whether his grown-up son's respect for him was diminishing: "When Daniel was young, I could sense that he respected me a lot whenever I taught him various subjects. But now that he's in college and expanding his knowledge rapidly, it feels like his respect for me has diminished. He's learning so much and becoming more knowledgeable, especially in his field, that it seems he knows more than I do now!" He interpreted the diminishing respect from his son as a consequence of the growing knowledge gap between them. With an awkward laugh, he added, "I don't think he respected me as a great person. He respected me because I knew more than he did."

Daniel's father's doubts seem to have some validity. Daniel was one of the few who discussed his conflicts with his parents: Toward the end of his interview, he admitted feeling ambivalent about his father's influence on his choice of major and career path. Although he initially resisted his father's strong push for him to become a doctor, Daniel eventually decided to apply for a neuroscience graduate program at an Ivy League college—a choice that still seemed to align with his father's preferences. But Daniel appeared to struggle with this decision, repeatedly questioning whether it was genuinely his own choice or if he was making it to please others, especially his father: "I like neuroscience. I really do. But sometimes I wonder if I'm studying it just because my dad wanted me to become a neuroscientist, like I'm his puppet. My dad and I do share a lot of interests, and I know I enjoy this major. But I sometimes question whether I truly chose this path for myself." Daniel's internal struggle did not lessen his respect and gratitude for his father. However, he was beginning to question the extent to which his tastes, interests, talents, and achievements were influenced by his father. He yearned to establish himself as independent and self-made, worried about the stigma of being seen as merely a dependent child of an elite family.

Locally Based Fathers

For locally based fathers, their children's education abroad complicated their fatherhood to some extent, leading them to question whether they were adequately supporting their high-achieving children from a distance. This reflection caused them to view their own efforts as relatively minimal, especially when compared to the more extensive involvement of other fathers they observed or heard about among the parents of Korean students abroad. For example, Heather's father considered himself and his wife "outliers" in this context. Recalling a visit to Heather's prestigious Korean boarding school, which had a special class for students aiming for colleges abroad, he mentioned, "One of Heather's teachers even called us too easygoing." He interpreted this term not as a compliment but as a sign of his perceived underinvolvement in his daughter's applications to elite colleges abroad, which often required substantial parental assistance.

While justifying his minority position, Heather's father criticized the fathers who were more engaged than he was: "You know, one of my friends sent his kid to a prestigious Korean boarding school, and I saw him spend every weekend supporting his son. He drove two hours from Seoul to pick up his son, then took him to his tutor in Seoul, and drove him back to school at night. I really don't understand why he felt the need to do that every weekend." By depicting other fathers' support as excessive, Heather's father sought to normalize his own more minimal paternal involvement. This often involved directly comparing himself to fathers with more resources, underscoring the class differences between him and other fathers. He shared another anecdote that underscored the disparity he perceived between himself and other fathers in his circle: "I once attended my coworker's son's classical music recital. My coworker invested so much time and money into organizing it. I was shocked by the extent of his efforts. It felt like he was just creating an impressive entry for his son's résumé. [*Laughs.*] You know what I mean?"

Calling himself an "outlier" did not imply that he felt completely detached from his daughter's upbringing. His perspective on his involvement in her education was ambivalent. Although he generally downplayed his academic input, especially in comparison to "other fathers," Heather's father occasionally worried that his advice might have been excessive or even coercive. Like many fathers in this chapter, he had suggested that his daughter pursue a major similar to his own—accounting and business management. He was concerned that this guidance might have been "too early." He remarked, "I think I talked too much about which field was promising or what she needed to do to enter the business world." Recognizing the potential impact of his advice on his daughter's career choices, he added, "I guess Heather chose the job she recently got in an accounting company because of my advice."

Like some highly transnational fathers, Heather's father was concerned about whether he had suggested the best path for her while also fearing that his guidance might have pressured her in a way that she might regret later. Reflecting on this, he admitted, "I wish I had just listened to her more carefully without making strong suggestions." This self-doubt led him to seriously rethink his entire fatherhood; when asked if he considered himself a "good" father, he responded with hesitation: "Well, I really don't know. Looking back, I wonder if I might have given Heather too much advice. I never insisted she follow my exact recommendations. I just presented her with options. However, since she was quite young, she might have felt pressured and perceived it as me pushing her. Perhaps I influenced her choices more than I intended."

Despite being deeply involved, many fathers in this chapter still viewed liberal parenting principles as crucial for defining "good" fatherhood, highlighting a societal acceptance of Western parenting norms in Korea. Heather's father, influenced by this ideology, found some justification for his relatively limited involvement. However, he was troubled by the persistent feeling that his support was inadequate compared to other fathers in his daughter's circle—a group of high-achieving Korean students studying abroad. This sense of inadequacy puzzled him, as he believed he was relatively engaged compared to many Korean fathers outside his social circle. Nonetheless, observing and hearing about fathers who were even more involved and resourceful left him feeling insufficient.

During his interview, Heather's father reflected on her graduation from an Ivy League college. After struggling to secure a job in the United States, Heather had chosen to return to Korea by the time of her father's interview. Knowing that many of her Korean peers at college were pursuing successful careers abroad, he felt responsible for her altered plans, seeing them as a "broken dream." He regretted some of the advice he had given her about which U.S. college to attend and was concerned that her departure from the transnational elite circles might reflect poorly on his guidance:

> Honestly, I wasn't financially prepared for life after retirement, so I shared everything about my situation with her, perhaps too openly. [...] When I met her college admissions counselor in high school, I told him I didn't want Heather to attend an Ivy League school. I was candid about wanting her to go to a public college with a scholarship. The counselor laughed because he had never encountered a parent with such a viewpoint and didn't even believe I was serious.

Given her struggles in the job market outside Korea, he attributed this to his own lack of financial and transnational resources: "Because I shared too much about my financial situation, Heather may have handled most of her [academic] work on her own and avoided seeking external help. There was a gap between what she truly wanted to pursue and what I was able to provide." While the highly transnational fathers rarely discussed the costs or only alluded to them vaguely, Heather's father highlighted the exclusivity of transnational fatherhood for high-achieving children. For him, the decision to send Heather to an Ivy League college represented a high-stakes choice with significant financial implications.

Holly's father, noted as the least transnational among those discussed in this chapter, refused to label himself a "good" father. He asserted, "I wasn't a particularly good father [to my children], which I regret now. I made a lot of mistakes." Unlike other fathers, Holly's was the only one to explicitly describe his actions as mistakes. He admitted, "To be honest, I think I've avoided many of my responsibilities as a father and made a lot of excuses. It made me a bad father."

In his view, a father's responsibilities went beyond merely providing substantial support to their children. Holly's father held a highly abstract and idealized concept of what it meant to be a "good" father, one that was even more idealized than those of highly transnational fathers. His ideal lacked any reference to elite individuals with abundant transnational resources. Instead, he based his paternal role on his relationship with his own father, aspiring to be both respectable and endearing: "My father was like a god to me. I don't recall many specifics about what he did for me, but I loved him deeply. He was always honest with me. Even though he didn't show affection with hugs, his love was palpable. If my kids see me the way I saw my father, then I'd consider myself a good father.[14]" He lamented his inability to meet this idealized vision of "good" fatherhood, noting that the decreasing frequency of conversations with his daughter abroad was one of the indicators of this gap.

Holly's father was unique among the fathers discussed for having never visited the United States. "I'm not sure if I'll ever visit Holly [in the United States]," he admitted. The growing cultural divide between him and his daughter made him feel that his role as a father was concluding earlier than he had expected, or earlier than the roles of many fathers of Holly's peers: "Now my daughter is truly on her own. Sometimes it feels like she's already married and all grown up. What more should I worry about? To be honest, I don't think about her much these days. [*Laughs.*]" His statement didn't imply a lack of paternal affection. As his daughter pursued a path to become a transnational elite—one he himself didn't or couldn't follow—Holly's father recognized that his role as a father was gradually diminishing. This perspective distinguished him from the majority of fathers discussed in this chapter, many of whom believed that their extensive involvement in their children's lives should continue, even after their college graduation.

Inequalities Among Elite Transnational Fathers

The concept of *extensive fathering*,[15] or "all-around" fathering, embraced by many men in this chapter involves taking on a variety of roles and responsibilities. None of the fathers believed that merely being successful breadwinners made them "good" fathers. Their vision of ideal fatherhood extended beyond traditional paternal roles. They aimed to take on—and felt they successfully did—the roles of education manager and emotional guide, which are typically associated with Korean mothers.

Fathers' deep involvement in their children's education, especially in transnational contexts, led them to measure their success as fathers by their children's academic achievements. This level of involvement was noteworthy given the usual imbalance in educational responsibilities in Korean society, where mothers often carry more of the burden.[16] However, the fathers in this chapter, particularly those with significant experience abroad, willingly assumed the role of the primary manager of their children's education. Many fathers observed that the achievement gap between themselves and their wives facilitated this unconventional gender division in parenting, and they believed it benefited their high-achieving children abroad. This gender-reversal was viewed as a unique aspect of their families but also a necessary outcome of their pursuit of ideal fatherhood.

In addition to closely managing their children's education, fathers aimed to embody the role of a "good" caregiver, skillfully balancing educational oversight with nurturing and friendliness. By broadening the traditional notion of a successful man and striving to "do it all," they redefined their roles as Korean fathers.[17] In willingly taking on educational responsibilities typically assigned to mothers in many Korean families, these fathers expanded the concept of "good" fatherhood through what can be described as "caring masculinity."[18] They dedicated their time and emotions to spending quality moments with their children, despite their demanding work schedules, thereby challenging the stereotype of the distant Asian father.[19]

This demanding yet rewarding approach to fatherhood largely depended on the fathers' class resources. While the benefits of flexible work arrangements for professional men are well-documented,[20] the advantages for the fathers in this chapter extended beyond that. With firsthand experience of life abroad, fluency in English, and success in their respective professions, these highly transnational fathers confidently guided their children's education overseas. Their ability to engage in extensive fathering was often supported by their wives, who dedicated themselves full-time to roles as wives and mothers. This support enabled their husbands to pursue a cosmopolitan elite lifestyle and ensure its careful transmission across generations.

Given their transnational elite backgrounds, the "all-around" fatherhood pursued by many fathers in this chapter expands the existing literature on "new" dads who redefine themselves beyond just breadwinners. While many "new" fathers reportedly limit their career aspirations or set clear boundaries between home and work to become more involved, the fathers in this chapter did not need to adjust or sacrifice their career commitments significantly. Instead, their immersion in work became a resource for their fathering role and a source of their children's respect. By leveraging their work-related knowledge and global connections, these men demonstrated how to integrate demanding yet rewarding careers with active fatherhood.

Such extensive fatherhood highlighted two forms of inequality. First, it exacerbated the achievement gap between the fathers and their wives, reinforcing the division between the fathers' public roles and the mothers' private responsibilities. Second, it marginalized fathers with fewer transnational resources, making it difficult for them to be recognized as "good" fathers within the circle of high-achieving children abroad. Many mothers, along with a few fathers, assumed a secondary role, concentrating on being "emotion experts" rather than educational managers or career counselors. Their emotional support often served as a substitute for the perceived lack of impactful academic support compared to their more transnationally engaged counterparts. Whether explicitly or subtly, their involvement was often undervalued by highly transnational fathers, who felt they were successfully managing *all* aspects of parenthood. Within these varying parental roles, another hierarchy emerged between academic and emotional support, mirroring the broader hierarchy between fathers and mothers.

Despite some children reporting conflicts with their fathers, most supported the positive views on their fathers' extensive involvement, indicating that meticulous paternal engagement was effective within their competitive school and work environments. The extensive transnational fatherhood discussed in this chapter suggests that fathers with resources and achievements can serve as teachers, mentors, and role models in the public sphere, often earning genuine appreciation and respect from their children.[21]

Conclusion

Classed and Gendered
Transfer of Mobility

Throughout this book, I explore how the intersecting identities of gender and class influence the perspectives of children, mothers, and fathers within elite Korean transnational families, particularly regarding their choices in family arrangements and parenting strategies for educating their children abroad. The central analytical framework of this book views elite transnational parenting as a form of gendered labor, both building on and challenging existing scholarship that characterizes middle-class parenting as intensive, demanding, and frequently centered on mothers. By detailing the specific ways gendered resources are utilized in raising "Asian globals"[1] by both mothers and fathers, this book aims to enhance understanding of the underexplored familial dynamics within elite Korean transnational families in the context of globalized higher education.

Drawing on interviews with children and parents, I undertake two tasks: Firstly, I analyze how each group—children, mothers, and fathers—interprets and represents their perspectives on elite transnational parenting, whether experienced, practiced, or observed. Simultaneously, I delve into the aspirations and senses of belonging of children, elucidating how daughters and sons from diverse familial backgrounds imagine and construct their life trajectories in distinctively nuanced ways. Secondly, by triangulating the narratives of mothers, fathers, and children, I explore the family dynamics of the subjects in this book—the underdiscussed transnational families of high-achieving Korean students at elite U.S. colleges.

Chapter 1, "Children Recount Public Fathering and Private Mothering," examined how children interpreted their transnational upbringing and family arrangements through a gendered perspective. The narratives revealed how the traditional gender division of labor, both within and outside the family, influenced children's views on their parents' roles and expectations in their high-achieving lives abroad. Children perceived their parents as fulfilling gendered roles and responsibilities in their elite transnational education. In their early years, children observed their mothers engaging in "concerted cultivation,"[2] often in a gender-segregated manner, aligning with societal expectations of Korean mothers. At the same time, they accepted their fathers as primary breadwinners and family achievers, which fostered a positive and appreciative view of their fathers' later involvement in their education and career preparation abroad.

In the children's narratives, gendered parenting patterns were closely intertwined with social class—particularly, the parents' transnational experiences and resources—and the structure of their transnational family arrangements. For high-achieving young adults, the hands-on support from parents was seen as crucial for thriving at an elite college abroad. The gender of a parent, reflecting societal expectations, defined the distinct roles of mothers and fathers within elite transnational families, with both engaging in intensive parenting in their own ways. Children tended to value the career-related support from their socially successful fathers more than the day-to-day care provided by their mothers for their physical and psychological well-being, perceiving this gendered division of roles as both compelling and unquestionable.

Chapter 2, "Who Learns to Become Cosmopolitan Better?" explored how gender and class simultaneously shaped children's views on life, career, family aspirations, and their sense of belonging. Except for a few children from less transnational backgrounds, the young adults in this book challenged reductive and pathologizing views of international students, demonstrating their ability to actively use their education abroad to meet their needs and aspirations. However, disparities and inequities remained among them, influenced by their gender and familial backgrounds.

Sons from highly transnational families actively rejected the Korean educational environment, embracing the philosophy of elite Western education, which they credited for fostering their creativity and liberal mindset. They engaged in "agency for becoming"[3] as they crafted their "choice biographies," detailing their ideal majors, degrees, occupations, places of residence, and marriages—choices they genuinely believed they had made independently. In contrast, daughters often created what might be described as "normal biographies," frequently constrained by prevailing gender norms related to their roles as daughters, mothers, and wives. Their narratives suggested that the employability of elite women abroad was significantly influenced by their gender, class, ethnicity, and citizenship, rather than by autonomous choices and "self-authoring."[4] Consequently, daughters across various majors and familial backgrounds commonly aspired to life stability and a "happy" marriage, in stark contrast to the sons' ambitions for social recognition and lucrative careers.

Despite achieving similar academic success, daughters often felt pressured to prioritize their families over their careers, while sons' aspirations typically aligned with societal and familial expectations: achieving professional success, serving as breadwinners, and making a positive impact on society. This underscores gender as a central factor in shaping children's transnational experiences and their consequential personal aspirations and achievements. However, class—defined primarily by parental and familial backgrounds—created significant within-group differences, particularly among sons. Sons with substantial resources, such as U.S. citizenship or permanent residency, enjoyed greater flexibility and opportunities, while a few sons from less transnational families did not overtly pursue grander ambitions, focusing instead on financial security. This perspective was also common among many daughters, regardless of class. Daughters from less transnational families, though a minority among the children in this book, were especially candid about the fear, anxiety, and loneliness they faced during their transnational upbringings, revealing various layers of discrimination against female Asian international students.

Chapter 3, "When Class Trumps Gender: Korean Parents' Views," explored how the intersecting influences of class and gender shaped parents' expectations regarding their children's elite education abroad. Fathers with experience studying abroad, along with mothers with similar backgrounds, shared common rationales for sending their children to schools overseas and had aligned expectations for academic and career success. Mothers who had spent extended periods abroad but had not studied there themselves also showed significant similarities to mothers and fathers who had studied abroad. By justifying their considerable investment in their children's elite education abroad, cosmopolitan parents actively reinforced the cultural hierarchy between the West and their home country. Their ambition to establish "mobile families," often accompanied by concrete plans, reflected their prestigious class position.

Despite their limited numbers, locally based parents with less mobility highlighted why children's elite education abroad and the resulting transnational family arrangements were considered high-stakes investments by many Korean parents. Rather than valuing mobility, these parents hoped that degrees from prestigious U.S. colleges would lead to lucrative careers in Korea. The ambivalence of locally based mothers was driven more by the significant emotional costs of transnational parenthood than by concerns about the cost-effectiveness of their children's education abroad—a concern more prominently expressed by the fathers. This group of locally based parents was notably opposed to transnational mobility and skeptical about their children settling in foreign countries, questioning whether it was more valuable than achieving success and happiness in Korea.

These findings suggest two key implications regarding the intersectional influence of class and gender on the intergenerational transmission of mobility through children's education abroad. Firstly, class—largely defined by educational and career backgrounds—emerged as the primary factor shaping parental expectations and evaluations within education-focused transnational families. Secondly, gender introduced nuanced yet significant distinctions. The gendered roles and responsibilities of parents affected their assessments of raising cosmopolitan globals: Fathers tended to emphasize the impact of elite education abroad on academic growth and career prospects, either implicitly or explicitly, while mothers focused more on their children's personal well-being and happiness.

Chapter 4, "What Makes for a Perfect Transnational Mother?" examined the various interpretations and practices of "good" motherhood among parents of high-achieving Korean students abroad. "Opt-out," full-time mothers adhered to traditional caregiving roles, reflecting and reinforcing the gender division of labor within the family. In contrast, employed mothers broadened the traditional concept of "good" mothering by integrating educational and, occasionally, career-related support for their adult children—roles typically associated with fathers in the context of high-achieving Korean students abroad. By striving to "do it all," elite professional mothers aimed to embody their own ideal of perfect transnational motherhood.

Mothers' educational and career backgrounds created significant differences and sometimes fissures among them. Those with professional occupations and, in some cases, degrees from abroad sought to blur the line between public fathering and private mothering. Their intensive educational and occasionally career-related support partially challenged the traditionally father-led support for adult children abroad, despite their continued view of their husbands as "better" role models in the public realm. In contrast, mothers with less education and work experience focused on providing around-the-clock, sacrificial care for their children rather than emulating their employed counterparts. This highlights how career and educational resources can serve as a rare but valuable mothering asset for high-achieving children abroad, potentially challenging the traditional gendered division of parenting within their elite circles.

Chapter 5, "Emerging Extensive Transnational Fatherhood," explored the underdiscussed role of fathers in elite transnational families, emphasizing what their extensive support for their children signified regarding their sense of manhood and fatherhood. These fathers generally saw their involvement as both extensive and fulfilling. Their high assessments of their fatherhood were influenced by several factors, including their educational credentials, career experiences, financial resources, and their children's academic achievements— all reflecting their privileged status. In this context, their masculinities aligned well with their paternal care. As men who had studied abroad with successful careers, they could leverage their resources, including a cosmopolitan lifestyle with fluent English, firsthand knowledge about life abroad, and connections with other elites, for their extensive transnational fathering. Their support for their children significantly hinged on their dominant status as transnational elite men, enabling them to fulfill the role of intensive caregivers for their high-achieving children abroad, who appreciated the rarity of such paternal support.

The narratives of less transnational fathers further illustrated the impact of classed resources in transnational parenting for high-achieving children. While their more transnational counterparts often felt they deserved respect and appreciation for their hands-on involvement, fathers with fewer transnational resources sometimes found their role overwhelming and emotionally draining. They frequently struggled to meet their children's high expectations for paternal support within the elite circle of families with children abroad. Instead of adhering to the dominant masculinity associated with being a successful and engaged father, these locally based fathers focused on emotional care—a role traditionally expected of mothers. This underscores how both fathers and children in elite transnational families reinforce the link between being a successful father and a high achiever.

Exclusive Intergenerational Transfer of Mobility

In analyzing the transnational family dynamics within Korean elite families—a collaborative effort involving mothers, fathers, daughters, and sons—I sought to unravel how class and gender intersect to create inequalities within these families. Class, particularly in terms of educational and occupational backgrounds, emerges as a primary source of differentiation and division among parents—both among mothers and fathers—more so than between the genders. Significant differences were observed between stay-at-home and employed mothers, as well as between highly transnational fathers and those who were locally based, especially in their perspectives on children's education abroad and their roles in transnational parenthood.

Despite these divisions, the parents and children in this book largely shared a common framework for understanding the gender divide in their transnational parenting. This framework reinforces traditional gendered expectations, with mothers assuming the roles of primary caregivers and "emotion experts,"[5] while fathers are seen as the main breadwinners and achievers. However, many families, especially those with high mobility, challenged the prevailing stereotypes about Korean mothers and fathers. Elite employed mothers not only provided daily care but also actively supported their children's professional ambitions, expanding their roles beyond traditional expectations. Meanwhile, cosmopolitan fathers demonstrated an intense level of involvement in their children's lives by providing comprehensive support, which aligns with but also extends the concept of "new age" fatherhood—traditionally associated with physical engagement during early childhood.

This book challenges the conventional stereotype of intensely involved mothers versus distant fathers in Korean—and more broadly East Asian—families. Often characterized as "too children-focused," Korean families are typically portrayed as centered around (middle-class) mothers who drive their children's education to maintain class status.[6] However, the families in this book reveal that the active involvement of elite fathers plays a crucial role in the success of their investment in their high-achieving children's education abroad, significantly influencing their family projects for mobility.

In this circle of elite transnational Koreans, the ideal of extensive motherhood and fatherhood was geared toward a single objective: the reproduction of transnational mobility. To achieve this, parents meticulously divided the parenting responsibilities of their high-achieving children according to their educational and career statuses, which in turn reinforced traditional gender expectations for women and men. This finding adds nuance to the understanding of Asian high achievement and parenting, providing a more contextualized view. Scholars have traditionally used the status attainment model to explain Asian achievements, focusing on socioeconomic and demographic variables such as family status, race, gender, and parenting styles.[7] Another approach, cultural frames, often assumes a universal "Asian fervor" for education across class lines.[8] However, these perspectives often overlook the classed *and* gendered dimensions of the familial motivations and aspirations that drive Asian achievements, especially within a transnational context. For the individuals featured in this book, the family acts as a gendered unit for class reproduction and the accumulation of cultural capital. By examining how Korean elites transfer transnational mobility and cosmopolitan lifestyles to their children, this book enriches our understanding of the cultural foundations of Asian high achievement, revealing it to be deeply intertwined with class and gender dynamics.

In contrast to the common portrayal of Asian families as having strained parent-child relationships—such as the stereotype of the "tiger mom" and her child yearning for more leniency—the families in this book present a different narrative. Here, parents and children describe their relationships as harmonious, cooperative, and built on mutual trust. The high-achieving young Korean adults featured in this book understand the purpose of their education abroad and the resulting transnational family arrangements. They generally accept and embrace their parents' extensive involvement in their lives, hoping that the family project will ultimately succeed, and sometimes even excuse their parents for any pressures they may have imposed. On the other hand, those who feel their parents lack the resources for such extensive parenting often express conflicts or disappointments, highlighting their own perseverance and independence as the primary factors in their achievements.

This class-based perspective further distinguishes the two groups, especially regarding their career and marriage aspirations. Children from more privileged families, particularly sons, often pursue careers beyond national and cultural boundaries. In contrast, those from less advantaged backgrounds may feel constrained or uncertain about how to leverage their elite U.S. degrees into successful careers outside Korea. Although this book does not extensively track the children's postgraduation trajectories, their envisioned biographies suggest that the outcomes of elite education abroad and the associated transnational family arrangements are uneven.

Further Inquiries on Korean (Asian) Family Strategies for Mobility

Throughout the book, I argue that class privilege, particularly through transnational mobility, is often perpetuated by the gender achievement gap within elite families. Many children perceive the gap between their mothers and fathers and the associated division of parenting as natural, unquestionable, and even effective. The critical questions remain, Will these children reassess their views when they become parents themselves? Will they continue the gendered division of parenting they observed, or will they adopt different approaches? More importantly, will they choose to replicate their parents' strategies, including the education-driven transnational family arrangements, to sustain or enhance their own mobility and perpetuate it across generations?

As discussed in the introduction, Koreans have practiced globalization primarily through education. In the 2023–2024 academic year, 123,181 Korean students were studying abroad, with the United States as the top destination, attracting approximately 33 percent (40,755) of them.[9] This makes Korea the third-largest country of origin for non-U.S. students in the United States. The number of Korean students abroad saw fluctuations during the early 2000s, paralleling the increasing trend of sending children overseas and the rise of wild geese families in Korea. However, despite these high numbers, the population of Korean students abroad has been declining or at least stabilizing since around the mid-2010s. By 2022, the number of Korean students studying abroad had decreased by approximately half compared to 2017, continuing a downward trend that began during the COVID-19 pandemic and persisted even as its impact lessened.[10]

The declining trend in Korean students studying abroad raises questions about whether Koreans' enthusiasm for education abroad is waning. Analysts who anticipate the continuation of this downward trend point to the difficulties faced by returning Korean young adults in the domestic job market. They argue that the benefits of studying abroad—such as improved domestic employment opportunities due to fluent English and the prestige associated with foreign degrees—are diminishing, which has led to a reduced perceived value of international education. An article published in 2015 recounts the experience of a Korean job seeker who had spent "half of [his] life" studying in the United States, ultimately earning a bachelor's degree from a state university in California. However, he found his global education less impactful and remunerative than anticipated, struggling to secure employment upon returning to Korea. The article concludes with a statement from a Korean Ministry of Education official, noting, "In the past, students believed that studying abroad would lead to better job opportunities. [. . .] However, those benefits no longer seem to exist."[11]

This trend may suggest the phenomenon of "credential inflation" in Korea, similar to what has been observed in other developed Asian societies like Hong Kong.[12] It could also highlight growing concerns among Korean businesses about the adaptability of graduates from foreign institutions to the specific demands of Korea's professional environment. These concerns might stem from a mismatch between the liberal environments experienced by students abroad and the distinct expectations of the Korean workplace. The decline in Korean students studying abroad is sometimes interpreted as a sign of "a weakening of the global mindset and tenacious spirit."[13] This observation can be compared to a phenomenon in Japan, where a sense of complacency emerged among youth following the economic prosperity of their home country. The growing number of Chinese students studying abroad further supports this theory, highlighting China's ongoing efforts to achieve global standards across various fields, given its relatively recent emergence as a significant player in the international education arena.[14]

I argue that the decrease in the number of Korean students studying abroad, particularly in the United States, must be understood within a broader context. First, the overall decline in international student numbers in the United States has significantly influenced the reduction of Korean students there. According to a report by the Institute of International Education, new enrollments of international students at U.S. colleges dropped by more than 10 percent between the 2015–2016 and 2018–2019 academic years.[15] This decline occurred while enrollment in other English-speaking countries, such as Canada and Australia, saw an increase. This trend likely reflects the impact of conservative U.S. immigration policies under the Trump administration, which likely contributed to the reduced international student numbers in the United States.[16]

This perspective supports the argument that the decline in the number of Korean students in the United States is primarily due to political shifts in U.S. immigration policies and changes in school administration rather than solely reflecting a diminishing enthusiasm among Korean parents for transnational education or the challenges faced by Korean students in the domestic job market. Additionally, the recent impact of COVID-19 has significantly contributed to the sharp decline in Korean students studying abroad, mirroring trends seen among students from other countries.[17] So while I acknowledge the ongoing decrease in *yuhak* (education abroad) among Koreans, I advocate for a more nuanced investigation into this trend, focusing on identifying specific demographics or groups that continue to drive the number of Korean students abroad, particularly in prestigious Western institutions.

Although the current number of Korean students pursuing degrees abroad, especially in the United States, is not as high as it once was, a significant cohort remains. I argue that transnational education in Korea is becoming increasingly stratified. In contemporary Korean society, where the trend of studying abroad has begun to wane, it is crucial to investigate which parents still aspire to, or successfully achieve, a transnational educational experience for their children. The elite Korean parents highlighted in this book, especially fathers, exemplify a leading group in the selective pursuit of international education, marked by their strong preference for prestigious Western institutions. What objectives do these parents aim to achieve through their costly transnational parenting? What does nurturing children with transnational mobility truly signify? If sending children abroad is about more than just career success in their home country, what are the broader aspirations driving this choice?

In examining elite Korean transnational families, a prevalent theme emerged: a strong desire to pass on mobility and cosmopolitan aspirations to future generations. Many students and their parents viewed studying abroad as profoundly transformative, believing that elite Western education not only enhances employability and career prospects but also fosters overall personal growth and the development of well-rounded, exemplary individuals. While a few families hoped their children would return to Korea and achieve success after graduating from prestigious U.S. colleges, the majority aimed to establish themselves in the United States or other "global cities"[18] after graduation. This perspective underscores the privileged motivations driving these families' dedication to their children's education abroad and the resulting transnational family arrangements.

The question then arises, What are the long-term effects of this intergenerational reproduction of transnational mobility? Future research would benefit from exploring the enduring impacts of (elite) education abroad and the intergenerational transfers of transnational mobility. Although I lack longitudinal data on children's life trajectories postgraduation, observations from participants who graduated and secured their first jobs during my data collection suggest a discernible pattern.

Despite the small sample size, a trend emerged among the observed cases. Students, often men, whose parents were elite professionals with degrees from abroad, frequently secured lucrative positions in the United States or global cities like Hong Kong and Singapore. In contrast, some children of locally educated and less affluent parents returned to Korea after facing difficulties in securing employment abroad. They often sought to leverage their English proficiency and foreign credentials within the Korean job market. However, articulating these decisions proved challenging for them, as they and many of their peers perceived returning to Korea as a form of failure within their circle.

This observation highlights a common aspiration among most participants: to launch their careers in the United States or other developed countries. Their overarching goal was to become transnational elite professionals, which was seen as the ideal outcome of their substantial investment in transnational education. This pattern indicates that transnational mobility is often successfully transferred between generations through education abroad, especially within prestigious contexts like upper-class families with socially accomplished parents who have also studied internationally.

The narratives of parents and children in this book illustrate that transnational education, especially between Korea and the United States, acts as a cultural bridge linking elite Korean parents with their high-achieving children. The shared experiences of studying abroad and their cosmopolitan aspirations create a strong bond between these parents and their children. In contrast, parents who have not studied abroad often struggle to connect with their children living overseas, leading to a widening cultural gap. These insights reveal that education abroad not only functions as a mechanism for class reproduction but also fosters familial connections in Korean society, where class inequalities are frequently highlighted as significant social issues.

The privileged context of the families in this book is crucial when considering the effects and consequences of studying abroad as an expensive family endeavor. This book focuses on the "successful" cases of education-driven Korean transnational families with children attending elite U.S. colleges. However, it does not explore the parenting and family dynamics of transnational families whose children achieved less than expected, both academically and culturally. This includes those who dropped out of high school or college abroad, as well as those who aimed for Ivy League admission but were unsuccessful. Additionally, this book provides limited insights into the experiences of individuals who returned to Korea after studying or working abroad, though it does include the stories of a few children who decided to return at the time of their interviews.

Some researchers have examined the experiences of Korean skilled returnees who return to Korea after exposure to education and labor markets abroad.[19] These studies highlight that returnees frequently encounter issues of exclusion and "in-betweenness," revealing "the irony in perceiving them as both agents of change and privileged transnationals."[20] While this book focuses on the upper tier of education-driven Korean transnational families and their children, future research that explores families and individuals across the entire class spectrum could offer a more nuanced understanding of the complexities and diversities within transnationally mobile high achievers.

The experiences of Korean, and more broadly, Asian women abroad also warrant greater academic scrutiny, as they tend to face heightened challenges in amassing the ideal capital to construct a "desirable self."[21] This "desirable self," as a form of cultural capital, is shaped by class, race, and gender judgments. For many Asian women, studying abroad can offer an "escape route" from the patriarchal and misogynistic cultures of their home countries, enabling them to pursue a "desirable self."[22] However, the narratives of some parents in this book reveal that familial pressures often continue to direct Asian daughters back toward traditional, family-oriented roles—a phenomenon Ulrich Beck referred to as "female status fate."[23] These gendered pressures, both within and beyond the home, underscore the need for further analysis of this issue.

The gender dynamics in Korea require urgent attention, particularly in light of the recent resurgence and popularization of feminism, often referred to as the "feminism reboot."[24] This movement may complicate the portrayal of elite Korean women and their career and family aspirations, raising questions about potential generational differences in these areas. Notably, none of the mothers or daughters in this book explicitly expressed a desire to challenge the unequal gender relations or the division of labor and parenting roles. Instead, they inadvertently supported the status quo, especially when it was seen as beneficial for maintaining their social class. This suggests that the gendered reproduction of privilege, facilitated by sending children abroad for education, is deeply intertwined with the existing achievement gap between women and men. In these families, where career and cultural resources are essential for effective and esteemed parenting, elite men often find themselves in a more advantageous position due to societal expectations for men to achieve more professionally than women. The question remains, Will this dynamic ever change?

Acknowledgments

This book builds upon my doctoral dissertation, which I began pursuing in earnest around 2015. At the outset, my interest in transnational families was broad and undefined. However, an opportunity to participate in a research project examining how college students' academic experiences in the United States varied by class and race led me to seek out Korean students both within and beyond the University of Massachusetts Amherst, where I was based at the time. As my research focus evolved, I eventually parted ways with the original project team. Nevertheless, my interactions with students not only from the large public university but also from nearby elite private institutions allowed me to undertake the qualitative research that became the foundation of my dissertation and, ultimately, this book. Like many qualitative studies, this research was not carried out according to a rigidly predetermined plan. Rather, it emerged organically at the intersection of my personal curiosity, academic aspirations, and, most importantly, the collaboration of my participants. While there were undoubtedly challenging moments at the time, nearly a decade later, as I await the publication of this book, what remain are only fond memories.

Throughout the process of conducting this research, my positionality has been an asset in many ways. As a first-generation scholar, navigating this entire journey without the intellectual guidance of parents or other family members was not something I found disappointing—it was simply expected. Yet as the research progressed, I came to realize that this position allowed me to approach the families I sought to understand from a more distanced and critical perspective. At the same time, my status as an international scholar in the United States provided a foundation for mutual understanding and solidarity with

175

many of the students and at times even their parents, who participated in this study. My identity as an unmarried woman in her early thirties further facilitated smooth communication with both the children and parents involved in the research. In many ways, this was a study I found genuinely engaging and enjoyable to conduct. It has remained close to my heart for nearly a decade since the first interview, and not once did I feel fatigued or lose interest in it. I am simply grateful and delighted that I was able to carry out this research, complete it successfully, and see it take shape as a book.

That this research, which began as a chance curiosity, could ultimately take shape as a book is due, above all else, to the invaluable cooperation of the participants—a point that cannot be emphasized enough. I am deeply grateful to the 74 students and 34 parents who shared their experiences with me, often speaking candidly about sensitive aspects of their lives that are not easily disclosed to others. Given the public scrutiny surrounding the privileges of elite transnational families, it would have been understandable for participants to feel hesitant. Yet the sincerity of those who told me, "Someone needs to study us," gave me the resolve to continue this project rather than abandon it midway. As someone who remained, in many ways, an outsider, I gained both personal and academic insight from their worldviews and experiences—perspectives I would not have otherwise encountered. Conducting research on elites is never an easy task, and I want to remember all my participants not just as subjects of study but as collaborators, even cowriters, in this endeavor.

I am forever grateful to my doctoral advisor, Naomi Gerstel, for inviting me to join the research project that became the foundation of this study and for her unwavering mentorship, even after I transitioned to an independent study. Her guidance allowed me to grow as a researcher early on, giving me both the freedom and confidence to pursue my work. Her perspectives and language have shaped my scholarship in ways even deeper than I had initially realized. I take this opportunity to express my sincere appreciation.

Beyond Professor Gerstel, this book would not have come to life without the support of numerous scholars who have accompanied me throughout my academic journey, from my graduate studies to the present. I am especially grateful to Joya Misra, a great mentor who always genuinely appreciated my research, and to Miliann Kang, who has been an inspiring role model as an Asian woman scholar. I also extend my gratitude and solidarity to the colleagues and friends with whom I shared both the joys and challenges of becoming an independent scholar at UMass Amherst. From the UMass sociology and women, gender, and sexuality studies community, I learned how precious and fulfilling it is to live a life of scholarship—to write, to present, and to engage in intellectual inquiry.

I am also heavily indebted to the professors and colleagues I have encountered at my academic home, Yonsei University, where I completed my undergraduate and master's degrees and later returned after earning my PhD. Special thanks go to Hyun Mee Kim, who guided me toward a life of research, and Wangbae Kim, whose support helped me navigate the challenges of completing my master's degree. I am also thankful to the Yonsei sociology department and the College of Social Sciences, where I found inspiring colleagues and students who have supported me throughout my writing.

Additionally, I sincerely appreciate all the reviewers and audiences of my journal publications and presentations related to this research. A special thank you to the members of AKSA (the Association of Korean Sociologists in America), including Hyeyoung Woo and Hyunjoon Park, for providing precious opportunities to share my work with broader audiences—an opportunity not always easily accessible to international scholars.

I am deeply grateful to Peter Mickulas at Rutgers University Press for his support for this book project and to Sam Martin, Hannah McGinnis, and Daryl Brower for all of their help during the production process. I also thank the editors of the Families in Focus series for the opportunity to include my book in such a fitting and valuable collection, as well as for their insightful feedback on earlier drafts.

Finally, I extend my deepest gratitude to my family. Never once have they questioned the source of my drive to learn and pursue an academic career. Rather than seeking to understand or justify it, they have offered me their unwavering support throughout this journey. Because of them, I have been able to study, write, and teach with joy and pride, free from guilt or obligation. I am especially grateful to my parents, Sun-Ok and Seongbok, for their love, patience and generosity. I also thank Haewon, whose wholehearted support extends to the publication of this book and every aspect of my scholarship and life. Last but certainly not least, I dedicate this book to my maternal grandmother, Guido Lee, who took immense pride in my achievements, both great and small. I look forward to reuniting with her and cherishing sweet moments together in heaven.

An earlier version of chapter 1 was previously published as Juyeon Park, "Public Fathering, Private Mothering: Gendered Transnational Parenting and Class Reproduction Among Elite Korean Students," *Gender & Society* 32, no. 4 (2018): 563–586. An earlier version of chapter 2 was previously published as Juyeon Park, "Unequal Opportunities in Becoming Cosmopolitan: Korean Students' Gendered and Classed Acquirement of Transnational Mobility Through Studying Abroad," *Gender and Education* 35, no. 8 (2023): 724–741.

Notes

Introduction

1 Throughout, I refer to South Korea simply as Korea.
2 Throughout, bracketed ellipses indicate omissions in quoted text rather than faltering speech or an incomplete thought.
3 Kuptsch and Pang 2006.
4 Skeldon 2008.
5 Findlay 2011.
6 Abelmann and Kang 2014.
7 [S.] Park and Abelmann 2004, 646.
8 [K.] Chang 2010.
9 Crystal 2003.
10 [S.] Park and Abelmann 2004, 650.
11 *HYPS* is an acronym for Harvard University, Yale University, Princeton University, and Stanford University.
12 Dillon 2008.
13 International Institute of Education 2024.
14 Yale Office of International Students and Scholars 2024.
15 Abelmann and Kang 2014.
16 See [Y.] Lee and Koo 2006; [J.] Kang and Abelmann 2011; Kim [Jongyoung] 2008; [S.] Park and Abelmann 2004.
17 Kim [S.] and Finch 2002.
18 Abelmann, Park, and Kim 2009, 270.
19 Cho [U.] 2004.
20 Lee [Jin-Young] 2001.
21 Some point to Confucianism, which holds learning and self-cultivation in high regard, and its influence on Korean culture as the primary reason for this educational fervor. See, for example, [Jeong-Kyu] Lee 2006.
22 Fenton 2015; OECD 2024b.
23 Horn 2014.
24 Koo 2007.
25 [H.] Park 2013.

26 See Kim [H.] and Okazaki 2014; [J.] Park 2009; [J.] Shin et al. 2014 for Korean students who do "early study abroad."

27 Lo et al. 2015.

28 Fewer than ten Korean high schools—including some foreign language high schools (selective special-purpose high schools) and private boarding high schools, such as the Korean Minjok Leadership Academy—offer special classes called *yuhakpan* to prepare students for elite colleges abroad.

29 Abelmann, Park, and Kim 2009, 277–278.

30 Hong 1993, 25; my translation.

31 Hong 1993, 290; my translation.

32 Park [W.] 2004, 55.

33 See Khan 2011; Mijs and Savage 2020.

34 *Yŏsŏngjungang* 2015; my translation.

35 *Yŏsŏngjungang* 2015; my translation.

36 Nonini and Ong 1997.

37 Ong 1999, 95, cited in Waters 2005, 359.

38 Skeldon 1994, cited in Waters 2005, 361.

39 According to Bourdieu (1986), capital can take three principal forms: economic capital, which is immediately and directly convertible into money and may be institutionalized in the form of property rights; cultural capital, which is convertible, on certain conditions, into economic capital and may be institutionalized in the form of educational qualifications; and social capital, made up of social obligations ("connections"), which is convertible, in certain conditions, into economic capital. In this context, migration is a means of "potential accumulation of different forms of capital at different geographical sites" (Waters 2005, 363).

40 Ong 1999, 18–19.

41 See Ley 2003; Ong 1999; Teo 2003.

42 Waters 2005.

43 Chee 2003; Ho 2003; Ong 1999; Pe-Pua et al. 1998; Waters 2002.

44 Bartley 2003; Eyou, Adair, and Dixon 2000; Ho 1995; Larmer 2017.

45 Chee 2003; [S.] Huang and Yeoh 2005.

46 For research on (advantaged) Korean transnational fathers, see [Y.] Kang (2012) and [Se Hwa] Lee (2021a, 2021b).

47 See Kim [Jongyoung] 2011, 2012.

48 Goh-Grapes 2009.

49 Cho [U.] 2004.

50 [Jeehun] Kim 2010.

51 Mazzucato and Schans 2011.

52 Onishi 2008.

53 Ha 2007.

54 Ly 2005.

55 [E.] Chang 2018, 213.

56 See [Se Hwa] Lee 2021b; Jeong, You and Kwon 2013.

57 [I.] Park and Cho (1995) argue that Confucian teachings dictated that Asians build father-centered households, with the central familial relationship being constructed not between spouses but between parent and child.

58 Abelmann, Park, and Kim 2009, 268.

59 For some examples, see Cheah, Leung, and Zhou (2013) and [G] Huang and Gove (2015).
60 Blair-Loy 2001.
61 Nader 1972.
62 Mazzucato and Schans 2011.
63 Bourdieu and Passeron 1977.
64 See Grinker 2008; [M.] Kang, Park, and Park 2020.
65 For similar approaches, see Bayer (1969) and Bertrand et al. (2016).
66 Khattab 2015.
67 See Griffith 1998.
68 Breen 2007.
69 See Kerstetter 2012.
70 Hewitt-Taylor 2002.
71 Shaw et al. 2020, 284. Also see Flores (2016) for the merits and payoffs of field research conducted by an "outsider-within."

Chapter 1 Children Recount Public Fathering and Private Mothering

1   See Hwang 2012; Lee [Eun A] 2013.
2   Hays 1996.
3   Chun [S.] 2002; [J.] Park 2009.
4   See [A.] Kim and Pyke 2015.
5   Chun [K.] 2018.
6   Josephson and Burack 1998.
7   See Christopher 2012.
8   Spending on private education in Korea has increased steadily in recent years, with the exception of 2020 (Statista 2024). According to OECD (2024a), Korea's private spending on education has been above the OECD average since 2015.
9   Lareau 2003.
10 As of 2023, only about ten high schools in Korea, characterized by a very low acceptance rate and expensive tuition, offer special programs and courses for students aspiring to apply to colleges abroad. Notably, Daewon Foreign Language High School, Hanyoung Foreign Language High School, Hankuk Academy of Foreign Studies, and Korean Minjok Leadership Academy are renowned for their students' outstanding results in international college applications. Most of the individuals mentioned in this chapter who completed high school in Korea were alumni of these institutions.
11 Papanek 1979.
12 Risman 1998.
13 Risman and Johnson-Sumerford 1998, 36.
14 Parents' emotional support can manifest in various forms, leading to different outcomes and assessments. See Gillies (2006) for further exploration.
15 Research indicates that sons with college-educated fathers tend to experience better relationships with them and to communicate with them more frequently compared to peers whose fathers are not as highly educated (see Ide et al. 2018).
16 Papanek 1979.
17 Korea mandates military service for all able-bodied men, typically requiring around eighteen to twenty-one months of service, depending on the branch. This

requirement is rooted in the country's ongoing security concerns, particularly its tense relationship with North Korea. While exemptions or alternative service options exist for certain individuals, such as elite athletes or classical musicians, they are rare and highly scrutinized. In recent years, there have been discussions about reforming the system, including potential reductions in service length and expanding alternative service programs. Despite debates, military service remains a significant social institution that shapes young men's education, careers, and social lives.

18 See Longlands 2014.
19 Ackelsberg and Shanley 1996; Crocco 2001.

Chapter 2 Who Learns to Become Cosmopolitan Better?

1   In 2023, about 33 percent of Korean students abroad (40,755) were studying in the United States. Ministry of Education 2023.
2   [Y.] Kang 2012.
3   Fong 2011.
4   Oberg 1960.
5   Lin and Yi 1997; Popadiuk 2010.
6   Stevenson and Clegg 2012; Woodfield 2019.
7   Burke 2011.
8   Santiago, Karimi, and Alicea 2017.
9   Ono and Piper 2004.
10 Kelsky 2001; Ono and Piper 2004.
11 The population of Korean students studying abroad in 2022 was predominantly female, with 89,819 men and 107,415 women (Korean Statistical Information Service 2024).
12 Mengwei 2018.
13 See Brinton (1994) for the long-standing tendency of Asian parents to invest more in their sons' education than in their daughters'.
14 Beck 1992.
15 Giddens 1991.
16 [Y.] Kim 2013, 139.
17 Beck 1992.
18 Studying international students in Australia, Tran and Vu (2018) coined these four terms for agency in mobility: "agency for becoming," "needs-response agency," "agency as struggle and resistance," and "collective agency for contestation."
19 Tran and Vu 2018, 170.
20 [J.] Lee and Zhou 2015.
21 The SAT and Suneung are both college entrance exams, but they differ in important ways. The Suneung is a high-stakes, single-day test that heavily influences admission to Korean universities, whereas the SAT is more flexible and used for U.S. and international college admissions. The Suneung relies more heavily on content memorization and can only be taken once a year (with nationwide measures ensuring a quiet test environment), while the SAT focuses more on reasoning and problem-solving and can be retaken multiple times in a given year. Finally, unlike the SAT's scaled scoring, the Suneung ranks students by percentile, making competition especially intense.
22 Khan 2011.

23 Yu 2020.
24 Useem and Downie 1976.
25 See Ninh 2011.
26 See [Y.] Cho et al. (2016) and Roh and Kim (2021) for male-centered corporate culture in Korea.
27 See Bayer (1969) and Bertrand et al. (2016) for similar approaches.
28 Khattab 2015.
29 [R.] Chang and Morris 2015; Ng, Pak, and Hernandez 2016.
30 See Khan (2011, 2018) for the culture of elite (American) schools and the construction of elites, and see Duran, McCready, and Goodman (2024) for masculinities and relational leadership attitudes in the collegiate fraternity environment.
31 See Lareau 2003; Golann and Darling-Aduana 2020.
32 Khan 2018, 100.
33 See Sherman 2018.
34 For class as morality, see Sayer (2007).
35 See Jack (2019) for discussion of students from disadvantaged backgrounds in the context of elite colleges.
36 Martin 2021.
37 [Y.] Kim 2013, 119.

Chapter 3   When Class Trumps Gender: Korean Parents' Views

1 See Jung, Koh, and Kim 2024; Lee [Sung-Suk] 2023.
2 For private agencies assisting Korean students who wish to study abroad, see Cho [M.] (2002).
3 As stated in the introduction, most parents in this book chose not to become wild geese parents, often opting to send their children alone to boarding schools abroad. They believed that the physical separation of the couple would harm their marriage and family bonding. Their ample financial resources afforded them the option of such an expensive transnational family arrangement, wherein parents could reside together and children could visit them often via international flights.
4 Visiting family members abroad often requires substantial financial resources. Consequently, frequent international travel is a class-based strategy for family unity, accessible primarily to middle-to-upper-class wild geese parents. For contrasting cases of lower-middle-class Korean wild geese parents, see [Jeehun] Kim (2010) and Kim [Ju Hyun], Song, and Lee (2010).
5 [Se Hwa] Lee 2019, 2021b.
6 Compared to students with U.S. citizenship or permanent residency, international students reportedly have fewer opportunities to receive scholarships or financial aid.
7 This was possible because colleges in Korea start their academic year in March, while U.S. colleges begin in the fall. Some children I interviewed attended a Korean college for one semester "for the experience" or to build a local network while waiting for their U.S. college to commence.
8 Self-sacrifice is often portrayed as a significant motive in Korean (and Korean American) family and marriage dynamics. For instance, Korean immigrant children typically feel a strong sense of gratitude and responsibility toward their parents, whom they believe have made considerable sacrifices for their families. This ideal of sacrificial parenting persists in Korea, closely linked with the expectation of filial

and obedient children who recognize their parents' sacrifices. This debt-bound sentiment has indeed defined Korean parent-child relations. For further discussion, see Hyun (2007) and Ninh (2011).

9   In Korean culture, parents are expected to make a substantial investment when their children get married and start a family, particularly for their sons, often by purchasing a house for the couple.

10   Sewell and Shah 1968; Spera, Wentzel, and Matto 2009.

11   See Sewell and Shah 1968.

12   See Kirk et al. 2011.

13   Veblen (1899) 2005.

14   [Y.] Kang 2012.

15   See Na (2014) for the persistence of breadwinner norms in Korean society.

Chapter 4   What Makes for a Perfect Transnational Mother?

1   Parreñas 2005.

2   See [M.] Chang and Darlington (2008) for an example.

3   See Hondagneu-Sotelo and Avila 1997; Parreñas 2005, 2013.

4   See Parke and Cookston 2021; Parreñas 2008.

5   See [Se Hwa] Lee 2021a; Carling, Menjívar, and Schmalzbauer 2012.

6   In 2021, approximately 17 percent of Korean women took a career break following marriage. Among the married women who quit their jobs, 42.8 percent (597,000) cited childcare as the main reason for leaving the workforce ([Claire] Lee 2022).

7   Lim and Mohd Rasdi 2019; Stone 2007.

8   Hays 1996.

9   See DeVault 1991.

10   Bowen and Devine 2011.

11   Blair-Loy 2001.

12   See Finch and Kim 2016.

13   The term *opt-out mother* refers to a highly educated professional woman who voluntarily leaves the workforce to focus on raising children. It has gained prominence in discussions about work-life balance, as some women exit demanding careers due to structural barriers, workplace inflexibility, or personal choice. While often framed as a choice, critics argue that societal expectations and a lack of supportive policies push women out, rather than offering true flexibility, and thus favor the term *pushed-out* instead. In this book, I use the term *opt-out* only when participants explicitly described their decision to leave the workforce as voluntary, while also acknowledging both their class privilege and the structural and cultural forces that encouraged their departure. For a more in-depth discussion, see Stone 2007.

14   [S.] Park 2006, 2010; Shin, Jahng, and Kim 2019.

15   See Kim [M.] and Sang 2015.

16   See [Jaerim] Lee and Bauer 2013.

17   Hays 1996.

18   Kehily and Thomson 2011; Cook 2009.

19   Hoschild and Machung 2012.

20   As Hays (1996) describes it, *intensive mothering* often involves expert-guided and professional engagement in children's development, a practice typically accessible only to middle-to-upper-class mothers.

21   Hays 1996, 8.

22 See Taylor 2011.
23 See [Hye Gyong] Park 2009.
24 Feminist scholars have explored how motherhood is essentialized through the belief that all women desire to be mothers and naturally assume the maternal role after marriage (see O'Reilly 2016). Building on this, I argue that the narratives of mothers in this chapter essentialize intensive mothering within the context of elite Korean transnational families, taking for granted mothers' undivided and often sacrificial support for their children.
25 See Josephson and Burack (1998) for a discussion of neotraditional families.
26 Their narratives demonstrate how intensive motherhood and intensive careers can complement each other. See Leung (2011) for a similar discussion on entrepreneur mothers who regard their motherhood as a major source of their entrepreneurial spirit.
27 Blair-Loy 2001.
28 See Tingey, Kiger and Riley (1996) for a discussion on how performing multiple roles can usually be stressful for working mothers.
29 Buxton (1998) describes the "mother war" in the Western world, where the adversarial climate arises from competing mothering ideologies: the Superwoman, who prioritizes business-world-like efficiency, and the Earth Mother, who pursues naturalistic approaches to raising children. For further discussion, see also Johnston and Swanson (2003).
30 See You and Nesteruk 2022.

Chapter 5 Emerging Extensive Transnational Fatherhood

1 Casper and Bianchi 2002; Craig 2006.
2 Mazzucato and Schans 2011.
3 Lan 2023.
4 See [Y.] Kang 2012; [Se Hwa] Lee 2021a, 2021b.
5 Marsiglio and Pleck 2005, 259.
6 Lareau 2003.
7 [Y.] Kang 2012.
8 LaRossa 1997; Parke 1996.
9 For the case of low-income fathers, see Summers et al. (2006). For the case of fathers in Germany, see Joshi (2021).
10 See Kim [A.] and Pyke 2015.
11 Dowd 2000.
12 Marsiglio and Roy 2012, 5.
13 Marsiglio and Pleck 2005.
14 See Dick (2011) for the influence of men's relationships with their own fathers on their concept of fatherhood.
15 For an explanation of the term *extensive* in relation to parenting, please refer to Chapter 1, where I redefine the concept of *extensive mothering*.
16 Hwang 2012; Lee [Eun A] 2013.
17 For discussions on the historically dominant type of paternal masculinity in Korean society, see Gu (2020) and [A.] Kim and Pyke (2015).
18 See Elliott 2016.
19 Ko, Jang, and Choi 2022.
20 See Gracia 2014.
21 See Furrow 1998, and Randles 2020.

Conclusion

1 [Y.] Kang 2012.
2 Lareau 2003.
3 Tran and Vu 2018.
4 Beck 1992.
5 Risman 1998.
6 Cho [U.] 2004.
7 Watkins, Ho, and Butler 2017.
8 For example, in her widely discussed autobiography *Battle Hymn of the Tiger Mother* (2011), Amy Chua attributed her children's educational success to Chinese parenting practices rather than to her family's financial, cultural, and educational resources. This perspective, like others that emphasize cultural factors, reinforces the "model minority" myth about Asian individuals and families, neglecting the underlying class dimensions of their achievements. Recent studies ([Jennifer] Lee and Zhou 2015) attempt to integrate both the status attainment model and cultural frames to provide a more comprehensive explanation of Asian achievements.
9 Ministry of Education 2023.
10 Han, Moon, and Chang 2023.
11 Yeo 2015.
12 See Waters 2005.
13 Han, Moon, and Chang 2023.
14 See Griner and Sobol 2014; Henze and Zhu 2012.
15 International Institute of Education 2024.
16 Anderson 2019; Redden 2019.
17 Svrluga 2021.
18 Sassen (1991) 2013.
19 [Jane] Lee 2011; [J.] Shin et al. 2014.
20 [Jane] Lee 2011, 233.
21 Locke 2006.
22 See Martin 2021 for the case of Chinese women students in Western societies.
23 Beck 1992.
24 Many report the emergence and spread of feminism among younger generations of Korean women, exemplified by the "4B movement." The acronym 4B stands for four Korean words, all starting with *bi* and meaning "no": *bihon* (the rejection of heterosexual marriage), *bichulsan* (the rejection of childbirth), *biyeonae* (the rejection of dating), and *bisekseu* (the rejection of heterosexual sexual relationships). For further discussion, see [Jinsook] Kim (2021), Sohn (2020), and Sussman (2023).

References

Abelmann, Nancy, and Jiyeon Kang. 2013. "Memoir/Manuals of South Korean Pre-College Study Abroad: Defending Mothers and Humanizing Children." *Global Networks* 14, no. 1 (February 12, 2013): 1–22. https://doi.org/10.1111/glob.12017.

Abelmann, Nancy, So Jin Park, and Hyunhee Kim. 2009. "College Rank and Neo-Liberal Subjectivity in South Korea: The Burden of Self-Development." *Inter-Asia Cultural Studies* 10, no. 2 (June 1, 2009): 229–247. https://doi.org/10.1080/14649370902823371.

Ackelsberg, Martha, and Mary Lyndon Shanley. 1996. "Privacy, Publicity, and Power: A Feminist Rethinking of the Public-Private Distinction." In *Revisioning the Political Feminist Reconstructions of Traditional Concepts in Western Political Theory*, edited by Nancy Hirschmann and Christine Di Stefano, 213–233. New York: Routledge.

Anderson, Stuart. 2019. "New International Student Enrollment in U.S. Has Fallen 10% Since 2015." *Forbes*, November 19, 2019. https://www.forbes.com/sites/stuartanderson/2019/11/19/new-international-student-enrollment-in-us-has-fallen-10-since-2015/#7d17abdf1ae9.

Barker, Chris. 1997. "Television and the Reflexive Project of the Self: Soaps, Teenage Talk and Hybrid Identities." *British Journal of Sociology* 48, no. 4 (December 1, 1997): 611–628. https://doi.org/10.2307/591599.

Bartley, Allen. 2003. "'New' New Zealanders, or Harbingers of a New Transnationalism? 1.5 Generation Asian Migrant Adolescents in New Zealand." PhD diss., Massey University.

Bayer, Alan. 1969. "Marriage Plans and Educational Aspirations." *American Journal of Sociology* 75, no. 2 (September 1, 1969): 239–244. https://doi.org/10.1086/224769.

Beck, Ulrich. 1992. *Risk Society: Towards a New Modernity*. London: Sage.

Bertrand, Marianne, Patricia Cortes, Claudia Olivetti, and Jessica Pan. 2016. "When Social Norms and Women's Opportunities Interact: Effects on Women's Marriage Prospects by Education." Accessed November 8, 2021. https://cepr.org/voxeu/columns/when-social-norms-and-womens-opportunities-interact-effects-womens-marriage-prospects.

Blair-Loy, Mary. 2001. "Cultural Constructions of Family Schemas: The Case of Women Finance Executives." *Gender & Society* 15, no. 5 (October 1, 2001): 687–709. https://doi.org/10.1177/089124301015005004.

Bourdieu, Pierre. 1986. "The Forms of Capital." In *Handbook of Theory and Research for the Sociology of Education*, edited by John Richardson, 241–258. New York: Greenwood Press.

Bourdieu, Pierre, and Jean-Claude Passeron. 1977. *Reproduction in Education, Society and Culture*. London: Sage.

Bowen, Ronni Lee, and Carol Devine. 2011. "'Watching a Person Who Knows How to Cook, You'll Learn a Lot': Linked Lives, Cultural Transmission, and the Food Choices of Puerto Rican Girls." *Appetite* 56, no. 2 (April 1, 2011): 290–298. https://doi.org/10.1016/j.appet.2010.12.015.

Breen, Lauren. 2007. "The Researcher 'In the Middle': Negotiating the Insider/Outsider Dichotomy." *Australian Community Psychologist* 19, no. 1 (January 1, 2007): 163–174. http://groups.psychology.org.au/assets/files/acp_19(1)-incomplete.pdf#page=154.

Brinton, Mary. 1994. *Women and the Economic Miracle: Gender and Work in Postwar Japan*. Oakland: University of California Press.

Burke, Penny Jane. 2011. "Masculinity, Subjectivity and Neoliberalism in Men's Accounts of Migration and Higher Educational Participation." *Gender and Education* 23, no. 2 (March 1, 2011): 169–184. https://doi.org/10.1080/09540251003674139.

Buxton, Jayne. 1998. *Ending the Mother War*. London: Macmillan.

Carling, Jørgen, Cecilia Menjívar, and Leah Schmalzbauer. 2012. "Central Themes in the Study of Transnational Parenthood." *Journal of Ethnic and Migration Studies* 38, no. 2 (February 1, 2012): 191–217. https://doi.org/10.1080/1369183x.2012.646417.

Casper, Lynne, and Suzanne Bianchi. 2002. *Continuity and Change in the American Family*. Thousand Oaks, Calif.: Sage.

Chang, Esther. 2018. "Kirogi Women's Psychological Well-Being: The Relative Contributions of Marital Quality, Mother–Child Relationship Quality, and Youth's Educational Adjustment." *Journal of Family Issues* 39, no. 1 (February 23, 2016): 209–229. https://doi.org/10.1177/0192513x16632265.

Chang, Kyung-Sup. 2010. *South Korea Under Compressed Modernity: Familial Political Economy in Transition*. New York: Routledge.

Chang, Man Wai, and Yvonne Darlington. 2008. "'Astronaut' Wives: Perceptions of Changes in Family Roles." *Asian and Pacific Migration Journal* 17, no. 1 (March 1, 2008): 61–77. https://doi.org/10.1177/011719680801700103.

Chang, Rong, and Sarah Morris. 2015. "'You Speak Good English': Stereotyping of the Perpetual Foreigner." In *Modern Societal Impacts of the Model Minority Stereotype*, edited by Nicholas Hartlep, 133–154. Hershey, Penn.: Information Science Reference/IGI Global.

Cheah, Charissa, Christy Leung, and Nan Zhou. 2013. "Understanding 'Tiger Parenting' Through the Perceptions of Chinese Immigrant Mothers: Can Chinese and US Parenting Coexist?" *Asian American Journal of Psychology* 4, no. 1 (March 1, 2013): 30–40. https://doi.org/10.1037/a0031217.

Chee, Maria. 2003. "Migrating for the Children: Taiwanese American Women in Transnational Families." In *Wife or Worker? Asian Women and Migration*, edited by Nicola Piper and Mina Roces, 137–156. Lanham: Rowman & Littlefield.

Cho Myung-Duk. 2002. "조기 유학 붐의 원인과 문제점 및 해결방안" [The causes of increasing young Korean students who go abroad to study]. *Hyŏnsanggwa inshik* [Phenomenon and cognition] 26, no. 4 (December 1, 2002): 135–152.

Cho Uhn. 2004. "세계화의 최첨단에 선 한국의 가족: 신글로벌 모자녀 가족 사례 연구" [Korean families on the forefront of globalization]. *Kyŏngjewa sahoe* [Economy and society] 64 (December 1, 2004): 148–173.

Cho, Yonjoo, Jiwon Park, Boreum Ju, Soo Jeoung Han, Hanna Moon, Sohee Park, Ahreum Ju, and Eugene Park. 2016. "Women Leaders' Work-Life Imbalance in South Korean Companies: A Collaborative Qualitative Study." *Human Resource Development Quarterly* 27, no. 4 (September 22, 2016): 461–487. https://doi.org/10.1002/hrdq.21262.

Christopher, Karen. 2012. "Extensive Mothering: Employed Mothers' Constructions of the Good Mother." *Gender & Society* 26, no. 1 (January 1, 2012): 73–96. https://doi.org/10 .1177/0891243211427700.

Chua, Amy. 2011. *Battle Hymn of the Tiger Mother*. New York: Bloomsbury.

Chun Kyung Ho. 2018. "대치동 교육에서는 '아빠의 무관심'이 중요하다고?" [In Daechi-Dong, Gangnam, dads must be indifferent to their children's education?]. Ziksir. Accessed July 2, 2024. http://www.ziksir.com/news/articleView.html?idxno=6297.

Chun Sun-Young. 2002. "'어머니되기'의 새로움" [The newness of mothering: Between desire and anxiety]. *Sahoeiron* [Social theory] 22 (January 1, 2022): 285–332.

Cook, Daniel Thomas. 2009. "Semantic Provisioning of Children's Food: Commerce, Care and Maternal Practice." *Childhood* 16, no. 3 (August 19, 2009): 317–334. https://doi.org/ 10.1177/0907568209335313.

Craig, Lyn. 2006. "Does Father Care Mean Fathers Share? A Comparison of How Mothers and Fathers in Intact Families Spend Time with Children." *Gender & Society* 20, no. 2 (April 1, 2006): 259–281. https://doi.org/10.1177/0891243205285212.

Crocco, Margaret Smith. 2001. "Women, Citizenship, and the Social Studies." *Educational Forum* 65, no. 1, 52–59.

Crystal, David. 2003. *English as a Global Language*. Cambridge: Cambridge University Press.

DeVault, Marjorie. 1991. *Feeding the Family: The Social Organization of Caring as Gendered Work*. Chicago: University of Chicago Press.

Dick, Gary. 2011. "The Changing Role of Fatherhood: The Father as a Provider of Selfobject Functions." *Psychoanalytic Social Work* 18, no. 2 (October 1, 2011): 107–125. https://doi .org/10.1080/15228878.2011.611786.

Dillon, Sam. 2008. "Elite Korean Schools, Forging Ivy League Skills." *New York Times*, April 27, 2008. https://www.nytimes.com/2008/04/27/world/asia/27seoul.html.

Dowd, Nancy. 2000. *Redefining Fatherhood*. New York: NYU Press.

Duran, Antonio, Adam McCready, and Michael Goodman. 2024. "Men, Masculinities, and Relational Leadership Attitudes in the Collegiate Fraternity Environment." *Journal of Women and Gender in Higher Education* 17 (January 26, 2024): 1–17. https://doi.org/10 .1080/26379112.2023.2294731.

Elliott, Karla. 2016. "Caring Masculinities." *Men and Masculinities* 19, no. 3 (March 12, 2015): 240–259. https://doi.org/10.1177/1097184X15576203.

Eyou, Mei Lin, Vivienne Adair, and Robyn Dixon. 2000. "Cultural Identity and Psychological Adjustment of Adolescent Chinese Immigrants in New Zealand." *Journal of Adolescence* 23, no. 5 (October 1, 2000): 531–543. https://doi.org/10.1006/jado.2000.0341.

Fenton, Siobhan. 2015. "President Obama Praises South Korea for Paying Teachers as Much as Doctors." *Independent*, July 18, 2015. https://www.independent.co.uk/news/world/ asia/president-obama-praises-south-korea-for-paying-teachers-as-much-as-doctors -10398802.html.

Finch, John, and Seung-kyung Kim. 2016. "The Korean Family in Transition." In *The Routledge Handbook of Korean Culture and Society*, edited by Youna Kim, 134–148. New York: Routledge.

Findlay, Allan. 2011. "An Assessment of Supply and Demand-Side Theorizations of International Student Mobility." *International Migration* 49, no. 2 (April 1, 2011): 162–190. https://doi.org/10.1111/j.1468-2435.2010.00643.x.

Flores, Glenda. 2016. "Discovering a Hidden Privilege: Ethnography in Multiracial Organizations as an Outsider Within." *Ethnography* 17, no. 2 (March 23, 2015): 190–212. https:// doi.org/10.1177/1466138115575660.

Fong, Vanessa. 2011. *Paradise Redefined: Transnational Chinese Students and the Quest for Flexible Citizenship in the Developed World*. Redwood City, Calif.: Stanford University Press.

Furrow, James. 1998. "The Ideal Father: Religious Narratives and the Role of Fatherhood." *Journal of Men's Studies* 7, no. 1 (October 1, 1998): 17–32. https://doi.org/10.3149/jms.0701.17.

Giddens, Anthony. 1991. *Modernity and Self-Identity: Self and Society in the Late Modern Age*. Redwood City, Calif.: Stanford University Press.

Gillies, Val. 2006. "Working Class Mothers and School Life: Exploring the Role of Emotional Capital." *Gender and Education* 18, no. 3 (May 1, 2006): 281–293. https://doi.org/10.1080/09540250600667876.

Goh-Grapes, Agnes. 2009. "Phenomenon of Wild Goose Fathers in South Korea." *Korea Times*, February 22, 2009. https://www.koreatimes.co.kr/www/nation/2023/10/113_40060.html.

Golann, Joanne, and Jennifer Darling-Aduana. 2020. "Toward a Multifaceted Understanding of Lareau's 'Sense of Entitlement': Bridging Sociological and Psychological Constructs." *Sociology Compass* 14, no. 7 (May 28, 2020). https://doi.org/10.1111/soc4.12798.

Gracia, Pablo. 2014. "Fathers' Child Care Involvement and Children's Age in Spain: A Time Use Study on Differences by Education and Mothers' Employment." *European Sociological Review* 30, no. 2 (April 1, 2014): 137–150. https://doi.org/10.1093/esr/jcu037.

Griffith, Alison. 1998. "Insider/Outsider: Epistemological Privilege and Mothering Work." *Human Studies* 21, no. 4 (October 1, 1998): 361–376. https://doi.org/10.1023/a:1005421211078.

Griner, Jessica, and Allison Sobol. 2014. "Chinese Students' Motivations for Studying Abroad." *Global Studies Journal* 7, no. 1 (January 1, 2014): 1–14. https://doi.org/10.18848/1835-4432/cgp/v07i01/40893.

Grinker, Roy. 2008. *Unstrange Minds: Remapping the World of Autism*. New York: Basic Books.

Gu, Miyoung. 2020. "Paternal Masculinity in Korean Films." In *Transcommunication Vol. 7-2*, edited by Mitsuhiro Yoshimoto, 73–92. Tokyo: Waseda University Press.

Ha, Michael. 2007. "'Kirogi' Families Weigh Risks and Rewards." *Korea Times*, October 31, 2007. http://www.koreatimes.co.kr/www/news/issues/2015/10/229_12942.html.

Han Sang-heon, Moon Ga-young, and Chang Iou-chung. 2023. "Decline in Korean Students Studying Abroad Continue Post-Covid." *Pulse*, July 11, 2023. https://pulsenews.co.kr/view.php?year=2023&no=524288.

Hays, Sharon. 1996. *The Cultural Contradictions of Motherhood*. New Haven, Conn.: Yale University Press.

Henze, Jürgen, and Jiani Zhu. 2012. "Current Research on Chinese Students Studying Abroad." *Research in Comparative and International Education* 7, no. 1 (January 1, 2012): 90–104. https://doi.org/10.2304/rcie.2012.7.1.90.

Hewitt-Taylor, Jaquelina. 2002. "Inside Knowledge: Issues in Insider Research." *Nursing Standard* 16, no. 46 (July 31, 2002): 33–35.

Ho, Elsie. 1995. "Chinese or New Zealander? Differential Paths of Adaptation of Hong Kong Chinese Adolescent Immigrants in New Zealand." *New Zealand Population Review* 21, nos. 1–2 (May/November 1, 1995): 27–49.

———. 2003. "Reluctant Exiles or Roaming Transnationals? The Hong Kong Chinese in New Zealand." In *Unfolding History, Evolving Identity: The Chinese in New Zealand*, edited by Murphy Nigel, 165–184. Auckland: Auckland University Press.

Hochschild, Arlie, and Anne Machung. 2012. *The Second Shift: Working Families and the Revolution at Home.* New York: Penguin.

Hondagneu-Sotelo, Pierrette, and Ernestine Avila. 1997. "'I'm Here, but I'm There': The Meanings of Latina Transnational Motherhood." *Gender & Society* 11, no. 5 (October 1, 1997): 548–571.

Hong Jung-wook. 1993. *7mak 7chang* [Seven acts, seven scenes]. Seoul: Samsung Press.

Horn, Michael. 2014. "What Koreans Wish Obama Understood About Their Schools." *Forbes*, March 31, 2014. https://www.forbes.com/sites/michaelhorn/2014/03/31/what-koreans-wish-obama-understood-about-their-schools/.

Huang, Grace, and Mary Gove. 2015. "Asian Parenting Styles and Academic Achievement: Views from Eastern and Western Perspectives." *Education* 135, no. 3 (March 22, 2015): 389–397. https://eric.ed.gov/?id=EJ1095381.

Huang, Shirlena, and Brenda Yeoh. 2005. "Transnational Families and Their Children's Education: China's 'Study Mothers' in Singapore." *Global Networks* 5, no. 4 (October 14, 2005): 379–400.

Hwang Jung Mee. 2012. "다문화 사회와 '이주 어머니'—모성 담론의 재구성과 어머니의 시민권에 관한 고찰" [Positioning migrant mothers in a multicultural society: Realities, discourse, and new perspectives in Korea]. *Asia Yŏsŏngyŏn-gu* [Journal of Asian women] 51, no. 2 (January 1, 2012): 103–142.

Hyun Jung Hwan. 2007. "한국의 부모자녀관계와 관련된 최근 연구동향과 과제" [A review on the recent trends in the parent-child relations in Korea]. *Han'gukpoyuk'ak'oeji* [Korean journal of child education and care] 7, no. 1 (January 1, 2007): 95–110.

Ide, Michael Enku, Blair Harrington, Yolanda Wiggins, Tanya Rouleau Whitworth, and Naomi Gerstel. 2018. "Emerging Adult Sons and Their Fathers: Race and the Construction of Masculinity." *Gender & Society* 32, no. 1 (January 1, 2018): 5–33.

International Institute of Education. 2024. "Open Doors International Students Data: All Places of Origin from the 2024 OPEN DOORS Report." Accessed March 31, 2025. https://opendoorsdata.org/data/international-students/all-places-of-origin/.

Jack, Anthony Abraham. 2019. *The Privileged Poor: How Elite Colleges Are Failing Disadvantaged Students.* Cambridge, Mass.: Harvard University Press.

Jeong, Yu-Jin, Hyun-Kyung You, and Young In Kwon. 2013. "One Family in Two Countries: Mothers in Korean Transnational Families." *Ethnic and Racial Studies* 37, no. 9 (January 17, 2013): 1546–1564. https://doi.org/10.1080/01419870.2012.758861.

Johnston, Deirdre, and Debra Swanson. 2003. "Invisible Mothers: A Content Analysis of Motherhood Ideologies and Myths in Magazines." *Sex Roles* 49 (July 1, 2003): 21–33.

Josephson, Jyl, and Cynthia Burack. 1998. "The Political Ideology of the Neo-Traditional Family." *Journal of Political Ideologies* 3, no. 2 (June 1, 1998): 213–231. https://doi.org/10.1080/13569319808420777.

Joshi, Meghana. 2021. "'I Do Not Want to Be a Weekend Papa': The Demographic 'Crisis,' Active Fatherhood, and Emergent Caring Masculinities in Berlin." *Journal of Family Issues* 42, no. 5 (March 1, 2021): 883–907. https://doi.org/10.1177/0192513X21994154.

Jung Ok Kyung, Koh Ohn Jo, and Kim Kyung-keun. 2024. "영어유치원 선택요인 연구: 텍스트 네트워크 분석" ["English language kindergarten" discourse in online parenting communities: Application of topic modeling and sentiment analysis]. *Kyoyungmunhwayŏn-gu* [Journal of education and culture] 30, no. 1 (February 1, 2024): 311–338.

Kang, Jiyeon, and Nancy Abelmann. 2011. "The Domestication of South Korean Precollege Study Abroad in the First Decade of the Millennium." *Journal of Korean Studies* 16, no. 1 (March 11, 2011): 89–118.

Kang, Miliann, Hye Jun Park, and Juyeon Park. 2020. "Teachers as Good Mothers, Mothers as Good Teachers: Functional and Ideological Work–Family Alignment in the South Korean Teaching Profession." *Gender, Work and Organization* 27, no. 3 (July 23, 2019): 395–413. https://doi.org/10.1111/gwao.12396.

Kang, Yoonhee. 2012. "Singlish or Globish: Multiple Language Ideologies and Global Identities Among Korean Educational Migrants in Singapore." *Journal of Sociolinguistics* 16, no. 2 (April 1, 2012): 165–183. https://doi.org/10.1111/j.1467-9841.2011.00522.x.

Kaufman, Gayle. 2013. *Superdads: How Fathers Balance Work and Family in the 21st Century*. New York: NYU Press.

Kehily, Mary Jane, and Rachel Thomson. 2011. "Displaying Motherhood: Representations, Visual Methods and the Materiality of Maternal Practice." In *Displaying Families: A New Concept for the Sociology of Family Life*, edited by Esther Dermott and Julie Seymour, 61–80. London: Palgrave Macmillan.

Kelsky, Karen. 2001. *Women on the Verge: Japanese Women, Western Dreams*. Durham, N.C.: Duke University Press.

Kerstetter, Katie. 2012. "Insider, Outsider, or Somewhere Between: The Impact of Researchers' Identities on the Community-Based Research Process." *Journal of Rural Social Sciences* 27, no. 2 (May 1, 2012): 99–117.

Khan, Shamus Rahman. 2011. *Privilege: The Making of an Adolescent Elite at St. Paul's School*. Princeton, N.J.: Princeton University Press.

———. 2018. "Privilege: The Making of an Adolescent Elite." In *Inequality in the 21st Century: A Reader*, edited by David Grusky, Jasmine Hill, 100–102. New York: Routledge.

Khattab, Nabil. 2015. "Students' Aspirations, Expectations and School Achievement: What Really Matters?" *British Educational Research Journal* 41, no. 5 (January 21, 2015): 731–748. https://doi.org/10.1002/berj.3171.

Kim, Allen, and Karen Pyke. 2015. "Taming Tiger Dads: Hegemonic American Masculinity and South Korea's Father School." *Gender & Society* 29, no. 4 (May 13, 2015): 509–533.

Kim, Hyun Joo, and Sumie Okazaki. 2014. "Navigating the Cultural Transition Alone: Psychosocial Adjustment of Korean Early Study Abroad Students." *Cultural Diversity & Ethnic Minority Psychology* 20, no. 2 (January 1, 2014): 244–253. https://doi.org/10.1037/a0034243.

Kim, Jeehun. 2010. "'Downed' and Stuck in Singapore: Lower/Middle Class South Korean Wild Geese." In *Globalization, Changing Demographics, and Educational Challenges in East Asia*, edited by Hannum Park and Goto Butler, 271–311. Leeds: Emerald Group.

Kim Jinsook. 2021. "The Resurgence and Popularization of Feminism in South Korea: Key Issues and Challenges for Contemporary Feminist Activism." *Korea Journal* 61, no. 4 (December 1, 2021): 75–101.

Kim Jongyoung. 2008. "글로벌 문화자본의 추구: 미국 유학 동기에 대한 심층 면접 분석" [In pursuit of global cultural capital: Analysis of qualitative interviews revealing Korean students' motivations for studying in the United States]. *Han'guksahoehak* [Korean journal of sociology] 42, no. 6 (October 1, 2008): 68–105.

———. 2011. "Aspiration for Global Cultural Capital in the Stratified Realm of Global Higher Education: Why Do Korean Students Go to US Graduate Schools?" *British Journal of Sociology of Education* 32, no. 1 (January 1, 2011): 109–126. https://doi.org/10.1080/01425692.2011.527725.

———. 2012. "The Birth of Academic Subalterns: How Do Foreign Students Embody the Global Hegemony of American Universities?" *Journal of Studies in International Education* 16, no. 5 (November 1, 2012): 455–476.

Kim Ju Hyun, Song Min Kyoung, and Lee Hyun Joo. 2010. "기러기 아빠의 분거가족 결정과 유지경험에 관한 연구" [A study of wild-geese fathers' experiences of decision-making and maintenance in separated families]. *Sahoebokchiyŏn-gu* [Korean journal of social welfare studies] 41, no. 4 (December 1, 2010): 107–133. https://doi.org/10.16999/kasws .2010.41.4.107.

Kim Misook and Sang Chongryel. 2015. "중산층 밀집지역에 거주하는 중산층 학부모들의 자녀교육문화" [Neighborhood effects and child education in a middle-class residential Area: A case of Boondang-Gu]. *Kyoyuksahoehakyŏn-gu* [Korean journal of sociology of education] 25, no. 3 (September 1, 2015): 1–30.

Kim, Seung-Kyung, and John Finch. 2002. "Living with Rhetoric, Living Against Rhetoric: Korean Families and the IMF Economic Crisis." *Korean Studies* 26, no. 1 (January 1, 2002): 120–139. https://doi.org/10.1353/ks.2002.0008.

Kim, Youna. 2013. *Transnational Migration, Media and Identity of Asian Women: Diasporic Daughters*. New York: Routledge.

Kirk, Chris Michael, Rhonda Lewis-Moss, Corinne Nilsen, and Deltha Colvin. 2011. "The Role of Parent Expectations on Adolescent Educational Aspirations." *Educational Studies* 37, no. 1 (February 1, 2011): 89–99. https://doi.org/10.1080/03055691003728965.

Ko, Kwangman, Youngjin Kang, and Jieun Choi. 2022. "Patterns of Paternal Involvement of Korean Fathers: A Person-Centered Approach." *Journal of Family Issues* 43, no. 9 (July 13, 2021): 2505–2528. https://doi.org/10.1177/0192513x211030936.

Koo, Hagen. 2007. "The Changing Faces of Inequality in South Korea in the Age of Globalization." *Korean Studies* 31, no. 1 (January 1, 2008): 1–18. https://doi.org/10.1353/ks.2008 .0018.

Korean Statistical Information Service. 2024. "유학생 관련 현황" [Current status of international students]. Kosis. Last updated 2024. Accessed March 31, 2025. https://kosis.kr/ statHtml/statHtml.do?orgId=111&tblId=DT_1B040A14&conn_path=I3.

Kuptsch, Christiane, and Eng Fong Pang, eds. 2006. *Competing for Global Talent*. Geneva: International Labour Organization.

Lan, Pei-Chia. 2023. "Navigating Childrearing, Fatherhood, and Mobilities: A Transnational Relational Analysis." *Sociological Review* 71, no. 1 (December 15, 2022): 3–26. https://doi .org/10.1177/00380261221143586.

Lareau, Annette. 2003. *Unequal Childhoods: Class, Race, and Family Life*. Berkeley: University of California Press.

Larmer, Brook. 2017. "The Parachute Generation." *New York Times*, February 2, 2017. https://www.nytimes.com/2017/02/02/magazine/the-parachute-generation.html.

LaRossa, Ralph. 1997. *The Modernization of Fatherhood: A Social and Political History*. Chicago: University of Chicago Press.

Lee, Claire. 2022. "More Women in South Korea Choosing to Leave the Workforce." *HRM Asia*, November 23, 2022. https://hrmasia.com/more-women-in-south-korea-choosing -to-leave-the-workforce/.

Lee Eun A. 2013. "도시 결혼이주여성의 어머니 노릇과 정체성: 자녀교육 경험을 중심으로" [Urban marriage migrant women's role of a mother and their identities: Focusing on the experience of child education]. *Han'gukyŏsŏnghak* [Journal of Korean women's studies] 29, no. 3 (January 1, 2013): 115–146.

Lee, Jaerim, and Jean Bauer. 2013. "Motivations for Providing and Utilizing Childcare by Grandmothers in South Korea." *Journal of Marriage and Family* 75, no. 2 (March 14, 2013): 381–402. https://doi.org/10.1111/jomf.12014.

Lee, Jane YeonJae. 2011. "A Trajectory Perspective Towards Return Migration and Development: The Case of Young Korean New Zealander Returnees." In *Korea 2011: Politics, Economy and Society*, edited by Rüdiger Frank, Jim Hoare, Patrick Köllner, and Susan Pares, 233–256. Leiden: Brill.

Lee, Jennifer, and Min Zhou. 2015. *The Asian American Achievement Paradox*. New York: Russell Sage Foundation.

Lee, Jeong-Kyu. 2006. "Educational Fever and South Korean Higher Education." *Revista electrónica de investigación educativa* 8, no. 1 (May 1, 2006): 1–14.

Lee Jin-Young. 2001. "한국성인 40% 교육이민 희망" [40% of Koreans wish to migrate for education]. *Dong-A Ilbo*, September 10, 2001. https://www.donga.com/news/article/all/20010910/7736011/9?comm.

Lee, Se Hwa. 2019. "Only If You Are One of Us: Wild Geese Mothers' Parenting in the Korean Immigrant Community." *Amerasia Journal* 42, no. 2 (February 4, 2019): 71–94.

———. 2021a. "'I Am Still Close to My Child': Middle-Class Korean Wild Geese Fathers' Responsible and Intimate Fatherhood in a Transnational Context." *Journal of Ethnic and Migration Studies* 47, no. 9 (September 1, 2021): 2161–2178. https://doi.org/10.1080/1369183x.2019.1573662.

———. 2021b. *Korean Wild Geese Families: Gender, Family, Social, and Legal Dynamics of Middle-Class Asian Transnational Families in North America*. Lanham: Rowman & Littlefield.

Lee Sung-Suk. 2023. "영어유치원에 자녀를 보내는 어머니들의 경험에 대한 현상연구" [A phenomenological study on mothers' experiences of sending their children to English kindergarten]. *Haksŭpchajungshimgyogwagyoyukyŏn-gu* [Journal of learner-centered curriculum and instruction] 23, no. 7 (April 15, 2023): 593–605. https://doi.org/10.22251/jlcci.2023.23.7.593.

Lee, Yean-Ju, and Hagen Koo. 2006. "'Wild Geese Fathers' and a Globalised Family Strategy for Education in Korea." *International Development Planning Review* 28, no. 4 (December 1, 2006): 533–553. https://doi.org/10.3828/idpr.28.4.6.

Leung, Aegean. 2011. "Motherhood and Entrepreneurship: Gender Role Identity as a Resource." *International Journal of Gender and Entrepreneurship* 3, no. 3 (September 27, 2011): 254–264. https://doi.org/10.1108/17566261111169331.

Ley, David. 2003. "Seeking Homo Economicus: The Strange Story of Canada's Business Immigration Program." *Annals of the Association of American Geographers* 93, no. 2 (April 1, 2003): 426–441. https://doi.org/10.1111/1467-8306.9302010.

Lim, Wee Ling, and Roziah Mohd Rasdi. 2019. "'Opt-Out' or Pushed Out?" *European Journal of Training and Development* 43, no. 9 (November 4, 2019): 785–800. https://doi.org/10.1108/ejtd-04-2019-0063.

Lin, Jun-Chi Gisela, and Jenny Yi. 1997. "Asian International Students' Adjustment: Issues and Program Suggestions." *College Student Journal* 31, no. 4 (December 1, 1997): 473–479.

Lo, Adrienne, Nancy Abelmann, Soo Ah Kwon, and Sumie Okazaki, eds. 2015. *South Korea's Education Exodus: The Life and Times of Early Study Abroad*. Seattle: University of Washington Press.

Locke, Kenneth. 2006. "What Predicts Well-Being: A Consistent Self-Concept or a Desirable Self-Concept?" *Journal of Social and Clinical Psychology* 25, no. 2 (February 1, 2006): 228–247.

Longlands, Helen. 2014. "Men, Masculinities and Fatherhood in Global Finance." PhD diss., University of London.

Ly, Phuong. 2005. "A Wrenching Choice." *Washington Post*, January 9, 2005. http://www.washingtonpost.com/wp-dyn/articles/A59355-2005Jan8.html.

Marsiglio, William, and Joseph Pleck. 2005. "Fatherhood and Masculinities." In *Handbook of Studies on Men and Masculinities*, edited by Michael Kimmel, Jeff Hearn & Robert Connell, 249–269. New York: Sage Publications.

Marsiglio, William, and Kevin Roy. 2012. *Nurturing Dads: Social Initiatives for Contemporary Fatherhood*. New York: Russell Sage Foundation.

Martin, Fran. 2021. *Dreams of Flight: The Lives of Chinese Women Students in the West*. Durham, N.C.: Duke University Press.

Mazzucato, Valentina, and Djamila Schans. 2011. "Transnational Families and the Well-Being of Children: Conceptual and Methodological Challenges." *Journal of Marriage and Family* 73, no. 4 (July 15, 2011): 704–712. https://doi.org/10.1111/j.1741-3737.2011.00840.x.

Mengwei, Tu. 2018. "For Chinese Women, Foreign Study Doesn't Bring Gender Equality." *Sixth Tone*, January 30, 2018. https://www.sixthtone.com/news/1001634.

Mijs, Jonathan, and Mike Savage. 2020. "Meritocracy, Elitism and Inequality." *Political Quarterly* 91, no. 2 (March 30, 2020): 397–404.

Ministry of Education, Republic of Korea. 2023. "Data of Korean Students Studying Abroad in 2023." Accessed March 30, 2025. https://www.moe.go.kr/boardCnts/viewRenew.do?boardID=350&lev=0&statusYN=W&s=moe&m=0309&opType=N&boardSeq=97338.

Na Sung-Eun. 2014. "남성의 양육 참여와 평등한 부모 역할의 의미 구성: 육아휴직제도 이용 경험을 중심으로" [Men's care involvement and the construction of equal parenting between genders: Focusing on the experience of parental leave]. *P'eminijŭmyŏn-gu* [Issues in feminism] 14, no. 2 (October 10, 2014): 71–112.

Nader, Laura. 1972. "Up the Anthropologist: Perspectives Gained from Studying Up." In *Reinventing Anthropology*, edited by Dell Hymes, 284–311. New York: Pantheon Books.

Ng, Jennifer, Yoon Pak, and Xavier Hernandez. 2016. "Beyond the Perpetual Foreigner and Model Minority Stereotypes." In *Contemporary Asian America: A Multidisciplinary Reader*, edited by Min Zhou, 576–599. New York: NYU Press.

Ninh, Erin Khuê. 2011. *Ingratitude: The Debt-Bound Daughter in Asian American Literature*. New York: NYU Press.

Nonini, Donald, and Aihwa Ong. 1997. "Chinese Transnationalism as an Alternative Modernity." In *Ungrounded Empires: The Cultural Politics of Modern Chinese Transnationalism*, edited by Aihwa Ong and Donald Nonini, 3–33. New York: Routledge.

Oberg, Kalervo. 1960. "Cultural Shock: Adjustment to New Cultural Environments." *Missiology: An International Review* 7, no. 4 (July 1, 1960): 177–182. https://doi.org/10.1177/009182966000700405.

OECD (Organisation for Economic Co-operation and Development). 2024a. "Private Spending on Education." Accessed July 3, 2024. https://data.oecd.org/eduresource/private-spending-on-education.htm#indicator-chart.

———. 2024b. "Korea: Student Performance (PISA 2022)." Accessed August 18, 2024. https://gpseducation.oecd.org/CountryProfile?primaryCountry=KOR&treshold=10&topic=PI.

Ong, Aihwa. 1999. *Flexible Citizenship: The Cultural Logics of Transnationality*. Durham, N.C.: Duke University Press.

Onishi, Norimitsu. 2008. "For English Studies, Koreans Say Goodbye to Dad." *New York Times*, June 8, 2008. https://www.nytimes.com/2008/06/08/world/asia/08geese.html.

Ono, Hiroshi, and Nicola Piper. 2004. "Japanese Women Studying Abroad, the Case of the United States." *Women's Studies International Forum* 27, no. 2 (June 1, 2004): 101–118. https://doi.org/10.1016/j.wsif.2004.06.002.

O'Reilly, Andrea. 2016. "We Need to Talk About Patriarchal Motherhood: Essentialization, Naturalization and Idealization in Lionel Shriver's *We Need to Talk About Kevin*." *Journal of the Motherhood Initiative for Research and Community Involvement* 7, no. 1 (January 1, 2016): 64–81.

Papanek, Hanna. 1979. "Family Status Production: The 'Work' and 'Non-Work' of Women." *Signs* 4, no. 4 (July 1, 1979): 775–781. https://doi.org/10.1086/493663.

Park Hye Gyong. 2009. "한국 중산층의 자녀교육 경쟁과 전업 어머니 정체성" [Competition over children's education and the "full-time mother" identity in Korean middle-class families]. *Han'gukyŏsŏnghak* [Journal of Korean women's studies] 25, no. 3 (September 1, 2019): 5–33.

Park, Hyunjoon. 2013. *Re-Evaluating Education in Japan and Korea: De-Mystifying Stereotypes*. New York: Routledge.

Park, Insook Han, and Lee-Jay Cho. 1995. "Confucianism and the Korean Family." *Journal of Comparative Family Studies* 26, no. 1 (March 1, 1995): 117–134. https://doi.org/10.3138/jcfs.26.1.117.

Park, Jin-Kyu. 2009. "'English Fever' in South Korea: Its History and Symptoms." *English Today* 25, no. 1 (March 1, 2009): 50–57. https://doi.org/10.1017/s026607840900008x.

Park, So Jin. 2006. "The Retreat from Formal Schooling: 'Educational Manager Mothers' in the Private After-School Market of South Korea." PhD diss., University of Illinois at Urbana-Champaign.

Park, So Jin, and Nancy Abelmann. 2004. "Class and Cosmopolitan Striving: Mothers' Management of English Education in South Korea." *Anthropological Quarterly* 77, no. 4 (September 1, 2004): 645–672. https://doi.org/10.1353/anq.2004.0063.

Park Wonhee. 2004. *Kongbu kudan ogi siptan* [Study at level 9 and persevere at level 10]. Seoul: Kimyoungsa.

Parke, Ross. 1996. *Fatherhood*. Cambridge, Mass.: Harvard University Press.

Parke, Ross, and Jeffrey Cookston. 2021. "Transnational Fathers: New Theoretical and Conceptual Challenges." *Journal of Family Theory & Review* 13, no. 3 (November 16, 2020): 266–282. https://doi.org/10.1111/jftr.12392.

Parreñas, Rhacel. 2005. "Long Distance Intimacy: Class, Gender and Intergenerational Relations Between Mothers and Children in Filipino Transnational Families." *Global Networks* 5, no. 4 (October 1, 2005): 317–336. https://doi.org/10.1111/j.1471-0374.2005.00122.x.

———. 2008. "Transnational Fathering: Gendered Conflicts, Distant Disciplining and Emotional Gaps." *Journal of Ethnic and Migration Studies* 34, no. 7 (August 6, 2008): 1057–1072. https://doi.org/10.1080/13691830802230356.

———. 2013. "The Gender Revolution in the Philippines: Migrant Mothering and Social Transformation." In *How Immigrants Impact Their Homelands*, edited by Susan Eckstein, Adil Najam, and Susan Eva Eckstein, 191–212. Durham, N.C.: Duke University Press.

Pe-Pua, Rogelia, Colleen Mitchell, Stephen Castles, and Robyn Iredale. 1998. "Astronaut Families and Parachute Children: Hong Kong Immigrants in Australia." In *The Last Half Century of Chinese Overseas*, edited by Elizabeth Sinn, 279–298. Hong Kong: University of Hong Kong Press.

Popadiuk, Natalee. 2010. "Asian International Student Transition to High School in Canada." *Qualitative Report* 15, no. 6 (November 1, 2010): 1523–1548. https://doi.org/10.46743/2160-3715/2010.1359.

Randles, Jennifer. 2020. "Role Modeling Responsibility: The Essential Father Discourse in Responsible Fatherhood Programming and Policy." *Social Problems*, January 28, 2019. https://doi.org/10.1093/socpro/spy027.

Redden, Elizabeth. 2019. "Number of Enrolled International Students Drops." *Inside Higher Ed*, November 17, 2019. https://www.insidehighered.com/admissions/article/2019/11/18/international-enrollments-declined-undergraduate-graduate-and.

Risman, Barbara. 1998. *Gender Vertigo: American Families in Transition*. New Haven, Conn.: Yale University Press.

Risman, Barbara, and Danette Johnson-Sumerford. 1998. "Doing It Fairly: A Study of Post-gender Marriages." *Journal of Marriage and Family* 60, no. 1 (February 1, 1998): 23–40. https://doi.org/10.2307/353439.

Roh, Kyung-Ran, and Eun-Bee Kim. 2021. "An Analysis of Male and Female Managers' Responses to Work Stress: Focused on the Case of South Korea." *International Journal of Environmental Research and Public Health* 18, no. 21 (October 22, 2021): article 11119. https://doi.org/10.3390/ijerph182111119.

Santiago, Ileana Cortes, Nastaran Karimi, and Zaira R. Arvelo Alicea. 2017. "Neoliberalism and Higher Education: A Collective Autoethnography of Brown Women Teaching Assistants." *Gender and Education* 29, no. 1 (July 14, 2016): 48–65. https://doi.org/10.1080/09540253.2016.1197383.

Sassen, Saskia. (1991) 2013. *The Global City: New York, London, Tokyo*. Princeton, N.J.: Princeton University Press.

Sayer, Andrew. 2007. "Class, Moral Worth and Recognition." In *(Mis)recognition, Social Inequality and Social Justice*, edited by Terry Lovell, 100–114. New York: Routledge.

Sewell, William H., and Vimal P. Shah. 1968. "Social Class, Parental Encouragement, and Educational Aspirations." *American Journal of Sociology* 73, no. 5 (March 1, 1968): 559–572. https://doi.org/10.1086/224530.

Shaw, Rhonda M., Julie Howe, Jonathan Beazer, and Toni Carr. 2020. "Ethics and Positionality in Qualitative Research with Vulnerable and Marginal Groups." *Qualitative Research* 20, no. 3 (April 16, 2019): 277–293. https://doi.org/10.1177/1468794119841839.

Sherman, Rachel. 2018. "'A Very Expensive Ordinary Life': Consumption, Symbolic Boundaries and Moral Legitimacy Among New York Elites." *Socio-Economic Review* 16, no. 2 (April 1, 2018): 411–433. https://doi.org/10.1093/ser/mwy011.

Shin Jung Cheol, Jisun Jung, Gerard A. Postiglione, and Norzaini Azman. 2014. "Research Productivity of Returnees from Study Abroad in Korea, Hong Kong, and Malaysia." *Minerva* 52, no. 4 (October 2, 2014): 467–487. https://doi.org/10.1007/s11024-014-9259-9.

Shin, Kyunghee, Kyung Eun Jahng, and Dongjin Kim. 2019. "Stories of South Korean Mothers' Education Fever for Their Children's Education." *Asia Pacific Journal of Education* 39, no. 3 (May 5, 2019): 338–356. https://doi.org/10.1080/02188791.2019.1607720.

Skeldon, Ronald. 1994. "Turning Points in Labor Migration: The Case of Hong Kong." *Asian and Pacific Migration Journal* 3, no. 1 (March 1, 1994): 93–118. https://doi.org/10.1177/011719689400300106.

———. 2008. "International Migration as a Tool in Development Policy: A Passing Phase?" *Population and Development Review* 34, no. 1 (March 1, 2008): 1–18. https://doi.org/10.1111/j.1728-4457.2008.00203.x.

Sohn, Hee Jeong. 2020. "Feminism Reboot: Korean Cinema Under Neoliberalism in the 21st Century." *Journal of Japanese & Korean Cinema* 12, no. 2 (July 2, 2020): 98–109. https://doi.org/10.1080/17564905.2020.1840031.

Spera, Christopher, Kathryn Wentzel, and Holly Matto. 2009. "Parental Aspirations for Their Children's Educational Attainment: Relations to Ethnicity, Parental Education, Children's Academic Performance, and Parental Perceptions of School Climate." *Journal of Youth and Adolescence* 38, no. 8 (July 29, 2008): 1140–1152. https://doi.org/10.1007/s10964-008-9314-7.

Statista. 2024. "Total Expenditure on Private Education in South Korea from 2012 to 2022." Accessed July 3, 2024. https://www.statista.com/statistics/1042853/south-korea-total-spending-for-private-education/#statisticContainer.

Stevenson, Jacqueline, and Sue Clegg. 2012. "Who Cares? Gender Dynamics in the Valuing of Extra-Curricular Activities in Higher Education." *Gender and Education* 24, no. 1 (January 1, 2012): 41–55. https://doi.org/10.1080/09540253.2011.565039.

Stone, Pamela. 2007. *Opting Out? Why Women Really Quit Careers and Head Home*. Berkeley: University of California Press.

Summers, Jean Ann, Kimberly Boller, Rachel F. Schiffman, and Helen H. Raikes. 2006. "The Meaning of 'Good Fatherhood:' Low-Income Fathers' Social Constructions of Their Roles." *Parenting, Science and Practice* 6, nos. 2–3 (May 1, 2006): 145–165. https://doi.org/10.1080/15295192.2006.9681303.

Sussman, Anna. 2023. "A World Without Men." *The Cut*, March 8, 2023. https://www.thecut.com/2023/03/4b-movement-feminism-south-korea.html.

Svrluga, Susan. 2021. "After Decades of Increases, a Drop in the Number of International Students in the United States." *Washington Post*, November 15, 2021. https://www.washingtonpost.com/education/2021/11/15/international-college-student-enrollment-covid/.

Taylor, Tiffany. 2011. "Re-Examining Cultural Contradictions: Mothering Ideology and the Intersections of Class, Gender, and Race." *Sociology Compass* 5, no. 10 (October 1, 2011): 898–907. https://doi.org/10.1111/j.1751-9020.2011.00415.x.

Teo, Sin Yih. 2003. "Dreaming Inside a Walled City: Imagination, Gender and the Roots of Immigration." *Asian and Pacific Migration Journal* 12, no. 4 (December 1, 2003): 411–438. https://doi.org/10.1177/011719680301200401.

Tingey, Holly, Gary Kiger, and Pamela Riley. 1996. "Juggling Multiple Roles: Perceptions of Working Mothers." *Social Science Journal* 33, no. 2 (June 1, 1996): 183–191. https://doi.org/10.1016/s0362-3319(96)90035-x.

Tran, Ly Thi, and Thao Thi Phuong Vu. 2018. "'Agency in Mobility': Towards a Conceptualisation of International Student Agency in Transnational Mobility." *Educational Review* 70, no. 2 (March 1, 2018): 167–187. https://doi.org/10.1080/00131911.2017.1293615.

Useem, Ruth Hill, and Richard Downie. 1976. "Third-Culture Kids." *Today's Education* 65, no. 3 (September 1, 1976): 103–105.

Veblen, Thorstein. (1899) 2005. *The Theory of the Leisure Class: An Economic Study of Institutions*. New Delhi: Aakar Books.

Waters, Johanna. 2002. "Flexible Families? 'Astronaut' Households and the Experiences of Lone Mothers in Vancouver, British Columbia." *Social & Cultural Geography* 3, no. 2 (January 1, 2002): 117–134. https://doi.org/10.1080/14649360220133907.

———. 2005. "Transnational Family Strategies and Education in the Contemporary Chinese Diaspora." *Global Networks* 5, no. 4 (October 1, 2005): 359–377. https://doi.org/10.1111/j.1471-0374.2005.00124.x.

Watkins, Megan, Christina Ho, and Rose Butler. 2017. "Asian Migration and Education Cultures in the Anglo-Sphere." *Journal of Ethnic and Migration Studies* 43, no. 14 (July 10, 2017): 2283–2299. https://doi.org/10.1080/1369183X.2017.1315849.

Woodfield, Ruth. 2019. "The Gendered Landscape of UK Higher Education: Do Men Feel Disadvantaged?" *Gender and Education* 31, no. 1 (February 20, 2017): 15–32. https://doi.org/10.1080/09540253.2017.1288859.

Yale Office of International Students and Scholars. 2024. "Statistics & Reports: 2023." Accessed June 19, 2024. https://oiss.yale.edu/about/statistics-reports-2023#students.

Yeo Jun-Suk. 2015. "Number of Kids Studying Abroad Falls 63% in 8 Years." *Korea Herald*, November 15, 2015. http://www.koreaherald.com/view.php?ud=20151117001034.

Yŏsŏngjungang. 2015. "조기 유학을 위한 관문, 보딩 스쿨: 입학부터 대학 지원까지" [Boarding schools as a starting point for early study abroad students]. Naver Post, August 1, 2015.

https://m.post.naver.com/viewer/postView.nhn?volumeNo=11235294&memberNo=24364462.

You, Soo-Bin, and Olena Nesteruk. 2022. "'It Is Not the End of Parenting': Extended Parenthood and Child Launching Experiences Among Middle-Aged Korean American Mothers." *Emerging Adulthood* 10, no. 3 (May 7, 2022): 712–724. https://doi.org/10.1177/2167696821990270.

Yu, Helen. 2020. "Revisiting the Bamboo Ceiling: Perceptions from Asian Americans on Experiencing Workplace Discrimination." *Asian American Journal of Psychology* 11, no. 3 (September 1, 2020): 158–167. https://doi.org/10.1037/aap0000193.

Index

About the Author

JUYEON PARK is a qualitative sociologist specializing in gender, family, education, and migration studies. Much of her research explores the intersectional impacts of gender and class on parenting and parenthood, work and achievement, and migration strategies of Asian women, particularly those who are highly educated. She currently teaches and conducts research as an assistant professor of sociology at Yonsei University in Seoul, Korea.

Available titles in the Families in Focus series: